Making Constituencies

which minimizes people's exposure and openness to competitive political discourse, does more damage to democracy than manipulation.

Chapters 6 and 7 provide the theoretical justification for the intuition that links the arguments of these various chapters together: that democratic political representation urgently requires plurality as its enabling condition. I build the architecture for this claim from two sources. Chapter 6 mines the political theory of Claude Lefort, who was the first to name indeterminacy—the irreducibility of political divisions to (putatively) given social differences—as the democratic legacy of the French Revolution. Chapter 7 features the work of Ernesto Laclau and Chantal Mouffe, the first political theorists to make a constructivist turn in the name of *democratic* political representation. In *Hegemony and Socialist Strategy*, they defend a constructivist account of representation that prioritizes a concern with preserving plurality over a preoccupation with detecting and disarming manipulation. Their classic work provides an important resource for theorists of democracy today who are pressed to respond to critics aligning constructivism with elitism, and defining "manipulation" as a central threat to democracy in mass societies.

In Defense of *Mobilization*

Mobilization is a term of art in every subfield of political science. As *voter* mobilization, it names various activities for stimulating turnout, typically among those whom a campaign has identified as its likely supporters. As *political* mobilization, it refers specifically to voter participation. Scholars of comparative politics speak of *ethnic* mobilization, an activity that is assumed to work *on* group identities. The same is true of *interest-group* mobilization as well.

These commonplace uses of the term exemplify the persistence of the "social determinism" that comparative political scientist David R. Cameron criticized in "standard" social-science conceptions of mobilization almost fifty years ago.[1] Then as now, social scientists said *mobilization* when they meant something that might be better termed *targeting*. Their use of the word implies a constituency, already formed but dormant, that mobilization activates. *Mobilization* as I use the term casts off this most basic intuition of both pluralist and participatory theories of democracy: that groups form around shared interests to demand laws and policies that serve those interests. I turn that model around by proposing a term—*constituency effects*—that registers the power of representation to divide the social field.

I do not use *mobilization* in the typical sense, to refer to the activities—such as canvassing, phone banking, and other forms of direct contact—that political parties and other organizations use to turn out their likely voters by "reminding [them] of their partisan identities."[2] My use comports with the robust conceptualization of mobilization first proposed by political behavior scholars Berelson, Lazarsfeld, and McPhee. Far from reducing it to targeting, they—in the eyes of at least one subsequent scholar—recognized mobilization "as a key mechanism that *fashions* group identities into political blocs."[3] So understood, mobilization brings an understudied aspect of political representation into focus: that acts of political representation solicit groups and constitute interests.[4]

Under this category of *acts* of political representation, I include the "claims" and promises of political candidates, the policies enacted by legislatures, and the declarations of party leaders and other elite opinion shapers.[5] I also include appeals by unelected and "self-appointed" representatives such as charismatic individuals, advocacy groups, political movements, and minor political parties.[6] Slogans—"we are the 99%," "Black Lives Matter," "#MeToo"—have group-defining effects as well, as do cultural objects like knitted pink hats and red baseball caps.[7]

I maintain that acts of representation can change the subject of politics in the fullest sense of the word: they change how people identify themselves by redefining what they care enough to fight for and whom they count as allies. Mobilization involves prioritizing and clarifying select lines of conflict from among a field of cross-cutting social divisions, then working them up into politically consequential group identities. My concept *constituency effects* registers this power.

This chapter reclaims *mobilization* from commonplace uses of the term that circulate in political science today. I turn first to an emergent and innovative field of research on organizing that has made *mobilization* the lever of a polemic. These authors, who reject the standard determinism about constituencies, and who insist that constituencies cannot simply be targeted but must be organized, undercut the force of their own argument by using *mobilization* in the conventional sense. With the help of Rogers Brubaker, who coined the striking phrase "commonsense primordialism" to characterize the beliefs about social divisions that typify much scholarship on political groups, I propose a nondeterministic rethinking of constituencies.[8]

I begin by exposing as "commonsense primordialism" the beliefs about social divisions that typify much scholarship on political groups and political mobilization.[9] I proceed to empirical research on public-policy feedback that turns primordialism around, demonstrating that social divisions and political groups are effects of acts of representation, not their basis.[10] This research, which demonstrates that key beneficiary groups of social-welfare policy follow from social divisions that the policies themselves introduce, lends credence to my concept of *constituency effects*. Feedback scholars do not frame their work as a contribution to theorizing political representation; I interpret it as doing exactly that.

From *Targeting* to *Constituency Effects*

Leading scholars in an emerging field of research on organizing have reduced the term *mobilization* to a derogatory label for a counterproductive shortcut: targeting groups to activate them in superficial ways.[11] These scholars do not think of constituencies as static or socially determined; they know constituencies need to be forged. That is precisely why it concerns them to see organizations—having once provided an important "pathway to action" for ordinary people—now avoiding the political work of constituency-making, instead shifting their resources toward lobbying, lawsuits, and public relations campaigns.[12] Such strategies make a false promise to substitute targeting for the painstaking work of organizing, as if constituencies form spontaneously by their "preexisting interest" in a cause and need only be summoned into action.[13] Jane McAlevey and Hahrie Han, two of the most prominent figures in this emerging field, undercut their own valuable, innovative work by resorting to a polemical framing that makes what McAlevey calls "shallow *mobilizing*" the enemy of "deep *organizing*."[14]

Han and McAlevey recognize that union or interest-group members are not like soldiers who stand ready to be drafted into political action; they need to be organized. This recognition, the very centerpiece of their argument, gets undercut by their resorting to dichotomy as a rhetorical shortcut to convey it. By juxtaposing mobilizing against organizing and equating mobilization with targeting, Han and McAlevey inadvertently affirm the very myth they seek to puncture, one that disavows the value and work of organizing in the first place: the myth of society as a field of already organized groups that stand ready to be activated.

Back in 1984, social psychologist Bert Klandermans made an argument similar to that of Han and McAlevey in less polemical terms.[15] Like them, he insisted that organization members are not like soldiers. Even a union, operating in a workplace that is "highly unionized and [has] a strong union network, cannot be "assured of [its members'] willingness to take action."[16] For the call to action to succeed, Klandermans argued that members have to own a problem—accepting that it is urgent, that it can be solved without unreasonable sacrifice, and that it is up to them to take on the fight. Klandermans called the task of catalyzing that ownership "consensus mobilization."[17] Organizations can and do engage in consensus mobilization without "action mobilization," or the call to action; but, Klandermans warned, they cannot do the reverse: "action mobilization *cannot* do without consensus mobilization."[18] I reach back to Klandermans's work for empirical affirmation of a presupposition of my argument, which is that organizing is an aspect of mobilization and not its opposite.

Rethinking Groups: Effects, Not Origins, of Political Action

Many of us, whether we are scholars or not, posit social groups as a political starting place. We think of political-group identities and interests as being determined by economic or other social interests that are fixed prior to politics, and we imagine that political groups emerge relatively spontaneously whenever those interests are at stake. Sociologist Rogers Brubaker calls this "commonsense primordialism," a way of thinking that takes "discrete, bounded groups as basic constituents of social life, chief protagonists of social conflicts, and fundamental units of social analysis."[19] Brubaker coined this vivid term as part of a counterargument contending that social groups are not given by economic interests or identities that are fixed prior to politics, and that they do not give rise spontaneously to political groups whenever those interests or identities are threatened. Rather, they take shape in response to the work of entrepreneurial political actors who deploy "categories" to "stir, summon, justify, mobilize, kindle, and energize" them into being.[20] A self-proclaimed "constructivist," Brubaker maintains that categories are not merely labels to be applied to groups once they have emerged; on the contrary, categories themselves actively solicit group formation.[21] Groups, as Brubaker theorizes them, are not foundations of politics but constituency effects, outcomes rather than origins of acts of political representation.

No doubt most people picture groups as basic social building blocks, imagine themselves belonging to groups, and believe groups to be basic units of political action and participation. Brubaker's point is that even if people subscribe to such a "folk sociolog[y]," scholars are not justified in doing so.[22] It is one thing for scholars to recognize that primordialist thinking exerts a powerful hold on political behavior and quite another to concede that groups are "things *in* the world."[23] The distinction is, admittedly, difficult to grasp. What can it mean to admit something is *consequential* but deny that it *exists*?

Brubaker recommends that we think about "groups" as we think about race. We may accept the fact that "racial idioms, ideologies, narratives,

categories and systems of classification . . . are real and consequential, especially when they are embedded in powerful organizations," but this acceptance in no way obligates us to "posit the existence of races."[24] Just as
"race"—when conceived as a real difference or natural basis for hierarchy—
gives little analytic purchase on white supremacy, "group" affords little analytic purchase on the phenomena of identity, loyalty, and mobilization that
primordialists use it to explain. Groups hold together not by any essential
property shared among their members, but by virtue of representations of
division and difference that position them in a social field.

Rethinking Mobilization as Cleavage-Making

Thirty years before Brubaker, comparative politics scholar David R.
Cameron picked up on the primordialism in the "standard framework
for research on mobilization."[25] His article "Toward a Theory of Political Mobilization" targeted the work of leading mobilization scholar Karl
Deutsch. Cameron faulted Deutsch for conceiving of "political mobilization [as] the end result or end product of certain types of social cleavage
and social change."[26] Deutsch made it seem as if these cleavages opened
spontaneously in response to changes wrought by such large-scale forces
as industrialization, urbanization, and (today) globalization.

Cameron turned Deutsch's model upside down. He argued that large-
scale forces do not register as political cleavages without the mediation
of "mobilizing agents," such as parties, whose policy choices and organizing strategies lend them "political meaning," determine their "impact" on
group identities, and shape their relations of alliance and enmity.[27] Mobilization scholarship depoliticized mobilization by treating "induction"
into a group "as passive and inevitable," and that depoliticization made
party organizations invisible as "agent[s] of mobilization."[28]

Cameron gave the example of a centuries-old linguistic and territo-
rial divide between the regions of Dutch-speaking Flanders and French-
speaking Wallonia that did not become a political cleavage until the 1960s
and 1970s. In 1958, a change in state policy that expanded public funding for private and religious education muted the long-standing political
cleavage that had divided Catholics against liberal secularists.[29] A series of
policy decisions in the 1960s politicized language as the new dividing line.
Those policy decisions—which fixed the borders of Flanders and Wallonia as "officially unilingual regions," established French as the majority

language in most of Brussels, and imposed restrictions on bilingualism—invested long-standing linguistic and regional identifications with political significance.[30] These political identifications gave rise to ethnonationalist parties that appeared to emerge from (and would claim) a primordial ground. Cameron's account showed these parties to be constituency effects, products of acts of representation that select particular lines of conflict out of a social field crisscrossed with antagonisms.

Cameron also analyzed the rise of the Nazi Party in rural Germany between 1928 and 1933, explicitly taking aim at primordialist scholarship that imagined farmers to have "some inherent predisposition or set of social conditions" that predisposed them to fascism.[31] Cameron countered that farmers were largely unorganized until the Nazi Party forged them into a political constituency. The party made itself the "only effective defender of the interests of the farmers and lower-middle classes" by politicizing "such everyday problems as price declines and property seizures," and then holding meetings in existing community institutions to organize collective action.[32] In this and other cases, Cameron counted mobilization as "a *cause* rather than an effect of the organizational bases of social cleavage."[33]

Mobilization, as Cameron used the term, forges social cleavages; it does not merely register them. This usage makes him likely the first empirical political scientist to describe political representation as mobilization in the sense that I define it. His various case studies narrate acts of policy and political parties participating in the "institution of the social."[34] They politicize lines of conflict that mute long-standing cleavages and form new ones to remake patterns of alliance and enmity.

Group Formation as Constituency Effect

Scholars of policy feedback today elaborate on Cameron's critique, although they neither cite his scholarship nor invoke the concept of mobilization. I count feedback scholarship among the most influential critiques of primordialism. It may be the most persuasive demonstration of political representation's *constituency effects*.

I propose this term to name the mark that acts of political representation leave on the field of political conflict. Constituency effects may be calculated results of deliberate and strategic acts, but they may also be unintended and unpredictable consequences of policy provisions or

institutional design. The US two-party system, an example from my previous research, combines both. Many scholars believe two-partyism to be an
unintended, inevitable effect of plurality elections. It is correct that plurality voting *tends* toward two-partyism, but party duopoly is not inevitable
in a first-past-the-post system. Guaranteeing duopoly required deliberate,
strategic action that occurred at the turn of the twentieth century, when
reformers enacted a round of ballot and electoral law both to root out
corruption and to thwart alternative political-party organizing.[35] In this
chapter, I demonstrate that policy-feedback scholarship—specifically on
civic participation by World War II veterans and on the high voting rates
of retirees—documents constituency effects, although feedback scholars
(of course) do not use this term. Their work is notable for its emphasis on
institutional design: they attribute what some might call civic-mindedness
to the design and eligibility rules of social-benefit programs rather than to
the character virtues of particular groups of people.[36]

Feedback scholarship poses a profound challenge to democratic intuitions about responsiveness with one simple organizing insight: that "policies produce politics."[37] The idea is that initial choices about program
design, typically neither fully intentional nor planned, become defining
logics over time. Policy-making is dynamic. Rather than being driven by
elite initiative or responsive to constituent "demand," it is conditioned by
the "legacies" of haphazard, innocuous, even corrupt features of its initial
design.[38] Public policies themselves are "not only outputs of but important inputs into the political process."[39] Such feedback effects not only
constrain the choices of elite decision makers; they make their mark on
mass publics, especially on the "target groups" of social-welfare policy.[40]

Initially, scholars theorized those effects in terms of mobilization in
the conventional sense. They emphasized the "incentives and resources"
that social programs provide, both for "beneficiaries to mobilize in favor
of programmatic maintenance or expansion" and for interest groups to
organize and lobby on their behalf.[41] Suzanne Mettler and Joe Soss argue
that this research has taken a "constructivist turn" to demonstrate that
social-welfare policy doesn't only "target" groups.[42] It constitutes social
relations, produces social "group identification and consciousness," and
brings social groups into being, calling them "into or out of the political
process."[43]

These are constituency effects. Feedback scholarship offers two distinct accounts of how they work. They may be indirect effects of the "size,
visibility, and traceability of benefits."[44] They may also be direct effects of

the way that social policy constructs beneficiary groups via eligibility rules that introduce frequently normatively charged divisions into a heterogeneous population.

Constituency Effects: Indirect

Jacob Hacker provides a classic account of indirect constituency effects with his counterintuitive account of how the US came to rely on "*private* social insurance" to provide such basic aspects of social welfare as retirement pensions and health care.[45] Note that these three terms— "private," "social," and "insurance"—sit uneasily together. Insurance is typically either private, exclusive, and voluntary, or social, universal, and mandatory—but not both. Hacker contends that their conjunction characterizes the genuinely exceptional feature of the US welfare system: not its *lack* of social provision as compared to industrialized democracies in Europe, Scandinavia, and Britain, but its status as a hybrid of public and private forms of subsidy for which disproportionate funding "comes from the private sector."[46] Hacker details not only the interests and groups that this curious hybrid has organized into politics, but also those whose formation it suppressed.

Hacker shows that the US ended up with its hybrid retirement pension system not by elite design and certainly not by popular demand but haphazardly, over time. He traces its provenance to an innocuous feature of the tax code that, since the mid-1920s, has exempted corporate pension contributions and the interest generated by pension trust funds from both corporate and individual income taxation.[47] Initially these were obscure provisions, created to solve an accounting problem, that were almost inconsequential: few individuals paid income tax, corporate tax rates were low, and pension contributions played only a small role in employee compensation. Hacker emphasizes that "the primary motive for creating this provision was almost certainly not a desire to encourage private pensions on a broad scale," nor did any group advocate for them in such terms.[48]

Circumstances that no actor could have foreseen amplified an accounting work-around into a consequential political force. As corporate and individual tax rates increased, the tax exemption became more lucrative for employers and individuals alike. Rather than being taxed to create a universal pension system, employees were spared taxation on the benefits they received (and employers on those they paid). During World War II, when wage controls made benefits packages the only lure that employers could use to attract skilled workers, workers and ultimately unions began to have a vested interest in them. In this context, the Social Security Act proved not to initiate a move toward universal publicly funded pensions but to carry the US further away from them. Hacker notes that because Social Security covered the low-wage workforce at relatively low cost, it freed employers to "target" their significant pension expenditures to workers at the upper end of their pay scale.[49]

Hacker wants to tell a story of "path dependence," not constituency effects.[50] He demonstrates that although the US ended up with employer-sponsored retirement pensions, publicly subsidized by tax expenditures (i.e., foregone tax revenue), that structure "*reflected* business interests" neither at the outset nor even by the 1940s.[51] Rather, the public-private hybrid gradually engendered unlikely alliances against universal publicly funded pensions. It gave conservatives an interest in supporting expanded Social Security coverage. It enrolled labor unions on the side of private rather than public pension provision because employer-sponsored benefits gave them a way to raise compensation and stimulate membership (pensions could be negotiated by the bargaining unit). These interests emerged from "a complex interplay between public and private interventions in which both public and private actors strategically responded to one another over time."[52] To cite the watchword of feedback scholarship, policy produced politics.

Hacker amends this watchword even as he affirms it. He points out that this peculiar hybrid, "private social benefits," creates politics of a specific kind: a "'subterranean' politics . . . far less visible to the broad public, far more favorable to the privileged," and far less vulnerable to attack than directly publicly funded social programs.[53] Hacker identifies program funding structure as a key factor in determining whether or not a social policy is likely to mobilize citizen surveillance or opposition. Because hybrid programs "induce private activities rather than deliver[ing] benefits directly," their costs to the public go unnoticed, and "the scope of conflict surrounding them tends to be more restricted."[54] Proposals to cut antipoverty programs are more popular and occur more frequently than attacks on Social Security. Politicians who dare to mount such attacks meet resistance. Social Security beneficiaries, who are "already organized and attentive," are sensitive to the threat of loss and well positioned to defend their interests.[55]

Hacker suggests that subterranean politics puts advocates for public pension provision at a double disadvantage. Not only is it more difficult for them to organize, it is difficult for them even to make the case that they have lost something. Hacker observes that "even students of social policy do not know exactly how the tax exemption of employer-provided health insurance or pensions has affected the development of private benefits."[56] How is the average citizen supposed to question whether this system is necessary and whether it serves the public interest?

Hacker's concern about subterranean politics can be forcefully voiced in my vocabulary of constituency effects. Private social-benefit provision troubles him not because it fails to reflect some objective measure of the public interest, but by virtue of its constituency effects. Indirect public funding intensifies familiar logics of collective action by favoring the already organized and making it quite unlikely that negatively affected persons will form groups: such persons recognize neither *that* they are affected nor *how* they are affected. Thus, indirect funding configures the political field asymmetrically to the disadvantage of the already disadvantaged.

This analysis has the potential to change the terms of the debate over questions of democratic representation, whether Hacker intends it to or not. Rather than assess public-policy outcomes by the measure of responsiveness, Hacker calls them to account for the constituencies they mobilize — and those they discourage.

Constituency Effects: Direct

Other work on policy feedback has attended directly to the constituency effects of public policy, and specifically to the ways that social-welfare policy constructs beneficiary groups. At critical moments in the development of the US welfare state, this work has shown, responsiveness plays out in reverse. Rather than demanding benefits, constituencies have responded to their disbursement. Feedback scholars offer two different accounts of the dynamics of constituency-making as they have played out in these critical moments. Some use the term "relational," in the manner of Iris Marion Young, who emphasizes that groups are not defined by a "common nature" that their members share but by their relations of enmity and alliance with other groups.[57] Others describe it working in a way that I will call "differential."

Relational and differential approaches to group analysis *both* call attention to how power works in and through groups, but they conceive this operation differently. Relational analyses hold that groups are caught up in relations of power with other groups, and cannot be analyzed in isolation from those power relations.[58] Differential analyses call attention not to the interrelations among groups but, rather, to the practices of division that delimit unities out of social heterogeneities. Differential analyses emphasize group-making, noting how "differences that have been socially recognized" as significant despite having no extrapolitical ground (e.g., race, sexuality, and gender) lend "distinctness and solidity" to identities that are otherwise neither bounded nor fixed.[59] The differential analyst sees power at work not merely *between* groups but in the very process of grouping.

Laura Jensen's work on group benefits in the early years of the US provides an exemplary differential analysis of constituency effects. Jensen argues that the very notion of group benefits was anathema in US politics until the early nineteenth century, when the Fifteenth Congress enacted pensions for veterans of the American Revolution.[60] Prior to the creation of those pensions, the "political and constitutional culture of early America . . . obligated legislators to respond directly to the petitions and claims of citizens on an individual, case-by-case basis."[61] Revolutionary veterans did not organize and agitate for pensions; such a notion would have been inconceivable. Rather, Congress initiated the program to respond to the practical and ethical dilemmas posed by the spectacle of military men aging in penury.

Jensen's work illustrates an important theoretical claim of radical democracy, which is that identities are not freestanding terms; they emerge from dynamic processes of differentiation and othering that acts of representation set in motion. "Veterans" posed a constituency paradox. They were neither organized as a social group nor even recognizable as a subject of ascriptive grouping. In addition, it proved "deceptively difficult" for legislators to specify who should count as a "'veteran' for national policy purposes," as the House and Senate proposals in this area defined this constituency differently.[62]

The House bill aimed to alleviate poverty among those who had served their nation at its birth. For that reason, its bill was "essentially universal," providing benefits to every "commissioned and noncommissioned officer, musician, or soldier" who had served and was poor or otherwise unable to work.[63] The Senate's bill focused not on poverty alleviation but on merit, as attained through military service. It "restricted pension eligibility to veterans of Continental forces *only*—and among them, to men who had served for a minimum of three years or until the end of the Revolution."[64] One might imagine that it would be easy to distinguish between civilians and military men. But such demarcations are not given in fact; they are shot through with values. Making them involves introducing divisions into a heterogeneous population.

Jensen points out that the House and Senate bills deployed different conceptions of desert—one poverty-based and one merit-based—to distinguish "both *between* and *among* particular groups of military men."[65] Jensen underscores the differences among potential beneficiaries and the arbitrariness of their categorization: the "particular categories of citizens that come to be designated in public policy initiatives . . . may not be contiguous with associated social groups."[66] Granting pensions required something unexpectedly more difficult than applying a self-evident distinction between soldiers and civilians. That line remained to be drawn (and would be drawn differently in different policy contexts); because doing so depended on *differentiating* within and among "groups of military men," those men whom the policy rendered ineligible for pensions were effectively marked as civilians despite their service. This is public policy's constituency effect: it brings one group into being by differentiating it against another. Group differences are not the starting point of politics but its project.

Jensen makes a more profound break from a primordialist understanding of groups than do Anne Schneider and Helen Ingram, whom scholars credit with inaugurating a constructivist turn in policy studies. Despite identifying as social "constructionists," Schneider and Ingram direct their attention not to the ways that the design and eligibility rules of social policy *make* groups but, rather, to the value judgments that public policies attach to groups.[67] Jensen emphasizes how the aims and eligibility rules of the first veterans pension carved that group—"veterans"—out of a heterogeneous population of military men. By contrast, Schneider and Ingram take groups for granted, and deem the "facts of group characteristics [to] be real."[68] They explicitly hold only the "evaluative component that makes them positive or negative [to be] the product of social processes."[69] Deborah Stone praises Schneider and Ingram for presenting the "difference *between* groups" as a "neutral description," showing how social construction comes into play only at the moment of their "hierarchical ordering."[70] This constructionism takes up the construction of groups *as* (e.g., deserving, undeserving) without attending to the construction of groups *per se*. This approach differs from that of Jensen, who demonstrates that granting pensions was not just a matter of constructing veterans *as* deserving but of (more or less arbitrarily) *differentiating* some soldiers from other soldiers in order to secure the category "veteran" in the first place.

Joe Soss observes constituency effects at work in much the same way as Jensen in two more recent programs for poverty relief, the now-defunct Aid to Families with Dependent Children (AFDC) and Social Security Disability Insurance (SSDI).[71] He argues that programs like these make differences within a heterogeneous population, and that those differences affect both the security of the benefits and the likelihood that their recipients will organize collectively to defend them.

The beneficiaries of the programs seem quite different, with AFDC having mitigated poverty among unmarried women raising children without financial means, and SSDI providing supplemental income to would-be workers whose disabilities disqualified them for wage labor. Soss emphasizes that "AFDC and SSDI clients actually come from overlapping populations that experience a diversity of vulnerabilities and needs."[72] The "poor" and the "disabled" are not groups, except insofar as they are constituted as such by "eligibility rules [that] cut a line through" a heterogeneous population.[73] Cleavage-making is no mere matter of words. AFDC clients had to endure degradation, intrusive questioning about their private lives, and arbitrary applications of program rules to receive their designated benefits. This treatment made them much less likely than recipients of SSDI to act collectively and politically to protect those benefits.[74] The constituency effects of eligibility rules have palpable "civic effects" on clients of both systems, producing material differences affecting their capacities to act.[75]

Soss's AFDC/SSDI study does more than simply demonstrate that the design of AFDC eroded the political capacities of its beneficiaries. As he emphasizes, it also shows that without programs like AFDC or its successor TANF (Temporary Assistance for Needy Families), the "potent symbolic group known as 'welfare mothers' would fail to exist."[76] Both programs dole out benefits to individuals who "qualify for aid by proving they have specific characteristics that set them apart from normal citizens. Their program participation is a signifier of difference (based on wealth or health), as opposed to an equal citizen's rightful claim on the common share."[77] As policy categories divide populations into groups, they imbue those groups with different discursive grounds on which to make political demands, and with differential capacities to succeed: "politically meaningful groups are not just constituted; they are constituted *as particular kinds of subjects*."[78]

My term *constituency effects* complements what feedback scholars call *civic effects*. The term *civic effects* refers to the ways that features of policy design—such as universality, categorical inclusion as opposed to inclusion by individual application, impartiality, and regularity in program administration—produce a sense of efficacy and civic obligation in policy beneficiaries. Leading studies by Andrea Campbell and Suzanne Mettler on the civic effects of New Deal social policies have demonstrated their constituency effects as well, without using the term. They establish, as Soss has observed, that civic effects are "second-order products" of constituent effects.[79]

Campbell's 2003 book *How Policies Make Citizens: Senior Political Activism and the American Welfare State* centers on the vibrant political participation of senior citizens whom she calls "über-citizens of the American polity" because they vote and make campaign contributions "at rates higher than those of any other age group."[80] She argues that this participation is an *effect* and not a cause of Social Security. Being "both universal and contributory," Social Security conveys to seniors a clear understanding of their economic interests and imbues them with a sense that they are entitled to defend those interests politically.[81] Campbell urges us to regard Social Security as "unusual because it inspires self-interested behavior, which is rare, and because it inspires it in a low-income group, which is rarer still."[82] She links these civic effects to a constituency effect, arguing that the program "fashioned for an otherwise disparate group of people a new political identity as program recipients": "without a government policy conferred on the basis of age, there is no politically meaningful senior 'group,' merely a demographic category."[83]

Actually, seniors had long been a bit more than a "disparate group." Campbell glosses over the constituency effects of the Townsend movement, a federation of clubs that "claimed nearly a fifth of Americans over sixty years old, 2 million altogether" from 1933 to 1935.[84] The movement united Townsend Club members behind the Townsend Plan, which called for a monthly pension to be paid to every citizen age sixty and older who had retired and lived an honest life. Historian Edwin Amenta argues that the "aged had existed as a demographic group with generic problems and issues well before the Townsend Plan came on the scene, but not until its appearance was there a mass organizational vehicle that identified injustices, expressed specific grievances, and made demands for the group as a whole."[85] The club movement and the plan transformed the aged from a "demographic group" to a political one, by inducing "members to think of themselves as a distinct group with a separate identity and interests, including the right to an unconditional, government-granted pension."[86]

Mettler has similarly credited the GI Bill, by way of its "inclusive design, its fair manner of implementation, and its transformative socioeconomic effects," with boosting the civic involvement of its beneficiaries, particularly among those from less advantaged backgrounds. The GI Bill also had constituency effects that resembled the dynamics of differentiation and othering that Jensen and Soss described. Southern states disbursed the benefits of the GI Bill in ways that deepened existing racial cleavages.[87] In addition, the GI Bill was the "first federal policy to directly exclude persons identified as homosexual from the benefits of the welfare state." Historian Margot Canaday has demonstrated how exclusions built into the GI Bill by way of a soldier's discharge status (among other things) created homosexuals *as a class of people* for the first time.[88] It also brought "entitlement and masculinity" together by steering benefits toward "male breadwinners" rather than "single individuals."[89] Its benefit structure not only turned "soldiers to citizens," as Mettler emphasized, but set "homosexuality in opposition to citizenship" and defined the citizen as a straight man.[90]

Civic and constituency effects are enmeshed. As Mettler and Soss have argued, constructions of "citizens' ideas about which groups are deserving or undeserving" not only affect the distribution of benefits, they also "influence how group members perceive and evaluate one another—a feedback effect that has major consequences for the likelihood that group members will want to join together in collective political action."[91] Mettler and Soss, like feedback scholars generally, conceive of policy design as creating groups more than responding to them. Studies like Canaday's on the GI Bill and Soss's on AFDC/SSDI focus on cases that put at stake the movement of a group from ascriptive—with its putative members "identified by outsiders"—to "social"—comprising members who identify with one another (and differentiate themselves against others)—to politically active—functioning as a collectivity that makes demands and defends its interests.[92]

Conclusion

When public-policy initiatives divide a heterogeneous social field into discrete groups, representation as mobilization is at work. Policy-feedback scholarship suggests an alternative way to evaluate whether such representation works for or against democratic ideals. Rather than measure whether a party or policy initiative has responded to group demand, feed-back scholars suggest assessing whether those initiatives have configured the field of conflict in ways that are consistent with democratic values of equality and fair play. My term *constituency effects* gives an explicit name to the effects of power that policy-feedback studies make visible. To ana-lyze constituency effects is to analyze the politics of conflict. It is to regard group mobilization as an index of the institutional biases that organize some groups into and others out of politics, rather than as the expression of a common interest or affinity.

Scholars of mass feedback effects have concerned themselves explicitly with the ways that features of policy design—such as universality, cat-egorical inclusions as opposed to inclusion by individual application, im-partiality, and regularity in program administration—produce a sense of efficacy and civic obligation in policy beneficiaries. Other components— disbursing meager benefits at a caseworker's discretion and making them contingent on intrusive monitoring of the recipient's personal choices— are demoralizing and depoliticizing. Analyses of these civic effects pro-vide one evaluative standard for representation as mobilization. They im-ply that democratic representation is systematically distorted when policy design so stigmatizes a social group that its members are reluctant even to identify with one another, let alone engage in collective political action.

Critics of representative democracy need to concern themselves not only with the stereotypes that get attached to groups but with the division of the social field that gives rise to groups in the first place. My concept *constituency effects* calls attention to the practice of division that Jensen, Soss, and Canaday document. Their work shows how policy initiatives cut lines through heterogeneous populations that could be divided other-wise. Line-drawing not only creates groups but gives material presence to norms about what counts as public service, as legitimate dependency, or as masculinity. I return to this insight in later chapters, where I promote this practice of differentiation or line-drawing as both central to demo-cratic politics and the proper focus of realist analysis.

From the Bedrock Norm
to the Constituency Paradox

Many democrats hold two equally powerful expectations that conflict with one another despite being equally valid. Democracy means nothing if those represented do not exert some form of control over those who speak in their names, yet it means nothing in turn if political representation merely plays out power relations that wealth and social connections fix in place. I maintain, with Nadia Urbinati, that political representation in modern democracies is "*not* meant to make a pre-existing entity—i.e., the unity of the state or the people or the nation—visible"; it cannot do so because such unities come about as effects of acts of representation in the first place.[1] Yet representatives need authorization from their constituencies if they are to govern democratically. Modern representative democracy seems to ask political representatives to do the impossible: defer to constituencies they have necessarily had a hand in making. This notion—that democratic representation must posit as a starting point constituencies and interests that can take shape only by its means—I call the *constituency paradox.*

This paradox casts doubt on interest representation, a commonsense notion about mass democracy that presupposes what I term the *bedrock norm.*[2] Interest representation holds that citizen preferences should serve representative democracy as the "bedrock for social choice" and that representative politics functions democratically so long as the system fosters responsiveness to constituent demand.[3] Interest representation and the norm that underlies it necessarily presuppose that citizens form and fix their preferences prior to engaging with political institutions, acts of representation such as policy initiatives, or the claims and initiatives of candidates, political parties, and elected officials. Political scientists have taken responsiveness to be an operational index and normative ideal of interest representation and have come up with various approaches to measuring it.[4] These studies, as James N. Druckman has observed, "ignore how citizens form policy preferences."[5] Studies of political knowledge and preference formation establish that policy preferences are not cast in stone; rather, constituencies form and interests emerge over the course of the representative process.

It cannot vindicate democracy to find legislators responding to preferences they helped to create. Nor can it be reassuring to observe "consonance" between policy outcomes and public opinion if policies shape preferences in the first place.[6] Responsiveness is hardly a reliable indicator that democratic representation is functioning well. Arguably, it has become quite the opposite—a measure that calls attention to representative democracy's failings rather than its success.

I name the constituency paradox to expose the bedrock norm as a foundationalist fantasy that sets representative democracy up to fail. To believe that citizen preferences ought to have the character of bedrock—and then to find that they do not—stokes prejudice against mass electorates. This chapter asks where that powerful norm originates and explores how a critical analysis of mass democracy might proceed without it. I focus on the work of influential theorists of political representation. Few subscribe to the fantasy of bedrock preferences and many attempt to complicate the unidirectional conception of responsiveness to which that fantasy gives rise.

Even Hanna Pitkin, who established responsiveness as both the ideal and the measure of representative democracy, exposed the bedrock norm as fiction. Pitkin—along with many theorists of political representation succeeding her today—expects people's preferences to change over the course of the representative process. Yet Pitkin and her successors have a specifically pedagogical vision of what such change should involve. They want the representative process to make people better informed and, ideally, more inclined to consider public interests alongside private demands. Despite wanting mass democracy to succeed, these theorists' model of politics as pedagogy flames concerns about voter manipulation that resurrect the fantasy of the bedrock norm and stoke antidemocratic prejudices about the competence of mass electorates.

Pitkin's Constructivist Turn and Retreat

Hanna Pitkin's 1967 classic *The Concept of Representation* is not quite the "standard account" of interest representation that so many scholars have taken it to be.[7] At its boldest, *Concept* sets up the constituency paradox without naming it. But Pitkin sold her own work short when she packed her argument into this nutshell: "representing here means acting in the interest of the represented, in a manner responsive to them."[8] Pitkin added that in democratic regimes, as opposed to fascist ones, the "represented must be somehow logically prior; the representative must be responsive to him rather than the other way around."[9] Representation, in Pitkin's summary formulation, boils down to responsiveness; responsiveness, in turn, must be linear and unidirectional. Pitkin's summary flattened the work that led up to it, a nuanced argumentation that largely called into question the orthodoxy that Pitkin is typically charged (or credited) with originating.

Pitkin set out not to affirm but to launch an intricately argued assault on the democratic "folk theory"[10] that holds that citizen preferences can and ought to be the "principal force in a representative system."[11] She interpreted the leading empirical research of the time as demonstrating that legislators respond to too "great a complexity and plurality of determinants" for citizen preferences to be a driving force in legislative decisions.[12] Even were a legislator to want to accord a constituency pride of place, she noted that constituents seldom hold articulate and well-formed preferences on the bills that actually come before Congress.[13] In the rare instances when they do, the discrete preferences of the members of a district typically do not add up to a "single interest" without autonomous and creative action on the part of their representative to make it so.[14] Pitkin made representation an activity without a model, without certainty, and—in her words—without "guarantee."[15]

If representation cannot take its bearings from the imagined bedrock of constituent preferences, then how is *democratic* representation possible? Pitkin argued that it isn't—at least, not on the model of a "one-to-one, person-to-person relationship" to which folkways and much political science scholarship remain captive.[16] Pitkin proposed that representative democracy should be conceived as systemic, impersonal, and anonymous.[17] For representation to take place, there does not need to be a meeting of the minds between representative and constituency, nor even so much as a meeting. Provided the system is well designed, acts of government may be democratically representative even though "many individuals, both voters and legislators, are pursuing quite other goals."[18]

These bold arguments could and should have dismantled the bedrock norm, as a handful of Pitkin's readers registered. Robert Weissberg emphasized that, following Pitkin, there would be "no historical or theoretical reason to limit analysis to *dyadic* representational relationships."[19] James H. Kuklinski and John E. Stanga recognized that Pitkin called scholars to abandon their static, preference-based model of democratic representation to conceive of it as dynamic, an "emergent property of a complex system of interactions among citizens and government officials."[20] Edward N. Muller suggested indexing representation to the "expressive" and noninstrumental measure of "support" rather than to that of explicit demand satisfaction.[21] Paul E. Peterson advocated that researchers take up a deliberative approach to assess the rationale for constituent support, assessing the "*quality* of the reasons the representative gives."[22]

Astute as they were, these readings had little impact on the way that scholars received Pitkin's text. It is worth asking: How can a text that was so widely read have its most important contributions so thoroughly fail to register? Academic reading habits probably had something to do with it. At least some of Pitkin's readers probably focused most closely on the two chapters of the book that advertised their relevance to debates in political science, sparing themselves the intricacies of her exhaustive survey of the analogies for representation or her critique of Edmund Burke. As these other sections were where Pitkin did most of her unconventional retheorization of representation, readers took her concepts out of the unconventional context in which she presented them.

It did not help matters that Pitkin chose to sum up her bold move with a pallid term—*responsiveness*. Eulau and Karps, two of her more careful readers, recognized that this choice virtually guaranteed that her work would be assimilated to the conventional, unidirectional principal-agent model she had done so much to dismantle.[23] A responsiveness model casts democratic representation in the terms of the bedrock norm, as a dyadic relationship driven by constituent preferences. It also conjures the typical fear that something has gone wrong with democracy when that relationship goes the "other way around."[24]

Even Pitkin could not quite get responsiveness, as a theoretical frame, to work for her. It practically squirmed in her conceptual grasp as she struggled to adapt it to suit her argument, qualifying it as a "potential" rather than a "constant activity," or arguing that government need not actually respond to its citizens but "may be conceived as" doing so "so long as we feel that [the citizens] could initiate action if they so desired."[25] Pitkin went so far as to suggest that responsiveness may be satisfied even if the constituency has not or not yet formulated an interest to respond to and is "unaware of what it [the government] is doing," which may be the case "most of the time."[26] Here Pitkin casts doubt on "responsiveness" as a normative ideal and operational index of democratic representation. She verges on posing my constituency paradox, that democratic representation must posit as a starting point constituencies and interests that often take shape only by its means.

Over the course of her argument, Pitkin amended interest representation in various radical ways. She redefined democratic representation from an interpersonal relationship to a systemic process that is anonymous and impersonal. She also recognized, in a striking departure from influential versions of group theory, that representation often involves acting for an "*unorganized* group."[27] Whereas pluralists like Dahl or Easton assumed that self-organizing was prerequisite to political representation, Pitkin held that group identities and interests emerge over the course of their representation.[28] She emphasized that the "national unity that gives localities an interest in the welfare of the whole is not merely *presupposed* by representation, it is also continually re-created by the representatives' activities."[29]

Wrestling with the various puzzles she engaged over the course of the text—responding to citizens who are "unaware" of their interests or to "unorganized" groups—seems to have brought Pitkin to recognize that democratic representation need not be as quite so unidirectional as she had insisted. In a pivotal passage, she affirmed that democratic representation, understood to require "only potential responsiveness," is "perfectly compatible with leadership and with action to meet new or emergency situations."[30] In such instances, constituencies know too little to give specific direction to their representatives. Responsiveness may well turn "the other way around" if it can be said to exist at all.

Having acknowledged this risky point, Pitkin was quick to caution that representation "is incompatible . . . with manipulation or coercion of the public," and then equally quick to recognize that it is not easy to tell them apart:

> To be sure, the line between leadership and manipulation is a tenuous one, and may be difficult to draw. But there undoubtedly *is* a difference, and this difference makes leadership compatible with representation while manipulation is not.[31]

Something has changed with Pitkin's unidirectionality protocol. No longer does the flow of responsiveness mark the "difference between democratic and dictatorial relationships between ruler and ruled."[32] That difference now rests on a "line" between leadership and manipulation that Pitkin's own arguments render "tenuous" and difficult to draw. She has eviscerated the notions of prepolitical intent, identity, and interest that rested such a dividing line on bedrock.

Or perhaps I take this passage too literally. Pitkin may have had no interest in attempting to specify criteria for drawing such a line, as a normative theorist would do. Jason Frank has suggested reading that "line" in light of Pitkin's commitments to ordinary language analysis: as a distinction that people make in speaking about politics. It is not something to go looking for because it is already in use; it gets invoked whenever engaged publics pose questions about their relationship to power.[33] Understood as such, this line need not give rise to a normative project. There is no need to specify the grounds on which it might be drawn; it exists already.

If Frank is right, Pitkin did not intend to send theorists off on a normative quest. No matter. Just as scholars of voting behavior set out to operationalize responsiveness by devising ways to measure the congruence between constituency preferences and a representative's votes, political theorists have attempted to specify the line between manipulating constituencies and leading them.

Adherence and Resistance to the Bedrock Norm Today

Contemporary empirical research into the formation of political knowledge and public opinion suggests that Pitkin's most radical insights were correct. It shows that in mass democracies people form opinions and political preferences in response to messages they receive from sources they trust.[34] Representatives, as Pitkin made clear, do not simply respond to constituent preferences. They are "active . . . in searching out and sometimes creating them."[35] By vindicating Pitkin at her most radical, this research also turns her protocol of unidirectionality in reverse. In mass democracies, political representation does not typically start from the "bedrock" of citizen preferences.[36] It begins with messaging to which *citizens* respond.

This empirical research, which testifies to the constituency paradox, poses normative challenges to interest representation that theorists of representative democracy today have attempted to answer. I argue that these theorists recognize unidirectionality as a false promise, even as they work from within an interpretation of Pitkin's legacy that sets a premium on education.

Mansbridge Draws the Line

Jane Mansbridge's 2003 article "Rethinking Representation" is method-ologically and conceptually pathbreaking, in part for identifying Pitkin's purportedly "general" account of political representation as just one among three models that can be distilled from empirical scholarship on representa-tive politics.[37] On Pitkin's *promissory* model of representation, voters hold elected officeholders accountable to the principles and policies put forth in their campaigns. Responsiveness matters and follows the protocol of unidi-rectionality: the "voter's power works forward" to hold representatives to the promises they made at election time and the "representative's attention looks backward" to the previously expressed preferences of the constitu-ency.[38] As none of these strictures holds for the other three models, Pitkin's general definition proves to be one among many—a *conception* of repre-sentation rather than a *concept*.[39]

Mansbridge's *anticipatory* representation, the variant that she de-rives from empirical research on "retrospective voting," propels her into the constituency paradox.[40] Retrospective voting is present-minded and backward-looking. Voters assess whether they are better off than they were the last time they voted, especially economically, and they evaluate candi-dates based on performance in office. Retrospective voting prompts antici-patory representation in this sense. It orients representatives not primarily to the "actual [past] preferences of the voter" but to "what they think their constituents will approve at the next election."[41] Rather than simply carry out "what they promised to do at the last election," they must act not only according to the "actual [past] preferences of the voter" but also accord-ing to their own "*beliefs*" about "the future preferences of the voter" at reelection time.[42] Anticipatory representation requires representatives to represent interests and preferences that have not yet taken shape.

Mansbridge emphasizes that legislators may respond to retrospective voting in one of two ways. They might attempt to gauge what a voting ma-jority will want at the next election, by using "public opinion polls, focus groups, and gossip about the 'mood of the nation'" to track and adapt themselves to the electorate's movement.[43] This approach holds true to the bedrock norm by keeping voter preferences paramount. Yet there is an even surer course to reelection: abandoning the norm and making themselves agents rather than followers of preference change. Retrospec-tive voting teaches legislators that their "initiatives have the potential to *change* as well as to anticipate voters[']" positions at reelection time.[44] By doing whatever they can to shape public opinion to accord with their own positions, legislators can prime voters "to approve of . . . actions" they did not authorize in advance.[45] Anticipatory representation turns Pitkin's responsiveness "the other way around" and activates the constituency paradox as it does so.

Mansbridge recognizes the paradox—and it perturbs her. She would like to frame anticipatory representation as a potential entry point for deliberative models of democracy to bear on empirical research. In her words, retrospective voting can allow for a reflexive understanding of " 'interests' (defined as enlightened preferences)" to enter into "what would otherwise be a purely preference-oriented model of political behavior."[46] Yet, insofar as anticipatory representation takes leave of citizen preference as its bedrock, it "encourages us to think of voters" in two distinct ways: "as educable (or manipulable)."[47] That parenthetical interjection— "educable (or manipulable)"—betrays her ambivalence. Mansbridge portrays representatives as at once educators and manipulators; she casts voters as at once learners and potential prey.

This ambivalence impels Mansbridge to a line-drawing project. Quietly amending Pitkin, she argues that empirical researchers bear a normative charge to assess whether any changes they may observe in public opinion "are best described as 'education' or 'manipulation.' "[48] She calls on political theorists to "help" them do so.[49]

Mansbridge transforms Pitkin's pivotal distinction in a small but significant way. She reduces Pitkin's broad category of leadership to a specific activity—education—that links political representation explicitly to competence-building. Education, as Mansbridge defines it, respects and fosters autonomy. It is a "form of influence" that meets two criteria: it "works through *arguments on the merits* and *is by definition in the recipients' interests.*" Manipulation, by contrast, is a form of " 'coercive power' " that is exercised "against the recipients' interests without their recognizing characteristics of the situation that might have led them to take another action."[50]

Mansbridge recognizes that the bedrock norm haunts these alternatives. For researchers to tell the difference between education and manipulation, they would need a politically neutral account either of "the recipients' interests" or of what would count as an argument "on the merits" of an issue. She concedes that "questions regarding voters' interest, in contrast to their preferences," do not have the character of bedrock because they are not "susceptible to certain resolution."[51] Rather than ground it on bedrock, Mansbridge proposes to marry democratic representation to deliberative processes of interest formation. She charges political theorists to help empirical political scientists observe "whether the process of mutual communication with the representative deepens the base on which the voters' preferences rest, or instead introduces misleading considerations or emphases that, given adequate information and the time for adequate reflection, the voters would reject."[52]

Mansbridge imposes a traditional pedagogical frame on political communication that empirical research suggests it cannot always bear. Research shows that political communication can make people more reflective about their preferences, particularly when they encounter frames in competition with one another.[53] But this research also emphasizes that framing aims as much or more to *move* people as it does to *educate* them.

Take an iconic test: people's tolerance for the free-speech rights of "hate groups" like the Ku Klux Klan.[54] One especially well-constructed laboratory experiment exposed college students to competing frames extracted from actual television coverage of a KKK rally that took place at a county courthouse south of Columbus, OH in the mid-1990s.[55] The experiment found that participants "who saw a [television news] story framing the KKK rally as a free speech issue expressed greater tolerance for the Klan than did those who saw a story depicting it as a potentially explosive clash between two angry groups."[56] Researchers built the study so that they could measure whether different frames merely triggered different responses, tapping whatever happened to be at the top of people's heads, or whether participants' views changed because they engaged in a "more deliberate integration process, [to] consider the importance and relevance of each accessible idea."[57] Put differently, researchers wanted to know whether "volatility" in public opinion should be put down to incompetence or its opposite. Should it be taken to indicate that mass publics are highly susceptible to changes in messaging, or that they express understandable "ambivalence" toward issues where competing values are at stake?[58] In the instance of the rally, the authors concluded that frames tapped a "dynamic tension" in popular belief.[59] People were torn between recognizing the paramount importance of free speech and appreciating that "unqualified and unyielding support for [it] may impede other values, such as preserving civic harmony."[60]

I raise this example to identify a tension between Mansbridge's normative impulse to draw a line between manipulation and education and her astute political sense. This study *does* affirm her sense that mass political communication, shaped by the apparatus of "opinion polls and focus groups," should not be written off as a mere "tool" of manipulation.[61] But it prompts unease regarding whether "education" is the appropriate contrast category. Any framing aims at *persuasion*—which, as the authors of the KKK study argue, involves moving people. They describe "political campaigns and persuaders of all stripes" exploiting ambivalence, "using frames as *levers* to move opinion in their direction."[62] People who support free speech cannot be converted to oppose it. They might, however, be persuaded to ban a hate group's rally if they can be moved to weigh considerations of "public order" more heavily than they do those of free expression.[63]

If a campaign succeeds in moving people will it have educated them, manipulated them, both, or neither? Was the free-speech frame in this example "misleading"? Was the public-order frame "educative"? Mansbridge makes an urgent and creative departure from Pitkin's unidirectional account of political representation. Yet she ends up supporting a traditional pedagogical model that ties democratic representation more tightly to voters' educated preferences than even Pitkin was willing to do. I suggest that Mansbridge poses the constituency paradox without engaging it. She has remarkable faith in mass democracy, but her argument proves to reaffirm a focus on individual competence and intensify fears of manipulation.

Saward Changes the Subject

Michael Saward's "representative claim" demonstrates how a (deceptively) simple shift of emphasis can transform a field of study. Saward appropriates Pitkin's classic, general definition of representation—"the making present *in some sense* of something which is nevertheless *not* present literally or in fact"—to emphasize what he terms the "prior" task of *making* the represented over that of making it *present*.[64] This shift from reflecting to making politicizes the aspect of democratic representation that political theorists "often tak[e] for granted—the character of constituency and the stability and ready knowability of a constituency's interests."[65]

The standard conception of representation as speaking and acting for a constituency rests on what Saward terms "an underlying view of representation as *presence*."[66] According to this view, representation is a fact or status conferred by election. It also assumes that "if someone is duly elected to office," they not only become " 'a representative,' " authorized to act for a constituency, but they also—by virtue of that status—become something more, as if by the benefit of the doubt: they now "*are* 'representative'" in the (aesthetic) sense of standing for something beyond themselves.[67] Saward suggests that it is important to prize these distinct aspects of democratic representation apart.

Any representative, whether official, lay, informal, or self-appointed, not only competes to be "a" representative but also struggles to be regarded "as" representative. Winning a free and fair election confers procedural legitimacy, which secures their status. Winning the hearts and imaginations of a constituency is a different endeavor. It involves succeeding in a "performative" sense at making a claim that brings what Saward calls its "object"—its constituency—into being.[68]

In contrast to "representation as *presence*," Saward proposes a rival "underlying view" of "representation as *event*" to bring this performative or "aesthetic and cultural" aspect of political representation to light.[69] Saward emphasizes the work that representatives do to "'make representations' of their constituents . . . to try to get the latter to recognize themselves in the claims being made."[70] Claims "construct verbal and visual" images of constituencies as "'hard-working,' 'good honest folk,' 'family-oriented,' 'patriots,' and 'concerned' or 'worried' or 'angry,'" terms that are metaphorical, evaluative, and comparative.[71] Representing involves acts of picturing to define the represented as possessing "key characteristic X," to establish the representative as "possessing capacity or attribute Y," and only then to lay claim to be representative "by virtue of a certain resonance between X and Y."[72] Tapping this resonance is the "event" of representation, and success is far from within the representative's control. Culture, biography, temperament, and racialized and ethnic differences limit the "links" between representative and represented that can "plausibly be made in a given context."[73] Party politicians pay their pollsters a fortune to sound precisely these limits.

Rather than aim at accuracy in relation to a referent (e.g., constituent interests), representative claims allege demands that people either do or do not step forth to own. As claims-makers, representatives tap existing beliefs and predispositions. They depict "a constituency *as* this or that, as requiring this or that, as having this or that set of interests," in order to distinguish it from and, frequently, put it at odds with some other group.[74] A successful claim may or may not make a persuasive argument. It must, however, create an *idea* about the constituency, about what it is *like*, and a complementary "portrayal" of the representative, that the solicited body both recognizes and accepts.[75] Claims-making can inflame deep-seated prejudices and stereotypes. It can also make visible new lines of conflict and alliance.[76]

Saward is best known for his theorization of claims-making. Many regard his "representative claim" as winning mainstream attention for constructivist approaches to political representation. Some welcome this breakthrough. Others have criticized Saward for proposing an "explicitly non-normative approach" that cannot do the important work of differentiating between acts of representation that promote constituent interests and mere symbolic posturing.[77] This approach leaves no basis on which to make Pitkin's all-important normative distinction between symbolic and substantive representation, the first of these involving a constituency's merely "feeling represented" and the second ensuring that they are actually "being represented."[78] It also renounces the project of "identifying criteria for distinguishing between persuasion and manipulation."[79] As these critics see it, the theorist's role is to make judgments about representative claims, to sort out those that are justifiable in claiming to stand for a constituency from those that are not. Justifiability would depend on whether a claims-maker appeals to demonstrable constituent interests or manipulates a constituency on the basis of its fantasies and fears.

Saward counsels political theorists against assuming this "first order" task of adjudicating among representative claims and constituencies' responses to them.[80] He argues that that those who want to assess the democratic legitimacy of representative claims in a democratic "way"—which, as democratic theorists, we should—must leave it up to the "would-be constituents of claims" to decide whether or not to accept them.[81] He observes that this "approach does not resolve this question [of manipulation] so much as *dissolve* it; if recipients of representative claims accept those claims," then the claims are representative regardless of the "provenance" of the targeted preferences.[82] Theorists who express reluctance to leave these judgments to constituents make themselves "adjudicator[s] of occurrence."[83]

Saward's critique of the theorist as adjudicator, one of the less remarked-upon aspects of his influential theory of the "representative claim," is one of its most powerful. Adjudication involves sorting out claims that are democratically legitimate from those that are not. Saward stands out among theorists of representation for taking constituencies (as he defines them) at their word. Adjudication rests on a pedagogical model where critics assess whether or not constituencies make good judgments about their interests and about the people best suited to represent those interests. Saward defines democratic constituencies as *effects* of claims rather than as their source points. Adjudication displaces the judgment of the constituency in favor of that of the analyst. The constituency will have either responded to, not responded to, or rejected a claim; the analyst presumes to know what the constituency *ought* to have done.

Saward counters that model with a political one based on his unusual differentiation between *audience* and *constituency*. Audience and constituency play distinct roles. The audience for a claim includes all those who "hear, hear about, [or] read" the claim and "respond to it in some way."[84] Audiences determine its *success* or *failure* by propagating, actively commenting on, repeating (retweeting or reposting), or even refuting it. A claim *succeeds* so long as the audience assesses it favorably; it *counts as democratic* only when the constituency takes it up.[85] The constituency includes those named by the claim, plus all those "who judge that the claim is indeed for and about them"—"*under reasonable conditions of judgment.*"[86] Those conditions include "pluralism, contestation, and alternative sources of information."[87]

Saward differentiates between *audience* and *constituency* to embed an empirical observation within a normative distinction. The empirical observation is simple: representative claims "can only work, or even exist, if audiences acknowledge them in some way, and are able to absorb, reject, or accept them, or otherwise engage with them."[88] Empirically speaking, a claim becomes representative when a public takes it up. Normatively, it matters *which* public takes it up: audience or constituency.

An audience can spread a claim but cannot legitimate it. It is not uncommon for audiences to propagate claims and empower claimants a constituency does *not* accept, as when "self-appointed" representatives like Bono or Oxfam claim to represent groups who have not elected them and cannot sanction them.[89] Claims by Bono and Oxfam have succeeded at persuading audiences to donate money or care about global relations of equality that they had previously ignored. On Saward's terms, however, such claims-makers are not democratically representative.

The constituency alone can say that the *subject* of the claim (the representative) speaks and acts for them. The constituency alone can validate the *idea* of the object (itself) that the claim puts forth; only the constituency can say that it recognizes itself as it is depicted or figured in the claim. For normative purposes, Saward calls the constituency the "ultimate judge . . . of the democratic legitimacy of representative claims."[90] For empirical purposes, he breaks the constituency into two parts. There is the *intended* constituency, which is explicitly targeted by the claim, and the *actual* constituency, which includes all those "who judge that the claim is indeed for and about them."[91] The intended constituency may be smaller or larger than the actual constituency. Its being larger indicates that the claim hit home, tapping into grievances even more widely shared than the claimant anticipated; its being smaller indicates that the "claim faces an uphill struggle to be accepted."[92]

Saward's audience/constituency distinction makes it possible for critics to assess claims without presuming to know what people's interests are and who would best represent those interests.[93] The "idea of representative claim-making and claim-reception" directs critics to assess "who may be likely to make claims, the materials out of which claims may be constructed, how they will be targeted, how they may be seen or heard, and what opportunities recipients may have to respond."[94] The claim concept points critics toward assessing a representative claim in terms of its constituency effects. Saward gives critics a tool to differentiate between successful claims and democratically representative ones by calling attention to instances where the response of an audience turns a claims-maker into spokesperson (think of the media response to Gloria Steinem, whom all feminists did *not* accept as representative), usurping for the audience the position that Saward intended to reserve for the constituency. From Saward's perspective, claims matter when they transform the terms of an existing debate or distribution of power. Occupy Wall Street's "We are the 99%" was not an especially accurate claim, voiced as it initially was by citizens of the wealthiest nation on the globe. Yet that claim broke open a public conversation about radical income inequality in the twenty-first century, galvanizing new constituencies and new demands and leading to measurable—if not revolutionary—political impacts.[95]

Saward's work also enables political analysis of claims that galvanize antidemocratic constituencies. Consider the racially stereotyped "Willie Horton" ad that ran during the 1988 presidential campaign to distort public perceptions of risk and inflame tough-on-crime sentiments. The infamous ad featured a mug shot of Willie Horton, a Black man who had been convicted of murder and who, when released on furlough as part of a program that Dukakis inherited from a Republican governor, committed a rape and stabbing. Besides playing into racist stereotypes of Black men and political stereotypes of "soft on crime" liberals, the ad egregiously distorted the facts about furlough programs.

Audiences played a crucial role in selling this ad. Produced by an outside spending group (supposedly without coordinating with the campaign), it aired only briefly on cable television.[96] It might never have found its full constituency had television news broadcasts not picked it up, mostly to excoriate it. Officially, the Bush campaign denounced the message; meanwhile strategist Lee Atwater welcomed it into the campaign arsenal, stating that to beat Dukakis he would "make Willie Horton his [Dukakis's] running mate."[97] Audience response gave this ad a second life that enabled it to reach its intended constituency—conservative voters who put a Black face on crime and despised liberals for being "soft" on it.

This claim, a bid to catalyze conservative identity by propagating a racist stereotype, roused and was accepted by a constituency. Saward's framework enables critics to ask whether that claim—clearly not an accurate representation of Black people, criminals, or furlough programs—was legitimately representative of the constituency it catalyzed without debating whether Bush voters fell for a racist stereotype that tricked them out of voting in their material interest. "Reasonable" conditions of judgment *did* exist. Journalists at the time fact-checked the ad and attempted to put the Horton example in perspective. They reported that Massachusetts was no outlier. Forty-five states, including George W. Bush's Texas, had furlough-granting laws on the books and many of them—including Texas—furloughed people who had received life sentences for first-degree murder. In addition, data gathered by the Massachusetts Department of Corrections showed that granting furloughs significantly *reduced* rates of recidivism.[98]

The Horton ad did its work even though the fact-checkers did their jobs. A conservative constituency emerged to own and validate the idea of itself presented in the ad—and such constituencies must be taken at their word. Rather than question the competence of these constituencies, democrats might instead reckon politically with the historical and cultural contexts that enable this kind of constituency effect. In a nation that Michelle Alexander has described as being "trapped in a cycle of racial reform, backlash and re-formation of systems of racial and social control," is it terribly surprising that constituencies for such ads exist?[99] Constituencies for such ads are readily called into existence. They do not need to be hoodwinked into being. Nor can they be informed or chastised out of existence. They need to be answered politically, by claims-making that aims to mobilize a counterforce.

Conclusion: Politics and Pedagogy

I opened this chapter with the paradox that political representatives in mass democracies have to stand for constituencies and interests that they cannot help but have a hand in making. I have argued that Pitkin and her successor theorists of democratic representation wrestle with the constituency paradox without naming it. They recognize that constituent preferences cannot serve as the bedrock of representation, but they want to count representation as democratic only when it informs constituent preferences. Their approach seeks to tame the paradox.

To Saward, the constituency paradox is no paradox at all but, rather, a relic of representation as presence. Representing simply is constituency-making; it does not need to be tamed. Representative claims count as democratic when they successfully solicit constituencies, whether those constituencies conform to democratic norms or not. A recent article by Vijay Phulwani on Saul Alinsky's realism elucidates a pedagogy of organizing that complements Saward's views.[100]

Alinsky famously maintained that "a community is not a classroom."[101] Residents of a community are not like students who have enrolled in a course they can be compelled to attend. The organizer, Alinsky emphasized, has to "create the conditions and climate in which people want to learn" by meeting them where they are.[102] Organizers for the Industrial Areas Foundation (IAF) are known for taking this stricture quite literally, holding meetings in neighborhood gathering-places and speaking to constituents' immediate concerns, all while resisting the urge to correct the nativist, sexist, or simply ill-informed views constituents may have developed to account for the structural forces that thwart them. IAF organizing begins with the wager that if "people were able to gain the power they needed to take control of their lives in small ways [at the local level], they would be driven by necessity to confront, step by step, the larger structures that limited the exercise of their newly acquired power."[103] There is a kind of competence-building at work here but its success does not depend on educating constituencies in the traditional sense of tutoring them about their interests. As Phulwani notes, Alinsky's first organizing venture with the Back of the Yards Council dramatically illustrates this important point.

Located on Chicago's Southwest Side, the Back of the Yards was populated in the late 1930s by ethnically divided white European immigrants who mostly worked together in the packinghouses and shared the same union but did not share each other's languages, churches, or schools. Alinsky built his first neighborhood council there, only to see it "travestied" a few decades later when members redirected the organization toward segregationist ends.[104] After an initial attempt to correct the council's course, Alinsky recognized that the Back of the Yards community could not be educated out of the property interests that inevitably entangled them—as they entangled all single-family homeowners in the US—in racially discriminatory law and policy. Choosing to counter power with power rather than pedagogy in the traditional vertical sense, Alinsky went to work in the Black community of Woodlawn, to "organize against the organization I set up."[105] Phulwani emphasizes that Alinsky's "solution to the abuse of organized, democratic power was . . . its extension to new groups of people whose interests would challenge those of the old organizations," and perpetuate new forms of domination in their turn.[106]

Representing and organizing are not the same. But organizing counters the theorist's impulse to strike an adjudicatory posture. Rather than sort democratic claims and constituencies from undemocratic ones, Alinsky suggests reading them as an index to existing identities and lines of conflict. Organizers, unlike representatives, see no paradox in the constituency paradox. They know that constituencies come to exist as an effect of organizing practices. They also know that competence is an effect of those practices and not a prerequisite for them. Consummate realists, organizers treat organizing as an activity that produces agents, not norm-conforming subjects. I develop the link between the mobilization conception of representation and realism over the next chapters.

CHAPTER THREE

Can the Realist Remain a Democrat?

Introduction

Political scientists have debated the question of "democratic competence" for decades.[1] Their assessments of the US public follow what Morris Fiorina describes as a "cyclical pattern: one cohort of researchers disparages our citizens and then a succeeding cohort attempts to rehabilitate them."[2] Achen and Bartels stand among the most recent and most influential of the disparagers. Their provocative book *Democracy for Realists: Why Elections Do Not Produce Responsive Government* presents a data-driven takedown of "*all* the conventional defenses" of mass democracy for their failure to "portray human beings realistically, or take honest account of our human limitations."[3] Achen and Bartels counsel those who want to see a "greater degree of *economic and social equality*" in the US to give up the "folk" theories that trust elections to bring those ideals into being.[4] They offer small-*d* democrats a dose of what they call realism: stop kidding yourselves, they admonish, about luring US electorates back into the liberal fold.

The 2016 US presidential election propelled the competence debate out of the academy and onto the front pages of newspapers.[5] Journalists and public intellectuals rushed to make sense of disgruntled white American voters as if to offer their liberal readers a window onto a distant world. Traveling to rural Republican strongholds, training their attention on (mostly) white conservatives, these writers seized the tools of portraiture journalism to unravel what one *New York Times* headline declared "one of the central political puzzles of our time": that citizens who are most likely to benefit from federal government antipoverty programs enthusiastically vote for Republicans.[6] These accounts breathed life into social-science abstractions.

Together, social-science realism and the realism of portraiture journalism set up a zero-sum choice: Realist? Or democrat?

Kristoffer Alhstrom-Vij voiced that zero-sum dilemma in his contribution to a forum devoted to Achen and Bartels's book.[7] Alhstrom-Vij asked, "Can the Realist Remain a Democrat?"[8] He answered "no," that a "realist of the Achen and Bartels type [cannot] still maintain a commitment to anything resembling democracy."[9]

I wonder whether a critic of democracy ought to be a realist "of the Achen and Bartels type" at all. Social science and popular journalistic accounts of incompetence represent themselves as realist in the simplest and most intuitive sense. They purport to accurately describe, either by means of social-science data or slice-of-life narration, the voting behavior of the low-attention, low-information voters who populate mass democracies. This work reduces realism to "being realistic," circumscribing expectations of democracy within the limits of what these authors (believe they) know to be real.

I count myself both a democrat and a realist and cannot imagine separating the two identities. By *realist* I do not mean that I am chastened, practical, pessimistic, cynical, or anything else that attaches to this term in casual usage. I define *realism*, with Jeffrey Isaac, as a critique of power. Rather than take human behavior as a given—a limit of politics—critical realism focuses analysis on the "structures within which behavior takes place."[10] Realists, as I use the term, ask what *motivates* us to act the way we do now, taking motivation to be an effect of institutional design, not a matter of will.[11] Such a definition makes realism a critical project, one that seeks to transform voter behavior via institutional change, change of the built environment, change to habits of thought, and more. Raymond Geuss, one of the more recent and influential advocates of this kind of realism, observes that realists need to be concerned with the "way the social, economic, political, etc., institutions actually operate in some society at some given time," and with the "powerful illusions" that move people to act as well.[12]

I doubt that work that remains stuck on competence as a problem of individuals should count as realism in the first place. It is difficult for people to display competence, or even acquire it, if they do not know that a policy affects them. The competence debate trains attention on the capacities of individuals that James N. Druckman suggests ought instead to be trained on the political communication system composed of "the mass media, interest and advocacy groups, and political elites," which he characterizes as helping "individuals affected by a policy to recognize that they are affected, and how they are affected," and then affording or restricting their opportunities "to take appropriate action in response."[13] Political communication serves first to engage people and then to inform (or misinform) them. The competence debate, which begins by criticizing what little people know, fails to ask important questions regarding whether and how the political communication system engages those people.

Debates about citizen competence take for granted the very assumptions that previous chapters have called into question. They assume that constituencies form around shared interests and identities, and that representation, if it is to count as democratic, normally involves responsiveness to constituent interest. I have argued that acts of representation more typically mobilize constituencies than respond to them, and that mobilization entails forming constituencies, not just activating them. I have introduced the term *constituency effects* to name the marks of identity, difference, and division that acts of political representation leave on the field of political conflict. This chapter brings that concept to bear on the competence debate and the definition of realism it uses.

I dispute social-science and journalistic portraits of mass political incompetence that produce a pessimism about mass electorates that the authors present as realism. I counter these portraits with the work of political scientists Katherine Cramer and Suzanne Mettler, whose analyses of the "politics of resentment" (Cramer) and the "submerged state" (Mettler) reframe incompetence as a constituency effect.[14] Cramer and Mettler detail representatives' self-conscious strategies regarding how to design and communicate public policy. Both theorists are less concerned with citizens' knowledge than with their engagement: whether and how they come to know that a policy affects them. Analyzing constituency effects without using the term, Cramer and Mettler forge an alternate realism—one that is safe for democrats.

Social Science Pessimism

Realist social science today participates in a twentieth-century tradition, exemplified by Walter Lippmann, that enumerates the shortcomings of the ideals of democracy in the face of the "brute facts of reality."[15] Both Achen and Bartels and Jason Brennan target the ideal—central to interest representation—that "preferences are the starting point and the foundation" of representative democracy.[16] They argue that this ideal rests not on reality but on the various "folk theory" versions of democratic theory that imagine "ordinary people" to be capable of forming preferences competently.[17] All three authors refute this notion from what they deem to be a "more scientifically accurate and politically realistic" psychological basis of "group theory."[18]

It turns out that few of us manage to think for ourselves when it comes to questions of policy and politics—even to the simple act of voting. At best, we cast our ballots based on partisan identifications that are more or less convergent with our material interests. In the worst case, we form these attachments *first* and adjust our policy preferences accordingly, selectively taking in evidence to cement the link between the two.[19] In the very worst case, which Brexit and the 2016 US presidential election seem to exemplify, we attach ourselves in that crucial first instance to leaders who channel our anger, appeal to our insecurities, and play up the "status threat" posed to traditionally dominant groups by demographic and social change.[20]

Achen and Bartels argue that it is time for that folk faith, an inheritance of "rationalistic Enlightenment assumptions," to cede to the "group theory" of politics that they trace back to James Madison.[21] Dating back to Madison, and elaborated by nineteenth-century sociologists of mass society Gabriel Tarde and Gustave le Bon, group theory finds its starting point in the "powerful tendency of people to form groups," and for group identities to become epistemological and ethical lodestars.[22] Today these theoretical speculations have earned the backing of "an enormous body of experimental, quantitative, and qualitative evidence" in the fields of social psychology and political psychology—a body of evidence which finds that arbitrary group identifications, not considered reasoning, are "the mainsprings of political attitudes and interests."[23] This work establishes not only that people conform to group cultures and favor in-group members over out-group members, but that they do so based on the most arbitrary distinctions (and even in the absence of conflict between groups).[24] Achen and Bartels emphasize that people derive their political preferences as they do their preferences for food, dress, and religion: not from their self-interests and still less from any commitment to a public good, but from group identities—"affective tribal loyalties" that are impervious to reasoned argument or factual challenge.[25]

Philosopher and policy scholar Jason Brennan derives the argument of his provocatively titled book *Against Democracy* from that same body of research.[26] Brennan divides citizens of mass democracies into two types. They may be "hobbits," who pay little attention to current events, lack the "social science theories and data" to properly evaluate them, and mostly don't vote.[27] Or they are "hooligans," who follow their favorite political party as they do their favorite sports team.[28] Hooligans are more informed and engaged than hobbits, but because they "process political information in deeply biased, partisan, motivated ways," political outcomes would be less "harmful" for everyone (the hooligans included) if they stayed home.[29] And that's what Brennan wants them to do. Rather than giving political incompetents free rein to impose badly made "decisions on innocent people," he calls for restricting voting to the informed.[30] Why shouldn't individuals be required to obtain a license to vote, just as they are in order to drive or to practice medicine, law, or any other expert field that has the potential to do life-altering harm to its patients or clients?[31]

It isn't that Brennan wants to curtail anyone's civil liberties. He simply believes that voting should be reserved to those who "earn" the right to exercise it by taking an examination, perhaps by passing a "voter qualification exam."[32] In an attempt to ward off the obvious parallel to the racially discriminatory citizenship exams of the Jim Crow South, Brennan argues that no one could be *prevented* from taking such an exam, "regardless of their demographic background," and that everyone would be *required* to take it, if they wanted to vote.[33] He suggests that it could be composed of questions from the American National Election Studies (ANES) or the US citizenship exam, or it might instead require basic political and social-scientific background knowledge that makes someone "a good voter" quite apart from their knowledge of specific political facts.[34]

Achen and Bartels do not go quite so far as to take voters' unreliable preferences as a reason to curtail the right to vote. They dredge up Robert Dahl's classic argument for "*minorities* rule," counseling democrats to rely on "interest groups and parties . . . to do the work" that voters are not capable of—asserting majority preferences and holding governments accountable to them.[35] Achen and Bartels serve up warmed-over Dahl without Dahl's cautious optimism. They recognize that interest groups will never serve majority preferences unless minority interests can be prevented from exercising "power in the policy-making process" as they do now, disproportionately "to their presence in the electorate."[36] They also recognize that such a transformation, if it could be successfully designed, would be "bitterly" opposed by the entrenched elites of today.[37] These concessions beg the question of what kind of realists they are—even on their own terms—to think it is realistic to invest faith in interest-group politics but give up on voting.

Brennan is an elitist. Achen and Bartels want democracy to succeed, although they are pessimistic about its prospects. All three theorists might be viewed as the latest in a long line of critics whom Harold Lasswell (counting himself among them) termed "despondent democrat[s]."[38] The discourse of despondency, of which the work of Walter Lippmann in the early twentieth century is iconic, emerged after World War I. Confronted with the power of propaganda to rouse support for that war, scholars leapt to "revise traditional democratic theory by removing the idea of a competent public from its center, replacing it with technocratic experts."[39] Those experts were supposed to teach democratic politicians to use the tools of propaganda for themselves, to "manage the public mind" in the direction of public goods while inoculating US citizens against "antidemocratic ideas and activities" seeping in from fascist Europe.[40] Like Achen and Bartels today, those postwar liberals counted themselves realists. In the 1950s, when right-wing populists appropriated those tools to wage a homegrown assault on civil liberties in the name of anticommunism, the liberals' realism proved stunningly naive.[41]

Achen, Bartels, and Brennan all fall well short of realism—even on their own traditional terms, whose standards require them to offer realistic accounts of voter behavior. All three critics put forth "contrarian" arguments in the name of realism that they justify by appealing to "generic claims about human psychology."[42] John Medearis warns that psychology makes a seductive (though misguided) interpretive lens because it focuses on the limitations of people's cognitive capacities and their emotional motivations at the expense of paying attention to how institutions stage "conflict" and organize relations of power.[43] In addition, Achen and Bartels propose a new *"group theory* of democracy" that treats the concept of *group* as if it didn't itself need to be theorized.[44]

Achen and Bartels depict group formation in primordialist terms, as an expression of *groupiness*, a psychological propensity which they claim is "fundamental to thinking about the beliefs, preferences, and political behavior of democratic citizens."[45] They scramble various "group memberships" together ("being a Protestant rather than a Catholic, a union member rather than not, or a white person rather than an African American or other minority") as if it makes no difference to democratic politics whether a group affiliation is self-chosen or ascribed, based in religion or demography, racialized or treated as normal.[46] They define *identity* as a group membership that is or becomes "central" to a person's "self-concept," without offering any account of how that occurs.[47] Their group theory is primordialist because it lacks a theory of groups *as political*.

This primordialism puts Achen and Bartels at odds with at least one of the founders of group theory, to which they lay claim as a "powerful realist tradition."[48] In his classic book *The Process of Government*, Arthur F. Bentley framed a theory of groups *as political*.[49] Bentley refused emphatically to take groups literally as the demographic foundation for identity. As Mika LaVaque-Manty has argued, Bentley insisted that "groups are irreducible" to the "private interests" or "biological, psychological, or demographic attributes" of the individuals who "make them up."[50] Bentley proposed a strikingly antifoundationalist account of groups emerging only when they become "salient" and "meaningful" in response to political activity; groups neither motivate nor drive that activity.[51] When scholars of political behavior today treat the link between opinion and identity as a psychological predisposition or fact rather than a political achievement, they introduce an essentialism into group theory that was not present at the start.[52] Taking aim at the folk theory of democracy, Achen and Bartels produce a folk theory of their own: a *"group theory* of democracy" that so thoroughly reduces groups to individual psychology as to rule the politics of group-making out of the scope of the analysis.[53]

Portraiture Journalism

The realism of the portraiture journalists writing in the 2010s differs from the realist scholarship of this time but is similarly flawed. Rather than proclaim their realism, these journalists perform it by transposing the naturalism of nineteenth-century painting into prose. They enter into the everyday lives of a disparaged subgroup, aiming for an accurate, sometimes sympathetic snapshot of life in rural America and hoping to convey what in that (remote and unfamiliar to their readership) world motivates the mostly white voters who live there to identify as "forgotten" Americans.[54] Some accounts feature towns whose residents survive off government benefits while voting for Republicans who promise to slash those benefits.[55] Work in this genre, which presents itself as an ethnography of white grievance, plays more explicitly to liberal readers' sense of superiority than Achen and Bartels's work does. These accounts picture Republican voters in rural counties as petulant adolescents who bite the government hand, unaware that it feeds them. Work in a second genre, a journalism of pathos, plumbs the suffering and disappointment that brought white rural Americans to such a point that they would vote for a party whose right wing has gone from more or less quietly dismantling to loudly and explicitly promising to retrench and repeal the very programs on which they depend.[56]

Whether it invites the reader to sympathy or scorn, work in both genres misses the realist mark as well. Portraiture, with its tight focus on subjectivity, has little to say about the institutions that condition subjects' choices. It proves to do surprisingly little to challenge the prejudices about these groups' competence and their lifestyles that some of these journalists set out to dispel. It feeds the incompetence narrative particularly well when it portrays working-class or rural voters forming opinions and preferences based on what "feels" true to them rather than on facts and evidence.[57]

The Pathos versus the Politics of Resentment

The journalism of pathos emerged in response to ethnographies of white grievance, which Thomas Frank launched in 2004 with *What's the Matter with Kansas?*[58] That book, especially its attention-grabbing title and ambitious subtitle—"How Conservatives Won the Heart of America"—promised revelations that his evidence could not redeem.[59] An exasperated Frank chastised the Democratic Party for turning to cultural issues popular with an educated middle class and abandoning the bread-and-butter concerns of working-class voters. This abandonment left those voters open to the "hallucinatory appeal" of a newly minted values conservatism, which lent Republicans a smokescreen for implementing an upwardly redistributive tax policy.[60] Frank's argument, though appealing, rested on an improbable conception of class and an unstated assumption that Larry Bartels laid bare in an academic review that got little popular play.

Bartels asked a telling question that few readers thought to pose: Who is Frank's Republican-voting "working class"? Frank defined class by the measure of educational attainment, not income. Then he quietly populated that category exclusively with *white* non-college-educated voters. Bartels observes that fully 40 percent of those voters "had family incomes in excess of $60,000," a figure which placed them solidly in the middle of the US income distribution.[61] Bartels emphasized that Frank's dramatic claims about Democrats losing working-class voters "depends critically on the assumption, implicitly throughout Frank's account but never stated, that he is writing about [a] *white* working class" defined by education rather than income.[62] Even with this focus on white voters, had Frank looked to the bottom third of the income distribution, the data would have disproven his title. Conservatives won next to nothing there and Democrats lost just 2 percent.[63] That decline would have been offset by including "the votes of *non-whites* without college degrees," who gave the Democrats a "two-point *increase*."[64] That gain would have cancelled out the slight loss among low-income whites.

Democrats did lose significant support among white, non-college-educated, middle-income voters in 2004, but not because Republicans took them on a hallucinatory trip. Bartels argues that non-college-educated white voters knew what they were doing. They genuinely cared about so-called cultural issues, registered the Democratic Party's leftward shift, and voted for Republicans because they felt represented by the Republican Party on issues of value to them.[65] Bartels suggests that Frank's title amounts to false advertising. It promises a sensational "story about [how] 'Democratic leaders . . . have lost touch with blue-collar America,'" when voters of the working class (as defined by income) remained solidly in the Democratic camp.[66]

False advertising or not, Frank's title became a powerful slogan that focused critics on two themes: first, liberal elitism in the Democratic Party; and second, the susceptibility of putatively working-class whites to "values" issues, race-baiting, and nationalism—tactics that make them vote incompetently; that is, against their own economic interests. Arlie Russell Hochschild wrote *Strangers in Their Own Land*, a study of Tea Party supporters in southwestern Louisiana, partly to debunk Frank's title claim—as if his text had proven it. Reframing Frank's narrative of a great con—low-education white voters hoodwinked into supporting a "rich man's 'economic agenda'" by "the 'bait' of social issues"—Hochschild proposes to unwind a "Great Paradox": white rural voters' alienation from government despite their acknowledgment that it pays their bills and battles the corporate polluters that damage their health and destroy the ecosystems on which their livelihoods depend.[67]

Hochschild opens with a compelling portrait of Lee Sherman, a pipefitter who made a dramatic revelation at a public hearing over a fish kill. Sherman disclosed that he had engaged in repeated acts of after-hour dumping of toxic waste into an adjacent waterway, on orders from his employer, a local petrochemical company.[68] Sherman personifies Hochschild's Great

Paradox: How could a pipefitter–turned–whistleblower and "ardent en-vironmentalist" become an equally ardent Tea Party supporter? Sherman bought the Tea Party's small-government agenda—and its attacks on the Environmental Protection Agency in particular—because he felt more "crossed" by the high taxes imposed on him by the federal government than he did by the industry that made him an accomplice in a felony.[69]

Hochschild argues that Tea Party supporters, like Frank's "working class," know their interests well. They want clean air, clean water, and sus-tainable livelihoods, and they know that oil companies have jeopardized all three. But they make a "principled refusal" of government help toward these goals because they see the world, as Hochschild emphasizes we all do, through a *"subjective prism*," a "deep story" or *"feels-as-if* story" that puts the federal government on the wrong side of the struggle for justice.[70] That story depicts people like them as "forgotten" Americans who wait patiently "in a long line leading up a hill," working their way toward the American dream, while others who neither work nor wait patiently cut "ahead of [them] in line."[71] Their Black president abets the cheating (he probably cheated himself to get where he is now) and chases away lucra-tive local jobs with his environmental regulations and Clean Power Plan.[72] Hochschild heard that story, wrote it down, and "tried it out on [her] Tea Party friends to see if they thought it fit their experience."[73]

This is what rural voters look like to people like Hochschild who dare to cross the "empathy wall" that divides them from liberal elites.[74] They rally to the Tea Party out of an *"emotional self-interest*" whose credibility as a source of action-orientation Hochschild affirms, even as she describes it as a "story feelings tell," one that "removes" both judgment and "fact."[75] Hochschild touts emotional self-interest as the "discovery" of her study.[76] It gives her a solvent to use on the "Great Paradox," which she claims no longer appears as a paradox when voters' story-driven motivations are properly understood and respected. She uses her discovery to amend the work of authors like Frank who count only material self-interest as valid.[77] In keeping with realism at its most positivistic, her posture toward this story remains purely descriptive. Yet even as she tells it, people could have drawn those battle lines otherwise, in ways that would have positioned them to side *with* the government in battling corporate irresponsibility and greed.

Hochschild does little to explain why the cleavage broke as it did, po-sitioning these citizens against their government rather than against their employers. Her empathy-fueled storytelling portrays Tea Party southerners voting in packs based on what feels true to them, and being disposed psychologically to feel that the government robs them worse than oil companies do. By defending one feels-as-if story, she ends up affirming a different feels-as-if story, the one she set out initially to debunk: that of rural people's democratic incompetence.

Compare Hochschild's journalistic portraiture to Katherine J. Cramer's study of rural identity in Wisconsin, *The Politics of Resentment: Rural Consciousness in Wisconsin and the Rise of Scott Walker*. Like Hochschild and the rest of the portraiture journalists, Cramer sets out to understand how people in rural areas think about politics. She poses the familiar puzzle— "why is it that many low-income voters who might benefit from more government redistribution continue to vote against it?"—but resists reducing these voting patterns to the psychology or ignorance of people who live in rural America.[78] Cramer attributes them to "rural consciousness," which she defines as an interpretive frame that couples a "strong sense of identity as a rural person" with "a strong sense that rural areas are the victims of injustice": they "do not get their fair share of power, respect, or resources" *because they are rural.*[79]

Cramer emphasizes that "the alliance of Republican and rural is not inevitable. Nor is the correlation between small towns and support for less government."[80] That alliance marks a political victory for national and, especially, state-level Republican politicians who do not "creat[e] . . . divisions" like the one between urban and rural people; they make them into political compass points. Portraiture journalists tend to naturalize those divisions; Cramer sets out to discover the "interpretations of the world that make [them] happen."[81]

Talk of a red state/blue state divide has served as shorthand for the diagnosis that Cramer's book most vigorously contests: the idea that people in the US live their political differences as differences of culture and that such differences are geographically determined and nonnegotiable.[82] For this gross generalization that differentiates *among* states, Cramer substitutes an urban/rural cleavage that forges lines of difference *within* them. That cleavage is neither determined by nor expressive of the facts of geography—even if the language of place makes it easy to naturalize.[83] Cramer recounts how urban/rural differences are made politically by dynamic interactions among rural people and between them and their representatives. The former urgently engage in making sense of their political and economic displacement, and the latter busily craft frames that cast the blame for that displacement on "other residents rather than broader structural forces."[84] Rural identification, as Cramer theorizes it, is a constituency effect.

Not so for Cramer's interviewees, who linked rural consciousness to the apparently straightforward facts of geography. They defined "rural" as everything north of State Highway 29, which they called, tongue-in-cheek, the "Mason-Dixon line." The highway, which runs east–west from Green Bay through Wausau to the Minnesota border, divides the part of Wisconsin that contains Milwaukee and Madison from the rest of the state.[85] Cramer warns that the "physical marker" is deceptive.[86] There's plenty of "rural" land south of Highway 29 in Jackson, Monroe, and Richland counties, which are home to towns like Argyle and Blanchardville (populations 822 and 798 respectively).[87] And "urban" neither refers to a place on a map nor simply expresses coded hostility toward racial minorities (though it is certainly a racialized signifier). Those whom rural people count as urban make up a heterogeneity that cannot be termed a group—"public employees but also liberals, academics, people of color, wealthy people, and people with a different work ethic."[88] The term encompasses everyone whom rural people imagine to be both culturally distinct from them and disrespectful of their way of life.[89]

Cramer studies how rural identity came to have political significance for residents of small towns in Wisconsin. She argues that being a rural person has less to do with what you are or where you live than with how you interpret the world, and speaks of "rural consciousness" rather than "rural identity" to underscore this point.[90] Rural consciousness is oppositional, oriented by "a significant rural-versus-urban divide."[91] It is also bound to "resentment," a term that Cramer uses to describe the emotion that arises from rural people's sense of injustice, their perception that urban people are "eating their share of the pie" and looking down on them as they do so.[92] Resentment involves making sense of power disparities and economic insecurities "as the fault of guilty and less deserving social groups," rather than "the product of broad social, economic, and political forces."[93] It also involves personalizing political differences so as to see them as reflecting not differing "points of view" but rather "fundamental differences in who we are as human beings."[94]

In Cramer's hands, resentment is neither an essential psychological propensity of rural voters nor a cause of group identification.[95] Throughout her book, beginning with its title, Cramer characterizes resentment as a *politics* and not a character flaw. Rather than treat resentment as a psychological root of rural voters' incompetence, she presents it as a "perspective[e] through which they encounter facts and conceive of possible solutions."[96] Each of us might view the world from any number of perspectives—as a partner, parent, or dog owner; as a shop owner, professional, or service industry worker; as a cyclist, swimmer, or cross-country skier; as a person who commutes by car, on foot, or by bus. Which of these perspectives come to matter politically and how they affect our political judgment depends on which questions of policy come up for debate, on the responses they provoke among our associates and friends, and on the messages we hear from both advocacy groups and elected representatives.

Wisconsin has always had a large rural population; that population has not always identified itself in opposition to cities. That oppositional identification has emerged not because rural people were impelled to it by "groupiness." Rather, they were hailed to it by politicians who tapped their perceptions of the protracted economic downturn that began in the 1970s and channeled those perceptions into political demands for smaller government.[97]

Over this period, Republicans turned rural areas red. Rural people registered: wealth disparity (correctly perceived but mistakenly attributed to the distribution of tax revenues);[98] environmental regulation (emblematic of distant government);[99] and a Black president carrying nearly every pedigree of city life (emblematic of their status as outsiders).[100] Cramer answers that familiar question about rural people voting Republican— why do people who "prefer less government when they might seemingly benefit from more of it"?—in an unfamiliar way, one that does not open a conversation about competence.[101]

Cramer acknowledges that the urban/rural divide, like others that have "physical markers," can be "easily exploited" to provoke resentment.[102] Nonetheless, Cramer refuses to put resentment down to geography, psychology, or some other supposedly prepolitical base.[103] She insists that resentment is a style of politics that codes political messaging in the language that ordinary people use to differentiate social groups, as with "the Mason-Dixon line." Rural consciousness affords a foothold for constituency effects, and Cramer devotes the later chapters of her book to detailing how Governor Scott Walker went out of his way to produce them using a combination of policy initiatives and representative claims.

Walker strategically "activated" the urban/rural divide by linking high-profile issues to rural consciousness and then "reap[ed] the benefits of the divisiveness" he helped to "create."[104] In 2010, he crafted arguments against an ambitious public project (a high-speed train linking Madison to Milwaukee) to "resonate" with precisely that rural consciousness, asserting that the project "would directly take money away from regions of the state outside the Madison and Milwaukee metro areas" and deplete resources for spending on "local roads and . . . bridges."[105] His "anti-city rhetoric" framed the train project as a distributive issue when the state might have claimed it as a victory—scoring more than three-quarters of a billion dollars from the federal government to fund transportation infrastructure that would boost the economy and mitigate carbon emissions.[106]

Walker also specialized in storytelling about abuses of overtime and sick pay which cast hard-fought workers' rights as scams of "overpaid public employees."[107] Cramer emphasizes the care he took to equate those employees with "places like Madison" to portray himself as "taking on" the cities.[108] Walker might well have renamed Act 10, the "Budget Repair Bill" that he implemented in January 2011, the "Urban/Rural Cleavage Act." The legislation severely limited the collective bargaining rights of most public employees, modified tenure protections for university professors, cut public employee benefits, and slashed the budgets of state agencies such as the Department of Natural Resources (DNR). It redressed rural people's sense of distributive injustice *without* delivering them any materialrelief.

Take Cramer seriously when she speaks of the *"politics of resentment"*: she presents it as a politics rather than a psychological pathology. She emphasizes that in-group/out-group thinking is learned (we teach it to "each other") and then put to work by elites who fan intergroup animosities to win votes.[109] If they win, they misrepresent their victories in ideological terms, as "evidence that the public has a principled stance on [limiting] the role of government."[110]

Cramer stands out among other political scientists who emphasize the role that social identities, as opposed to issues or ideologies, play in politics for refusing either to treat group differences as primordial or to reduce identification to primitive psychological mechanisms. She explains the puzzle of rural people's preference for smaller government in terms of an urban/rural divide that she does not take literally, as an expression of hostility between demographically determined groups, but represents as an interpretive frame. That frame develops in rural people's interactions with one another and gets taken up by Republican politicians like Scott Walker, who fashioned it into representative claims that rallied support for his budget bills.[111]

Scott Walker neither invented popular animosity toward public employees nor taught locals to refer to a state highway as the "Mason-Dixon line." But his policies made these divisions "readily available for people to grasp onto" as they struggled to make sense of economic and political change.[112] He did not create rural people but "mobilized" rural consciousness into a consequential political force.[113] He endowed it with constituency effects.

The Ethnography of White Grievance versus the Submerged State

Ethnographies of white grievance have appeared in prominent national publications such as the *Atlantic Monthly* and the *New York Times*. Rather than validate the claims of self-proclaimed forgotten Americans, these stories set out to debunk those claims by portraying white rural voters in broad strokes, as people who indulge an ungracious disavowal of the publicly sponsored programs on which they live. Such portrayals are noteworthy because, like Frank's, they oversell their evidence.

In 2018, the *New York Times* devoted many column inches to a profile of Harlan County, Kentucky, which then ranked fifth in the nation for dependence on federal programs. The *Times* oversold its contents with a sensational headline—"Where Government Is a Dirty Word, but Its Checks Pay the Bills"—that invited liberal readers to condescend to the county's approximately 26,000 residents, who reportedly derived more than half their income from Social Security, Medicaid, food stamps, and the earned-income tax credit. Meanwhile, deep within the story, the reporter buried the telling fact that cast its supercilious headline into doubt: The people who benefit most from government programs are not voting Republican.[114] Most likely, they are not voting at all.

The story of Harlan County, Kentucky is not that voters bite the hand that feeds them. It isn't even that voters bite the hand that feeds their low-income neighbors. It isn't a story specific to Harlan County at all. (And if there is a character flaw at work, it afflicts voters from the middle to the upper end of the income spectrum, in blue states as well as red.) What Harlan County's story does feature is the "submerged state" that—by delivering public benefits without fanfare—shapes many US voters' opinions about social policy in general and redistributive programs in particular.[115]

Political scientist Suzanne Mettler's *submerged state* builds on Jacob Hacker's *subterranean politics*.[116] Mettler coined the term to refer to the many costly forms of government aid that operate either indirectly, "by subsidizing private actors to provide social benefits," or through social tax expenditures that benefit individuals "in the form of smaller tax bills or refunds."[117] These forms of aid, which include guaranteed student loans, tax-exempt employer-sponsored health insurance, and the home mortgage interest deduction, cost the federal government much more than it spends on direct-transfer programs to low-income households.[118] Yet being submerged, these state programs rarely come under attack as do their direct and visible counterparts. On the contrary, during a period where "Pell Grants, unemployment insurance, and welfare . . . have deteriorated in value" or "grown more restrictive" in their coverage, the programs of the submerged state have increased in value.[119] Their beneficiaries reap federally sponsored opportunities and capitalize on federally subsidized financial advantages mostly without recognizing them as social programs.[120] Although the submerged state was initially created "by happenstance," in recent decades both Republicans and Democrats have enlarged it, strategically, to deliver public goods and services to key voting blocs without having to bloat the federal bureaucracy or battle the opposition that direct spending provokes.[121]

Mettler reframes citizens' misconceptions about social welfare as being not a problem of competence peculiar to less-educated rural whites, but rather a constituency effect of institutions that miseducate the public across the board. When policy design strategically hides federal government participation, especially in such popular items as employer-provided health insurance or the home mortgage interest deduction, Mettler writes that people "are likely to assume that markets are more autonomous and effective than they are in actuality, and they may well fail to give government due credit for addressing society's problems."[122] If people do not see the federal government providing goods to them, "it makes sense if they conclude that [government] is not responsive to them."[123] That the costs of tax expenditures are mostly invisible while those of direct transfers are broadcast and exaggerated "confounds citizens, blinding them to [the] size, growth, and upwardly distributive effects" of the submerged state.[124] This confounding dynamic persists—even grows—when politicians and advocacy groups draw voters to the polls by rousing anger toward the direct-transfer programs that serve the most vulnerable, while doing nothing to solicit debate over submerged-state policies, the groups they benefit, and the inequities they entrench.[125]

This is a realist analysis, attuned to how structures motivate people to act, and to the misconceptions those structures produce. For the state to surreptitiously sponsor so vast a tapestry of policies and programs makes it difficult for people to assess crucial questions about the role and ethos of government spending: Where would I get a better return on my tax dollars—government or markets? Does the distribution of my tax dollars accord with my judgments about merit, need, and desert? Some submerged-state programs certainly do serve middle-income job-holding homeowners; many of them, however, redistribute social wealth upward to the richest of the rich.

Mettler emphasizes how submerged-state programs frustrate judgment and opinion formation in voters of all kinds. I emphasize that her *submerged state* concept also calls attention to what E. E. Schattschneider would call a *bias* in the organization of conflict that leads to undemocratic constituency effects.[126] That bias shelters government spending programs that benefit easily organized, well-represented groups by making such programs unrecognizable as forms of social subsidy, while exposing to political challenge the programs that benefit the dispersed, disaggregated masses. Compare the home mortgage interest deduction, which persists without a murmur (for two homes, no less), to the perpetual debates over cuts to Medicaid or the Children's Health Insurance Program (CHIP), whose design requires its funding to be periodically extended. Such bias not only distorts democratic judgment and opinion formation but warps political participation by intensifying the elitist dynamics of collective action.

Being highly visible to the organized interest groups that reap its richest rewards, the submerged state amplifies the "political voices of the rich and powerful," whom it equips with both the financial means and self-regarding incentive to protect the status quo.[127] At the same time, it "does little to engage either" the average beneficiary or the general public.[128] These groups carry a distorted picture of the winners and losers from government programs that explains their disinclination to rally around proposals like the Affordable Care Act. Operating in a context defined by submerged programs and aiming to satisfy unmet needs by creating new submerged mechanisms, the ACA faced unfavorable institutional odds: it sought "to transform policies that Americans barely know exist, and to create some new policies that they [would be] unable to see."[129]

Mettler's analysis reframes the phenomenon of people voting against programs on which they depend. No contradiction, paradox, or problem of competence, it is a constituency effect of strategically confounding policy design. She takes a realist perspective on the supposed problem of "uninformed" or "misinformed" democratic decision-making by looking at what politics brings out in people, not what they bring to politics. She attributes people's resentment of government and reluctance to enlarge it to their everyday hands-on encounter with benefits or services whose public provenance is "submerged." She sees no failure of cognition nor expression of tribalist propensities as do Achen and Bartels. If a "feels as if" story is at work here, that story does not begin with low-educated, low-income individuals' perceptions of alienation and betrayal induced by the line-jumping of fellow citizens and a government that abets it. It begins with the distorting effects of the submerged state, which work to convince large swaths of people in every demographic category—including the well-educated upper-middle class—that government is not doing anything for them.

Conclusion

I opened this chapter with a question: Can the realist remain a democrat? Democrats cannot be realists if realism requires accepting the deficient competency of mass voters as theorized by political psychology and measured by survey research and journalistic ethnography. Cramer and Mettler make it possible to be a realist and a democrat by shifting realist analysis of the failings of mass democracy away from a focus on voter competence and onto constituency effects.

Cramer presents her work explicitly as a counterpoint to pessimistic social science. Contrary to the widespread prejudice that "members of the white working class vote for Republicans" out of "ignorance, or perhaps, a lack of sophistication," Cramer documents that rural people correctly judge their economic disadvantages relative to urban life.[130] In rural places wages are lower, people drive greater distances and spend more on gasoline, some expenses (such as the cost of food, electricity, health care premiums, and mortgage rates) tend to be higher, and, particularly in tourist areas, "infrastructure . . . like more highways and larger sewage and water systems, and more police officers, firefighters, and paramedics" costs more than it would in a "nonrecreational county of the same size."[131] Even so, their resentment against city dwellers is not fully justified.

Urban areas do not—as the strategic framings of Scott Walker and other politicians invite them to believe—rob them of their share of taxpayer monies. Per capita, rural people receive about the same amount in public dollars as people in urban areas do—and because they typically receive more from state and federal coffers than they pay in, it could be argued that they end up with the long end of the stick, not the short one, where tax dollars are concerned.[132] Alternatively, it could also be argued that government has done far too little to respond to the economic and technological shifts that have devastated rural people's livelihoods and compromised the ecosystems on which those livelihoods depend. Cramer centers such debates in her book. I draw attention to a different aspect of the story she tells: her account of the politics of resentment as a constituency effect.

Cramer details how Republican candidates tapped rural people's assessments of their situation, whether accurate or not, and crafted a causal narrative to suit the kind of advocates they wanted to be—champions of smaller government and of reining in the privileges of public employees. Some may read her account as redeeming rural people's competence; I read her as resisting the competence debate altogether by deflecting attention away from what individuals know in order to focus on how they come to identify themselves in response to political messaging.

Mettler's *submerged state* concept further enriches this dialogue. First, she shows that rural people are neither uniquely disposed to misperceptions about the public benefits they receive, nor uniquely susceptible to resentment. The submerged state, a phenomenon peculiar to the US, cultivates misapprehensions in everyone who lives here about government functions and the distribution of government benefits.

Second, Mettler demonstrates that constituency effects act on the public and politicians alike. The surreptitious delivery of social benefits contributes to working people's perception that they are not getting their share and motivates them to favor cuts to public spending. That resentment, in turn, motivates policymakers to deliberately enlarge the submerged state rather than publicize government spending, even when such spending delivers broadly advantageous public benefits. The submerged nature of those benefits' public source stokes resentment still further. Thus, acts of political representation produce constituency effects that act back on the representatives themselves.

The next chapter builds on this one by drawing on the work of two mid-century political scientists, E. E. Schattschneider and Jack Walker. Schattschneider and Walker may have been the first architects of democratic realism. They displaced the competence debates of their time by arguing that phenomena such as nonparticipation should be read not as evidence of incompetence but, rather, as a means to "shed light on the bias and the limitations of the political system."[133] I reach back to Schattschneider's work for a portfolio of terms directing attention to the forms of organization that motivate (and suppress) popular participation in mass democracies, and to Walker—who put Schattschneider's analysis to use—for a radical analysis of the institutional biases of pluralist democracy.

CHAPTER FOUR

Realism for Democrats

D emocrats cannot be realists if realism requires accepting that voters are ill-informed and "ripe for manipulation."[1] This chapter argues that it does not. I build a realism for democrats out of E. E. Schattschneider's *The Semisovereign People: A Realist's View of Democracy in America*—a remarkable battle cry of a book that belongs on the field of combat today, sixty years after its publication in 1960.[2]

Schattschneider crusaded against the competence framing of his time. Although he did count as "simplistic" definitions of democracy that put forward "preposterous" expectations about the political activism and engagement of mass publics, Schattschneider adamantly refused to fault voters for what (little) they know.[3] He maintained that "conflict . . . involves the people in politics and the nature of conflict determines the nature of the public involvement."[4] By *conflict*, he meant everything from a riot in the street, to an electoral campaign, to a contest over the direction of social policy. People engage in politics or disengage from it depending on the "bias" of conflict, a term Schattschneider used in an unconventional sense.[5] Rather than describe an attitude in favor of or against a person, group, or thing, *bias* names a structural power inherent in "forms of political organization" to "favor . . . the exploitation of some kinds of conflict and the suppression of others."[6]

Schattschneider's *bias* concept puts forward one crucial tenet of political realism by making it clear that political institutions do far more than simply host political battles; they "discriminate among conflicts."[7] He offered a second tenet by drawing attention to division as a practice of power. Against the primordialist notion that political outcomes are determined by an "equation of forces [that] is fixed at the outset," Schattschneider insisted that cleavage-making comes first.[8] He affirmed that "what happens in politics *depends on the way in which people are divided* into factions, parties, groups, classes, etc.," and that political outcomes depend "on which of a multitude of conflicts gains the dominant position."[9] Politically constituted divisions, by deciding the nature and number of the forces that come to battle, shape the outcome.

Peter Mair, one of the few political theorists to treat *Semisovereign People* to a close reading, rightly credits Schattschneider with proposing "a conception of politics in which the structure of politics itself, and the structure of political competition or political conflict, in particular, helps determine the *terms of reference* for the development and processing of political ideas and demands."[10] Mair credits Schattschneider with identifying how a "prevailing *language of politics*" provides the discursive constraints within which political actors frame their demands.[11] I argue that Schattschneider understands the structure of conflict to do even more than this. It solicits—and discourages—those actors' very formation.

I turn to Schattschneider in this chapter because his work shifts the focus of the debate over mass democracy away from citizen competence and onto *bias*. That focal shift means that rather than ask what citizens bring to politics, it is important to ask what politics brings out in citizens. Schattschneider builds a conceptual vocabulary to call attention to the ways that institutions, with their in-built preferences for particular kinds of conflict and modes of organization, solicit action by some groups and suppress that of others. He counts as a realist in Jason Frank's terms, a critic of democracy who emphasizes the "conflicts, constraints, and possibilities faced by historical actors" as opposed to their psychological dispositions and cognitive (in)capacities.[12]

This chapter elaborates a realism for democrats that draws from Schattschneider's work and from that of an unlikely ally, Jack Walker, who is best known as a scholar of interest groups. Schattschneider battled the group theorists of his time, whom he accused of expecting groups to form and individuals to engage in politics by "spontaneous generation . . . at the grass roots."[13] Walker took aim at a similar stereotype of spontaneity. Like Schattschneider, Walker registered the force of institutional bias. He wanted to explain how some groups could emerge, organize, and establish themselves, while other "elements of the population who are experiencing great distress remain without representation," because they remain unorganized or they organize but are unable to persist.[14] Walker did not juxtapose interest conflict against party conflict as Schattschneider did. He credited interest groups with fostering political engagement, which Schattschneider did not.

In these respects, scholars rightly count Walker a critic of Schattschneider; I establish the two theorists' shared democratic realism.

Democratic Realism and the Autonomy of Politics

Schattschneider's conflict-centered account of politics and his insistence that institutions, not electorates, set the terms of engagement with mass democracy place him squarely in political theory's "new realism."[15] Realism in political theory is quite unlike that in social science, despite their both having emerged out of a similar impatience with political theorists crafting abstract ideals as yardsticks for political practice. Social-science realists like Achen and Bartels ground themselves in empirical findings about voters' tribalism, cognitive limitations, and attention deficits to debunk the "folk theory" that bases expectations for democratic citizenship on an eighteenth-century ideal of deliberative reasoning that twentieth- and twenty-first-century mass electorates cannot hope to meet.[16] Realists in social science trade *ideal thinking* for its opposite, *limit thinking*, premised on "brute facts" regarding democratic incompetence.[17] They make a primordialist move to put the incapacities and failings of citizens first and trim their political expectations accordingly.

By contrast, realists in political theory promote the "autonomy of the political" as a signature tenet.[18] That tenet, Alison McQueen aptly observes, can be more precisely understood to mean "that politics is *not reducible* to other fields or domains" than that it is free of constraints.[19] Political theory realists campaign for the "nonreducibility of politics to ethics" in a field that Bernard Williams describes as characterized by "political moralism," and Raymond Geuss criticizes for "ethics-first" argumentation.[20] Williams coined "political moralism" to identify the habit of treating moral principles either as ends for or "severe constraints . . . on what politics can rightfully do," which depoliticizes conflict in three distinct ways.[21] First, political moralists treat disputes over rival courses of action as akin to "rival elaborations of a moral text"; second, they cast opposed convictions as "autonomous products of moral reason" rather than positions motivated by "historical conditions" and worldly stakes; and third, they engage political opponents as partners in argument rather than rivals in struggle.[22] In "ethics-first" argumentation, political theorists elaborate arguments from abstract ideals rather than in response to the specific constraints imposed by "contexts of action."[23]

Some of the most arresting new realist work reconstructs such icons of "ethical puris[m]" as Mahatma Gandhi and Martin Luther King as realist exemplars.[24] Karuna Mantena and Marc Stears cast nonviolent direct action in Schattschneider's terms, as a political confrontation that aims to change the bias of existing institutions by exposing as contingent such seemingly "immutable and endemic" forms of violence as colonialism and apartheid.[25] Mantena argues that "militant and direct political action" served Gandhi's realist analysis of the bias toward violence that colonial institutions manifest not only in blatantly coercive acts but in beliefs and practices of social hierarchy that have "attain[ed] moral and political legitimacy" over time.[26] Under conditions where violence commands "people's emotional and psychological attachment," Gandhi recognized that argumentation cannot convince an opponent that you are right; it can only "escalate" conflict, charging their attachments with fresh intensity.[27] Gandhi advocated mass civil disobedience to create an "antagonistic relationship" to social hierarchy, to make it show its violence, reveal its contingency, and turn people from "active (even if unwitting) collusion" with authority to active resistance against it.[28]

Marc Stears has demonstrated that Gandhi's realism, and not just his ethics, influenced the Black civil rights movement in its practice of nonviolence. Though movement activists are often credited for taking up nonviolent resistance out of faith in basic American ideals and the American people, Stears argues that as much as those activists may have "longed" to live in a just, fair, and equitable society, they "understood the prevailing American order . . . [to be] characterized by domination."[29] Direct action for them as for Gandhi served to "reveal the fact of domination and . . . illustrate its locations and its mechanisms."[30] It enacted what McKean calls "oppositional" utopianism by using imaginative (and dangerous) strategies of collective action—the lunch counter sit-in, the Freedom Ride, Freedom Summer, and the Freedom Vote—to provoke "surprising reversal[s] of power."[31] This new realist scholarship aims neither to ground political theory, thinking, and action in reality, nor to bring it within the limits of what we know to be real. It aims to make theory an ally of the democratic movements that have struggled to *redefine what people take as real.*

In the mid-twentieth century, E. E. Schattschneider made himself an exemplary democratic realist. He challenged the group theorists of his time to treat nonparticipation as an effect of the bias of privatized conflict rather than a symptom of the cognitive shortcomings, psychology, or even

contentment of mass electorates. As Peter Mair has argued, Schattschneider advanced the notion of the "autonomy of the political" well ahead
of its time.[32] In contrast to the new realists, who defend that autonomy
against the reduction of politics to ethics, Schattschneider insisted that political power is not reducible to social determinants. In battle with midcentury theorists of pluralism, he defended the autonomy of politics against
those pluralists' primordialist or social deterministic tendencies.

Why Voters Abstain: Schattschneider versus the Pluralists

Schattschneider seized his readers' attention with a vivid title—*The Semisovereign People*—that accurately advertised his project. He undertook
to challenge the "schoolbook" notion that in a democracy the people can,
should, and "really do decide" questions of public policy—and that if
they cannot or do not, democracy fails.[33] Equally important is the "often
forgotten subtitle": "A Realist's View of Democracy in America."[34] Schattschneider identified as a "realist," unlike many of the thinkers whom political theorists have canonized in the "revival of political realism" today.[35]
But he did not specify what he meant by the term. He certainly did not use
it to endorse the notion that *power*—not morality, ethics, or ideology—
explains political outcomes. Nor was realism as Schattschneider practiced
it merely reproductive or validating of the status quo. High rates of voter
abstention in mass democracies bothered him. Rather than attribute that
abstention to voters' failings, he asked the realist's question: What motivates it?

Prominent midcentury scholars found an answer in apathy. They took
low turnout rates and other typical indicators of voter indifference as evidence that politics makes scant claim on most people's attention and time.
This premise supplied the ontological foundation for what Lipset named
the "'elitist' theory of democracy."[36] These scare quotes are significant to
Lipset's meaning (although it is typical for his interpreters to leave them
out).[37] Lipset put them around "elitist" to draw a distinction between
elitist *democrats*, who thought mass democracy could survive despite
its tendencies toward elite rule, and *antidemocratic* elitists like Michels,
who framed his own "iron law" of oligarchy as a condemnation of mass
democracy.[38] According to Michels, the gap that inevitably emerges between party leadership and party members makes representative democracy an oxymoron by thwarting members' participation and assuring their

disempowerment.[39] Lipset criticized Michels for subscribing to an idealized and antiquated notion of democracy that counted *"any separation* between leaders and followers as *ipso facto* a negation of democracy."[40] By holding mass democracy to an anachronistic standard, one that the representative system was bound to fail, Michels made himself an *antidemocratic* elitist. Lipset recognized that thinkers like Dahl wanted to rescue mass democracy by rejecting anachronism and accepting a division of labor between representatives and voters. Modern democracy, in such a framing, need not conform to the "ideal of the Greek city state or of small Swiss cantons" to count as democratic.[41] The mass-elite separation could even be mass democracy's "distinctive and most valuable element," provided that elites engage in "competitive struggle for the votes of a mainly passive electorate."[42]

Self-proclaimed democratic "elitists" like Lipset and pluralist or "empirical" democrats like Dahl share an aim and a belief. They aim to defend mass democracy, but they believe that voter passivity is a given. Dahl did not welcome voter passivity. He regarded electoral participation rates in the US as "deplorably low."[43] Although nonvoting troubled him, Dahl doubted that increasing voting rates alone would shore up US democracy. He and other midcentury scholars hoped that a competitive political system with protections for free speech and a free press could compensate for the reduction of participation in voting.

Schattschneider shared Dahl's concern over nonparticipation but he approached it in a strikingly different way. He regarded nonparticipation not as a social fact about mass electorates but as an effect of the ways that "conflict, competition, leadership and organization" work to structure popular choice.[44] When Schattschneider objects to versions of popular sovereignty that "attribute to the people a mystical, magical omnipotence," he emphatically maintains that the limits of popular sovereignty are structural, not cognitive.[45] In the debate between empirical democrats, who take the limitations of mass electorates as givens, and classical democrats, who overestimate those electorates' levels of attention and engagement, Schattschneider strikes an unconventional position. He calls it an "outrage" for survey researchers "to attribute the failures of American democracy to the ignorance and stupidity of the masses," and a "disservice" for theorists to take "no cognizance of what very large numbers of people cannot do *by the sheer weight of numbers.*"[46] Just as a "locomotive can do [little] without rails," Schattschneider argues that mass publics cannot be expected to choose meaningfully—much less act spontaneously—without "a tremendous effort to define the alternatives, to organize the discussion and mobilize opinion."[47]

A Conceptual Framework for Realist Analysis: *Conflict System*

Take the locomotive image as a metaphor for realism as Schattschneider understands it. The rails are the policy alternatives at any given moment that solicit some groups and individuals to ride the train and discourage (or even prohibit) others from doing so. The network of railways and stations makes up the "conflict system," a phrase Schattschneider uses to make visible power that operates through the way the "political system is organized and structured."[48] It denotes the principles (such as universal rights or particularistic demands), governing mechanisms (such as markets and states), and modes of organizing (party, movement, interest group) that either foster or "plac[e] obstacles in the way of organizing the electorate."[49]

Schattschneider emphasized that acts of representation aim first and foremost not to *reflect* constituencies but to *shape* them. He centered his account of democratic politics on what he termed the "conflict of conflicts," the struggle by representatives to solicit constituencies by substituting a dominant "cleavage" (such as sectional conflict) with a new "antagonism" (such as conflict that purports to be based on race) in order to bring "subordinated conflicts" to the fore.[50] He held that conflict over the "direction and location" of lines of "cleavage" determines "the place of each individual in the political system"; it establishes possibilities for alliance and opposition that—because deciding what the "opposing sides are" determines how large they can be—practically decide "who wins."[51]

Schattschneider made himself a renegade in his time and remains one in ours with this argument that interests do not motivate individuals to organize groups and participate in politics; conflict does.[52] He argued that politics is neither a straightforward "conflict of interests" nor a high-minded "intercollegiate debate in which opponents agree in advance on a definition of issues." Rather, politics involves struggle to *define* the issues—"because power is involved in the[ir] definition" and because the nature of the definition in turn affects how "contagious" those issues can be.[53] He illustrates this realist maxim with the charged example of a Harlem riot, which he wields not to warn against the dangers of unruly mobs but to disclose what he terms the "central political fact in a free society": the "tremendous contagiousness of conflict."[54]

Public conflict mobilizes popular action. Private conflict suppresses it. In private conflict the outcomes can be fairly reliably predicted from the start because the "relative strengths of the contestants are likely to be known in advance."[55] Public conflict is different. Its outcome is "determined by the scope of its contagion."[56] Enlarging the "scope" of conflict, by including more people or by altering its frame, "changes [its] nature" and "changes the balance of the forces involved."[57]

The "nub of politics" in a free society, Schattschneider argued, is managing "the processes by which the unstable relation of the public to the conflict is controlled."[58] Schattschneider redirected scholars' attention to the battles that representatives of all kinds—elected officials, social movements, advocacy groups, media outlets—fight to determine which issues to bring to the fore and which to sideline. Schattschneider inspired the *bias of pluralism* tradition of realist analysis in political theory. These arguments, notably by Peter Bachrach and Morton S. Baratz,[59] William E. Connolly,[60] Peter Euben,[61] and Steven Lukes,[62] were important precisely because they did not equate wealth with power; they understood Schattschneider's "conflict of conflicts," which Bachrach and Baratz elaborated theoretically and empirically through their concept of "the *nondecision-making* process."[63]

Groundbreaking as all that work was, Jeffrey C. Isaac has argued that it remained constrained by the behavioralist premise that "power is the empirical causation of one actor's behavior by that of another actor."[64] Although they pointed toward the need to specify the "structural dimension of power," Isaac argues that these various theorists all shared the notion that power is necessarily held by an actor and necessarily exercised "in interaction" with others.[65] Isaac asserts that a genuinely realist social science would understand political power not causally but "relationally," on the model of realist philosophy of science, as an "enduring capacity" that inheres in the nature of a thing.[66] Just as scientists ascribe "conductivity" to copper by virtue of its "atomic structure," Isaac provocatively contends that "social science [should] be similarly concerned with the ascription of powers to social agents, and with the explanatory reference of these powers to agents' intrinsic natures."[67] By "nature," Isaac does not mean an inherent property or essence but a "capacity to act" that is "distributed by generalized and enduring social relations . . . to those who participate in them."[68]

Isaac presses two points against the political theory realists of his time. First, he insists that power exists regardless of whether it can be observed in a manifest conflict of interest or display of action-reaction. One-party rule gives the "Soviet Communist Party apparatus . . . power over Soviet workers and peasants even though it clearly does not prevail over them in situations of actual conflict of revealed preferences"; in capitalist societies, working-class people seek employment rather than revolution; the teacher-student relationship is "one of domination and subordination" even when teachers exercise that power in the students' best interests.[69] Second, he maintains that such relations are "negotiated in the course of everyday life," not permanently fixed.[70] Bosses enjoy a structural power "to supervise production, but tomorrow the workers may strike."[71] Teachers enjoy a structural power in the classroom, "but tomorrow the students may boycott class and conduct their own teach-ins."[72]

Schattschneider's *conflict system* concept pointed beyond transactional power to relational power as Isaac theorized it, as the power distributed by "forms of political organization" that need not be manifest.[73] Agenda-setting focuses on issues. By contrast, forms of organization direct attention to the relations of alliance and enmity that affect whether an issue stalls or commands a following. Schattschneider gave the examples of both "legislative procedure" and—notably—"sectionalism."[74] Paying attention to the institutional biases that convert resources like wealth or Facebook friends into weapons of partisan combat clarifies the counterpart to nondecision: demobilization.

Schattschneider's conflict system represents mass political institutions first and foremost as systems of crowd control, a state of affairs he suggests is not necessarily bad. Schattschneider acknowledges that "the reduction of the number of conflicts is an essential part of politics," because "any political system which attempted to exploit all of the tensions in the community would be blown to bits."[75] But crowd control can serve to exclude as well as stabilize. When it does, the exclusion runs much deeper, behaves far more insidiously, and inflicts more pervasive harm than do the franchise limitations that are spelled out explicitly in law. Exclusion that discourages group formation, "by extralegal processes, by social processes, by the way the political system is organized and structured may be far more effective than [exclusion by] the law."[76] Schattschneider eloquently declared that the "struggle for democracy" doesn't end with winning the right to vote, for the "vote can be vitiated as effectively *by placing obstacles in the way of organizing the electorate*" as by denying people the ballot.[77] Activists who battle *for* campaign-finance reform or alternative ways of voting and *against* voter suppression take this to heart.[78]

Many readers know Schattschneider for calling out the "flaw in the pluralist heaven" (that the "heavenly chorus sings with a strong upper-class accent"). Fewer have registered his insistence that power—whether of elites or masses—is mediated by the conflict system; specifically, any power is mediated by whatever biases in the organization of conflict manage the extent of that power's contagion. Like Herbert Croly, Schattschneider believed that democratic institutions "should be organized so as to stimulate the liveliest possible political interest over the widest practicable political area."[79]

Schattschneider's *conflict system* concept turns the reigning group theories of politics (of his time and ours) upside down.[80] He reframes nonparticipation as an index not of apathy, ignorance, or consent but one of organizational bias. In his words, "abstention reflects the *suppression* of the options and alternatives that reflect the needs of the nonparticipants."[81] Those currently in power have every interest in ensuring that potential opponents remain "self-disenfranchised" by their nonparticipation because their organization and entry into politics could "produce the most painless revolution in history."[82] Battling over "contested terms of reference" will do some of the work.[83] But to change entrenched patterns of participation requires more than a change in the way that issues are framed; it requires a change in the very topography of the fight, the introduction of "a new kind of political system based on new cleavages and *about* something new."[84]

Democratic Realism

The question of how power can "be acquired and exercised by as many people as possible, starting from conditions of widespread inequality and popular disempowerment" preoccupied both E. E. Schattschneider and Jack Walker.[85] According to Vijay Phulwani, the same question also defines democratic realism, by linking "a realist approach to political theory and a radical commitment to democratic politics."[86] Walker forged that link by taking up Schattschneider's conception of conflict as a mobilizing force, setting aside his romantic myths about political parties, and arguing for the value of social protest to democracy in precisely the terms most scholars of the time used to warn against its danger: its capacity to challenge the institutional biases that depoliticize the concerns of society's most "restless elements."[87]

In the 1980s, Walker made his reputation as an interest-group scholar by theorizing the role that "patrons of political action"—federal government agencies, private corporations, foundations, labor unions, wealthy individuals and more—play in political mobilization.[88] Walker's patronage thesis broke a deadlock between the predominant accounts of group formation that dominated the "post–World War II dialogue over group theory."[89] On the one hand, Walker rejected what he termed "Truman's theory of . . . spontaneous generation," which describes groups forming and self-propagating wherever individuals discover common interests, with the emergence of one group frequently touching off "waves" of group formation by others.[90] On the other hand, Walker took issue with the more pessimistic view of Truman's leading rival, Mançur Olson.[91] Olson's "logic of collective action" spelled out the instrumental calculus that depresses political action, particularly where the public interests of large, diffuse groups are at stake.[92] When people can expect to benefit from a collective good whether or not they join the fight to win it, Olson argued that they will choose not to join.

Walker recognized both Truman and Olson as realists of different stripes whose opposing group theories cancelled each other out. If Olson's irresistible logic, realist by virtue of its instrumental calculus, "undermined" Truman's simplistic assumptions about grassroots democratic action, Walker observed that the dramatic post–World War II increase in US interest groups "suggest[ed] that Truman ha[d] the data on his side."[93] Faulting both men for basing their theories on the "psychological and social characteristics of individuals," Walker's patronage thesis shifted the focus of the debate over group formation onto the conflict system—a shift which enabled him to propose a realist insight in Schattschneider's mode.[94] He cast group formation "as the result of the incentives, constraints, and opportunities created by the society's legal system and the intervention in political life of its largest economic, social, and governmental institutions."[95]

Walker's research on interest-group politics shows perceptible affinities to Schattschneider's ideas; the ties are even more visible in the work Walker did at the beginning of his career. Walker studied grassroots social protest, a research agenda that, in the discipline of political science in the early 1960s, was genuinely radical.[96] Walker's controversial 1966 article "A Critique of the Elitist Theory of Democracy" posed an urgent political question: What is the significance of social protest for democratic politics?[97] Imagine the power of such a question at a time when a liberal, representative theory of democracy predominated, characterized by a "marketplace" model that edited violence and other strong passions out of public life.[98]

Many political scientists, including Walker, find that marketplace model most eloquently expressed by Robert Dahl. In 1956, Dahl famously praised pluralism as a stable system for two reasons. First, it is based on "an underlying consensus on policy."[99] Second, "all the active and legitimate groups in the population can make themselves heard at some crucial stage in the process of decision."[100]

It is hard to imagine how any reasonably attentive person could have written such confident words in the mid-1950s, a time when southern whites responded to active organizing by Black Americans with a brutal violence that denied Black people their humanity—let alone their legitimacy. As Dahl published *A Preface to Democratic Theory* in 1956, he likely finished writing it as much as a full year earlier. The year his book spent in press proved cataclysmic. In 1955, white Americans launched their decades-long backlash against *Brown v. Board of Education* (1954). The August murder of Emmett Till sparked southern Black activists to coordinated civil rights organizing. By year's end, activists in Montgomery rallied around Rosa Parks to launch the bus boycott that put the movement on the national stage.

Dahl could not possibly have anticipated these events. Yet is difficult not to be struck by the incongruity between his classic statement of pluralist democracy and the burning South. In 1966, Walker dared to state the obvious, writing that "it is hard to believe, in these days of protest demonstrations, of Black Muslims and the Deacons of Defense and Justice, that the mood of cynical apathy that affects so many American Negroes is an indication of their *satisfaction* with the political system."[101]

This is Walker's thesis about US democracy: that its party system and interest system alike have a bias against "sharp conflict" that is antidemocratic.[102] Party leaders in a "fragmented society" composed of "numerous geographic, religious and racial conflicts" build "*ad hoc* coalitions" around "specific programs."[103] Sustaining those fragile coalitions requires leaders to sideline "highly controversial, politically explosive issues."[104] The interest system further constrains officeholders at all levels of the political system by catching them up "in a web of cross pressures which prevent them from making bold departures in policy."[105] Business leaders' "indirect influence" on politicians keeps them from proposing legislation or even broaching issues that they anticipate would provoke opposition from the business community.[106]

Today's readers should not equate simple *polarization* with Walker's *sharp conflict*. Polarization stalls problem-solving; sharp conflict advances political innovation. Walker praises sharp conflict for introducing new institutions, securing new rights, and encouraging new "political and social mobilization."[107] He defends the social movements that are its agents against those whom he terms "elitist theorists," who picture social protests as "manifestations of 'political extremism.'"[108] Given the bias of the party and interest-group systems, Walker asserts that "it becomes difficult to explain how significant innovations in public policy, such as the social security system, the Wagner Act, the Subversive Activities Control Act of 1950, or the Civil Rights Act of 1964, ever came about."[109]

Walker's biting thesis about sharp conflict should have been the aspect of this article to make a stir. Instead, he was taken to task by an offended Robert Dahl for "compress[ing] the views" of self-proclaimed elitists together with those of pluralist democrats like himself (Dahl) under the misleading phrase "elitist theory of democracy."[110] Dahl had good reason to take offense. Walker attributed to the "democratic elitists" claims that Dahl certainly did not endorse: that "democracies have good reasons to fear increased political participation" and "that a successful (that is, stable) democratic system depends on widespread apathy and general political incompetence."[111] Dahl protested the "appropriateness of the label" in a footnote that he prefaced with an apology for what might "appear to be nitpicking."[112] Dahl acknowledged that Walker could not be blamed for coining the phrase "the elitist theory of democracy."[113] Walker had picked up the "expression from Lipset"—who, Dahl noted parenthetically, "may have had his reasons while writing a preface to the major work of Michels for applying this phrase to Weber, Schumpeter, Parsons, and James Burnham," theorists so heterogeneous they could not possibly constitute a group.[114] Lipset's rationale, whatever it was, did not excuse Walker's "stretching" the term to "cover others" like Dahl himself.[115] Although it bothered Dahl that Walker mischaracterized his views, he seemed even more exercised by Walker's recirculating the expression in the discipline's flagship journal. Doing so lent credence to a dubious intellectual tradition and treated "a pejorative, even . . . polemical epithet" as legitimate scholarly discourse.[116]

The furor over Walker's polemical intervention into contemporary debate regarding where to draw the line between pluralist, elitist, and 'elitist' democrats overshadowed what I believe made his article genuinely disturbing and radical. Take the list of "innovations" Walker credits to social movements' sharp conflict: the Social Security system, the Wagner

Act, the Subversive Activities Control Act of 1950, and the Civil Rights Act of 1964. Note the incongruity in Walker's placing the anticommunist McCarren Act in the company of victories for collective bargaining and Black civil rights. Walker's realism shows itself here, in his frank recognition that not all popular movements conduce to liberal gains. It is also evident in his conviction that conflict is not neutral but, rather, an institutional force that mobilizes *and* demobilizes popular participation. Like Schattschneider, Walker maintained that nonparticipation should be an "intense concern" of democratic theory.[117]

Against the midcentury theorists of democracy who premised their "group theories" of politics on the activities of voters and legitimate, organized interests, Walker read urban uprisings like that in Watts, Black nationalism, and the Deacons of Defense and Justice (a group that organized in 1964 to provide armed protection to southern civil rights activists, and that engaged in armed struggle against the Klan), as indices to the biases of liberal pluralism. Following the realism of Schattschneider and anticipating that of the New Realists, Walker called attention to the "tangible deterrents" that (violently) discouraged African Americans from the simplest acts of registering to vote and turning out to the polls, and to the "weak, essentially meaningless alternatives" that the party system "usually present[ed]to them."[118] He reframed as "elements of rigidity and constraint" features that sustained what the pluralists sold as a stability-creating "underlying consensus."[119] Tight constraints on what Schattschneider would call its "contagion" left conflict to be expressed in forms of protest that Walker characterized in terms he borrowed from the then-groundbreaking work on popular uprisings by British Marxist social historians George Rudé[120] and Eric Hobsbawm.[121] By contrast to theorists in the political science discipline, which Walker faulted for addressing social protest—if it registered at all—as a pathology, Hobsbawm and Rudé were the first to treat riots and mobs with sociological precision and scholarly dispassion. They studied riots and mobs as a sociologist would any other group phenomenon: by specifying their membership, identifying their conditions of emergence, and enumerating their tactics and goals. Walker drew on their work because it enabled him to set aside the moralizing and outraged responses to social protest that were common among scholars and citizens alike; setting those responses aside allowed him in turn to propose a realist analysis that made social protest an index to the biases of the conflict system.

Hobsbawm and Rudé took aim at a persistent stereotype, inherited from nineteenth-century French conservative Gustave LeBon, that characterized the crowd "as irrational, fickle, and destructive; as intellectually inferior to its components; as primate or tending to revert to an animal condition."[122] Both theorists committed themselves to decriminalizing what Hobsbawm termed "primitive rebels."[123] They did so by taking the "disembodied abstraction" of the "crowd" or "mob" and rendering its participants in their particularity as men and women of various occupations, located at various geographical sites (rural and urban), and reacting to varied political contexts (feudal and revolutionary).[124] Their work is striking for the fact that neither one treated these actors to a republican whitewash. On the contrary, Hobsbawm and Rudé deliberately resisted glorifying their subjects as popular heroes or precursors of the working class.[125]

The "crowd" (Rudé) and the "mob" (Hobsbawm) are difficult to register as democratic actors. They are not organized, as workers would come to be with the advent of the labor movement. Participants lack an explicit ideology or "specific language in which to express their aspirations about the world."[126] Rudé claimed that the language would come later, as the revolutionary "ideas of the 'rights of man' and 'popular sovereignty' . . . gripped the popular imagination" in 1789.[127] The food riots that erupted repeatedly in the early eighteenth century as a pressure tactic leveraged feudal expectations about the responsibility of "rulers . . . to control princes and to distribute work or largesses."[128] Hobsbawm also described the dynamics of popular action changing with the eighteenth-century democratic revolutions, which brought about new expectations, inaugurated what Schattschneider would have termed a new conflict system, and eventually saw the institutionalization of both the industrial working class and a style of protest nearly opposite to that of the mob: The "very being" of that protest style, Hobsbawm claimed, "is organization and lasting solidarity, [where]as that of the classical 'mob' is the intermittent and short 'riot.'"[129]

By contrast, primitive rebels were *pre-political.*[130] Hobsbawm coined this term, which Walker took up, neither to denigrate the "mob and its riots" nor to dismiss them as politically insignificant.[131] He and Rudé intended to register the contribution of "social protest" to democratic struggle in situations where there is "no question of overthrowing the government or established order, of putting forward new solutions, or even of seeking redress of grievances by political action."[132] Although primitive rebels did not stand for (or against) anything, and did not aim for much beyond "limited or short-range objectives," Hobsbawm and Rudé held that they did not need to aim far in order to make democratic

gains.[133] To assess such primitive rebels instrumentally, by policy outcomes, risks missing their import in bringing what Schattschneider would
call society's "restless elements" into its conflict system.[134] Walker picked
up Hobsbawm's concept of the prepolitical to characterize a range of
movements—"the Negroes' drive for civil rights, or the Midwestern farmers' crusade for fair prices in the 1890's, the Ku Klux Klan, or the 'radical
right' movements of the 1960's"—that pluralist and empirical theories of
democracy either "overlooked" or denigrated.[135]

From Rudé, Walker took the phrase "trials of strength," which Rudé
introduced to praise "the crowd" for its "legacy to succeeding genera-
tions."[136] Rudé framed a narrative of progress that tied "the sans-culotte,
small freeholder, and cottager . . . to the factory worker and farm laborer,"
and "the machine wrecker, rick burner, and 'Church and King' rioter . . .
to the trade unionist, labor militant, and organized consumer of the new
industrial society."[137] Rudé affirmed, "it is perhaps not unreasonable
to see these earlier, immature, and often crude *trials of strength . . .* as
forerunners of later movements whose results and successes have been
both significant and enduring."[138] Walker borrowed the phrase "trials of
strength" but set its triumphalism aside to credit various social actors,
whether emancipatory or not, who sound out cleavages and give rise to a
fresh division of "factions, parties, groups, classes."[139] Walker described
protesters as instigators of "sharp conflict" whose value cannot be captured when assessed by the instrumental measures of pressure politics:
"By confronting the political authorities, or by locking themselves in
peaceful—or violent—conflict with some other element of the society,
social movements provoke *trials of strength* between contending forces or
ideas."[140] Walker did not credit Rudé specifically for the phrase (he did
list Rudé's work in the bibliography). Still, he used "trials of strength"
largely as Rudé did: to name a disruption with the power to change the
"agenda of controversy" and spark the "political and social mobilization"
of previously marginalized or excluded groups.[141] Social protest succeeds
on Schattschneider's terms, in introducing a new system of conflict "based
on new cleavages" that engages new participants because it is "*about
something new.*"[142]

Walker aimed to do for the social protest of his time something akin
to what Hobsbawm and Rudé had done by decriminalizing the mobs and
riots of the past.[143] Rudé romanticized his "machine wrecker, rickburner,
and 'Church and King' rioter" by casting them as precursors to emancipatory interests (labor, consumer) in advanced capitalist society. Walker

proposed a realist analysis. He took a lesson about power from social protests regardless of whether such protests could be linked to emancipatory democratic ends. He grouped the KKK and " 'radical right' " together with the civil rights and populist movements because he saw all these groups as equally democratic—not in a normative sense, but with respect to this power: all of them could test lines of cleavage that might prove "sharp" enough to change the topography of politics by transforming "friends [into] enemies and enemies [into] friends."[144] Walker did not idealize change as progress. He recognized that sharp conflict can just as readily mobilize groupings by appealing to fear and prejudice as by proposing emancipatory new rights.

It may seem to denigrate these groups to characterize them as prepolitical. Why not argue that rioting *is* politics—particularly for those who are excluded from politics' conventional arenas? Piven and Cloward, also drawing on Rudé, made a forceful case against the impulse to "normalize" social protest and thereby edit out of the picture precisely those controversial movements that featured centrally in Walker's account.[145] They argued that whereas marginalized populations are "easily . . . ignored" when they form coalitions and otherwise cooperate with mainstream actors, those same populations gain real leverage through strikes, protests, and riots—which afford them "some possibility of influence . . . if their actions violate rules and disrupt the workings of an institution on which important groups depend."[146] Protest politics need not be violent, just disruptive. They point to nonviolent civil rights protests in the South that "changed the political calculus" of the national Democrats regarding the importance of holding on to the Dixiecrats. By "activating northern liberals and the growing concentrations of black voters in the northern cities, and especially by enlarging the tide of southern white defections," those protests consolidated both political parties on new geographic bases, completing a process that had begun with the New Deal.[147]

Conclusion

Leading political scientists construct a trade-off: Be a realist or be a democrat. Political theorists today frame an imperative: The democrat cannot *not* be a realist! E. E. Schattschneider and Jack Walker elaborated central tenets of democratic realism well in advance of these contemporary debates.

The autonomy of politics is first among these tenets. Schattschneider maintained that every democrat has to welcome the irreducibility of political conflict to prepolitical divisions. He and Walker both characterized as democratic any action that aims to substitute an existing cleavage for a rival one, so as to transform patterns of enmity and alliance. Both theorists (implicitly) identified political representation as this activity of reshaping the social terrain, but they disagreed regarding where such actions were likely to be found. Schattschneider placed his faith in political parties. Walker valued, and undertook to validate, social movements and social protest.

Schattschneider and Walker alike refused the idea of spontaneous political action. A harmful stereotype that expects political action to materialize without "rails" (to recall Schattschneider's metaphor), this idea disposes critics to see inaction or misguided action as proof of civic incompetence. Democratic realism shifts the incompetence narrative to focus on the bias of conflict. Both Schattschneider and Walker argued that conflict draws people into politics. They both maintained that political institutions do not simply host conflicts but select among them. The incompetence debate treats the effects of institutional bias as immutable conditions of politics—something no democrat can afford to do.

Schattschneider and Walker let me flip Achen and Bartels's title around: By their focus on conflict as a mobilizing and demobilizing political force, Schattschneider and Walker sketch the contours not of *democracy for realists*, but of a *realism for democrats*. Rather than charge democrats to give up on mass political institutions, such a realism foregrounds the in-built preferences of the conflict system and its effects on political cleavages and political mobilization. Democratic realism values the irreducibility of political conflict to social cleavages. It celebrates as a central strategy of mass-democratic politics the "displacement" of conflict from one antagonism to another, given the potential of such displacement to activate what Schattschneider called the "relatively invisible people."[148]

Mair has argued that Schattschneider worried above all about the "process of consolidation" that occurs every time the conflict system re-forms around a new political cleavage.[149] Schattschneider understood that modern democracies have a tendency toward "inertia" that Walker theorized with his argument about sharp conflict.[150] The work of these two scholars is enormously important today for making plain the democratic threat of *sorting* as Levendusky describes it—a self-fulfilling thesis about political division. A representation of the field of politics as divided into opposing camps that are said to be socially determined, claims about sorting reduce political conflict to the primordial. As political acts that deny their own political character, such claims forge divisions that develop an especially pernicious inertia. The next chapter develops the point to which this one has led: that democratic realism calls critics to worry less about manipulation than about sorting.

CHAPTER FIVE

Manipulation

How Will I Know It When I See It?
And Should I Worry When I Do?

That friends of mass democracy should feel a profound concern about manipulation is easy to understand. These scholars inherited that concern from Pitkin; empirical research into "framing effects" on political knowledge and public-opinion formation subsequently stoked their fears.[1] Political scientists are voicing those fears . . . and political theorists are attempting to come to their aid. Most recently, concerns about manipulation have sparked collaborative efforts between political theorists and political scientists who imagine, as Pitkin did, that precision in conceptual analysis could clarify both empirical observation and normative judgments about politics.

In 1980, political theorist Robert Goodin wrote a prescient and insightful book, *Manipulatory Politics*, refuting exactly that idea. Goodin argued that many of the most perplexing observational challenges derive from "ethical ambiguities" that cannot be resolved by a more precise definition.[2] Goodin gave the example of political scientists taking "false cues" from political philosophers about power.[3] They "go off searching for concentrations of social power in full confidence that, if and when they find them, they will have revealed something ethically important about their societies," as if power were "necessarily evil" and "normative conclusions follow immediately and necessarily from its discovery."[4] Power, according to Goodin, raises ambiguities that cannot be resolved by definitional fiat. People welcome power when they commit themselves to break a bad habit or start a healthy one, submit to a contract, or even fall in love.

Anyway, issuing fiats is not political theory's job. Casting off the "piggy-back" model that pictures empirical observation taking its marks from the "well-established conclusions" of political theory, Goodin proposed that political theorists might instead slow that rush from discovery to condem-nation.[5] He picked a hard case on which to put his alternative model into practice: manipulation.

Few democrats regard manipulation as ambiguous in any way—ethical or otherwise. Goodin made a counterintuitive argument, affirming that lies, propaganda, and other "familiar modes of manipulation present fewer problems than commonly supposed."[6] Either they do not "qualify as manipulatory at all," or, if they are manipulatory, they are neither so persistent in their effects nor so uniquely available to the powerful as to be genuinely worrisome.[7] The really troublesome forms of manipulation go "largely unnoticed," Goodin argued, because they tend to be "impersonal and self-perpetuating."[8] They "cannot be traced to the activities of any-one in particular but only to the relentless workings of systemic bias" that affect us all, not just those whom the educated imagine to be especially vulnerable.[9]

Forty years ago, Goodin proposed a conception of manipulation as an "impersonal" exercise of power that is enabled by the organization of political institutions rather than by the cognitive failings or psychological vulnerabilities of citizens.[10] This decoupling amounts to a realist shift in Schattschneider's sense of the term, redirecting attention away from the failings of individuals and onto the biases of institutions. This work carries a lesson for those thinkers who worry about the content of political mes-saging today. Rather than attempt to sort the educative from the coercive in political communication, Goodin directs critics' attention to the com-petition *among messages*. He advises critics to pay attention to "who wins regularly," to use those patterns to determine the "biases of the political system," and to focus on those biases rather than on the content of the messages or the particular vulnerabilities of targeted subgroups.[11]

I enlist Goodin's work in this chapter to argue that manipulation as it is commonly understood presents a misplaced worry. It results from ex-aggerated claims about elites' capacity to shape public opinion as well as from a too-tight focus on the quality of "individual level opinion," a focus that distracts critics from analyzing the forces motivating those opinions.[12] With respect to the collaboration between political scientists and politi-cal theorists, Goodin aims to lay the "foundation for empirical studies with a sharper *evaluative* focus."[13] This evaluative focus involves adding to the empirical scholars' question—"How will I know x when I see it?"—a question that they frequently do not think to ask: "How worried should I be when I do?"

The Ambiguities of Manipulation in Democracies

It may seem impossible that targeted messaging could worry democrats too much in this twenty-first century, where strategic deception has played such a large role in several defining events to date. Think of the Iraq War, launched by US president George W. Bush (with the cooperation of British prime minister Tony Blair) on the false pretext that Saddam Hussein's regime harbored illegal weapons of mass destruction. Or recall the political consulting firm Cambridge Analytica, whose coupling of psychological profiling to viral disinformation may or may not have influenced the outcome of the Brexit vote and/or the 2016 US presidential election.[14] The Cambridge Analytica story as it was initially reported made many people feel that online marketplaces and social media—that vast communications and commercial network that is also a vast data dragnet—have swept even the world's most mature democracies into a consummate era of lies and propaganda: manipulation as it is commonly understood.[15]

Targeting may make a compelling story but empirical research on opinion formation suggests that worry over targeting is misplaced. Leading political-psychology scholars have argued that the "whole body of studies on framing" has "gone terribly wrong."[16] By testing framing effects on individuals in experimental settings devoid of context, this work has made "citizens look like puppets."[17] In the real world of policy and election campaigns, framing meets resistance from people's "established views, sentiments, political orientations, or values," and must compete against messages from opposing camps.[18] Dennis Chong comments that researchers' many "examples of how public preferences are susceptible to framing effects and heresthetic, or agenda-setting, maneuvers," amount to "discoveries . . . made after the fact."[19] In real time, framing is fraught with uncertainty. After-the-fact reconstructions make the process of influence look too easy and exaggerate the power of elite communications. Whatever the consulting firms promise, politicians quickly learn that they can do little to influence what people believe. Framing strategies are most successful at affecting which issues attract people's attention and influencing the considerations people bring to bear on those issues. But framing cannot make people care about things that do not matter to them, nor push them to form opinions in light of values they do not hold.

Political theorists have similarly questioned the assumption that equates strategic speech with manipulation. It seems obvious that to be *against* strategic messaging is to be *for* democracy. Even if frames do no more than prioritize "our thoughts and actions," the effect will still be to make us seem "unfree," with "our autonomy . . . threatened."[20] Terence Ball argues that politics is a rhetorical practice. It centrally involves "using language to move people to think and act in ways that they might not otherwise."[21] Contrary to those who hold that "only truth-telling and 'the forceless force of the better argument' should hold sway," Ball insists that "manipulation of a certain sort has its proper place in democratic politics," particularly in moments that turn the course of history.[22] James Bohman extends a similar argument to the "speech of the social critic," which he contends can neither be analyzed nor appreciated for its democratic contributions so long as one assumes that the "rhetorical effects of speech are the result of manipulation or power."[23] When a public or polity is in the grips of ideology, the social critic needs recourse not principally to argument but to "irony . . . , metaphors, jokes, and other jarring means of formulating utterances, so as to restore the conditions of possibility of communication itself."[24]

Just as speech that moves people has democratic uses, so too the critique of manipulation has undemocratic ones. Ball warns that a preoccupation with manipulation as "disinformation, appeals to prejudice," and demagoguery has been "one of the stock weapons in the arsenal of aristocrats and other opponents of democracy."[25] George Eliot brings this abstract counsel to life in her lesser-known historical novel *Felix Holt: The Radical.*

Eliot's novel takes place at a time of struggle over the franchise in Britain that stoked fears of the effects persuasive speech might have on less-educated populations. She composed the book during the lead-up to the Second Reform Act of 1867, which doubled the electorate in England and Wales by enfranchising many working-class renters, small landholders, and tenants. But she set it in 1832, just after the passage of the Great Reform Act. That first act left workers unsatisfied and restive; it enlarged the House of Commons to provide representation for working-class towns but stopped short of reducing property qualifications for voting or standing for office. Eliot's title character, Felix Holt, gets caught up in that unrest. In an election-day riot on the local manor, he ends up mistakenly charged with manslaughter. Holt appeared to have led the assault when, in fact, he had attempted to divert the crowd onto a harmless course.

Felix's predicament illustrates the problem of framing messages for an unlettered public. Eliot lets her readers in on the thoughts of Holt's ally, Reverend Rufus Lyon, as he reflects on the warnings he has received from his own political backers that Lyon's word is not likely to help sort out an affair limned by an already-confounding discourse:

> Lyon "cared intensely for his [own] opinions, and would have liked events to speak for them in a sort of picture-writing that everybody could understand. The enthusiasms of the world are not to be stimulated by a commentary in small and subtle characters which alone can tell the whole truth; and the picture-writing in Felix Holt's troubles was of an entirely puzzling kind: if he were a martyr, neither side wanted to claim him."[26]

Eliot's Lyon might be read as posing the dilemma of manipulation in conventional terms, expressing concern that it is easier to move "the enthusiasms of the world" with "picture-writing" in broad brushstrokes than with the "small and subtle characters" of truth. But he also might be heard to affirm, with Ball, that language moves publics to judge and act.

Maybe it does not trouble Lyon that publics are susceptible to picture-writing so much as it does that Holt's "troubles" do not lend themselves to it. No portrait of Felix is likely to sell him to the Tories or the reformers as their "martyr."[27] Possibly Lyon laments not popular incompetence but his own impotence. A minister who is no master of picture-writing in any case (let alone in a case so "puzzling" as this one), Lyon is ill-equipped to persuade and "stimulate" a following for Holt's defense.

To accept that political speech moves people as much or more than it educates them is to acknowledge the irreducible "ambiguities" of manipulation as a concept.[28] Yet political theorists yearn to separate *manipulation* from *leadership*, and they do so pedagogically. Mansbridge identifies *manipulation* with deceiving others about their interests or creating "conditions of choice leading others to make a choice not in their interests," and contrasts it with *education*.[29] James Fishkin defines it as persuasion by "misinformation or strategically incomplete arguments," and contrasts it to *deliberation*, which persuades by "a dialogue or debate in which accurate information is available" and the other side has its say.[30]

The worry that politicians deceive people about matters of truth and fact drives leading political-theoretic accounts of manipulation.[31] Even

Ball, who so astutely identifies concerns about manipulation as the discourse of an elite, remains committed to drawing a line between acts of manipulation that serve democracy and those that undermine it.[32] He falls back on the familiar opposition between deception and education to frame "*democratic manipulation*" as speech that "educates and inspires [people] to be better democratic citizens," and aligns "*undemocratic manipulation*" with secrecy, lies, disinformation, and "playing to (and upon) the fears and prejudices of the citizenry."[33] Each of these scholars dwells on exactly the forms of manipulatory politics that Goodin believes democrats need least to fear.

Manipulation as Acting Deceptively

Goodin's *Manipulatory Politics* defines what ought to concern democrats about manipulation in strikingly political terms: not that people are misled but that one person or group exercises an unchallenged hold on the will of another. For Goodin, being for or against the interests of a subject is not intrinsic to the "*concept* of 'manipulation' as such," nor is "withholding or distorting information."[34] These are *methods* of manipulation, to be sure. But to build them "into [its] very definition" is to end up with an "unduly narrow" conceptualization of the term.[35]

Goodin defines manipulation as "power exercised 1) deceptively and 2) against the putative will of its objects."[36] By setting aside the noun *deception* for the adverb *deceptively*, Goodin makes a conceptual leap with a fine distinction. Ball, Mansbridge, and Fishkin assume that manipulation involves deceiving someone *about* something, specifically their interests or a present or future state of affairs. Goodin argues that manipulation involves *acting* deceptively. The deception lies in the way that the manipulator conducts him- or herself, exercising power over someone while contriving to conceal that he or she is "doing something to them that they should be resisting."[37]

In Goodin's account, lying is incidental to manipulation; the critical component involves "bending another's will."[38] The proper contrast is not with providing education or information but with an "open display of power."[39] Manipulation at its core involves getting someone to do something that it is generally understood they would not have done otherwise, by employing "techniques" of power that hide its exercise "at the time of the act."[40]

For Goodin, lying, rabble-rousing, disinformation, even playing to the symbolic politics of racial identity and resentment—these practices either do not count as manipulation or give little cause for concern if they do. Take the "Kansas" narrative about white rural voters' manipulation by identity politics. Should playing up the symbolic rewards of white identity count as manipulation? Goodin recognizes that those rewards are no less real than "any material commodity," particularly when they are associated with marked forms of status, like titles in eighteenth-century France or whiteness in the US.[41] People are not manipulated into desiring or defending such markers of status; they genuinely (and understandably) desire them. Although they cannot simply be educated out of their desire, they will stop wanting those markers when the markers no longer count for anything, when the structures of privilege that anchor them have been dismantled.

Goodin also maintains that "dog whistle" politics is neither as secretive nor as subliminal as it is made out to be. Those who identify with whiteness know perfectly well what they are meant to hear in references to "forced busing" or "American carnage."[42] As for those who unknowingly respond, the signal often loses its power once the tactic is revealed.[43]

Lying and secrecy, two other highly charged topics, count as manipulation by Goodin's definition, but he argues that neither one is particularly worrisome. In modern bureaucracies, secrecy was difficult to maintain even before the internet made it possible to leak classified files with a keystroke.[44] Lies may be effective in the short term, but they can and in many cases will be exposed by journalists, advocacy groups, and political rivals, all of whom have incentives and resources to do so.[45] Even when lies are "difficult to expose," Goodin observes that "they can often be counteracted by other lies."[46] This statement, surprising to those who define manipulation in terms of lying, is consistent with Goodin's principal concern, which is to ensure that no one person or group monopolizes the power of messaging and framing. As he sees it, democrats need worry less about politicians lying than about their opponents not being able to counter-frame those lies, whether by correcting them or just telling a rival story.[47]

Goodin reaches similarly deflationary conclusions about another mode of manipulation that looms large in the popular imagination: that of the spellbinding speaker who so skillfully plays on the emotions of the audience that they are "swept away by stirring words before they know what is happening to them."[48] According to Goodin, rhetorical manipulation of this kind would be worrisome if more speakers could pull it off, but few orators are that good.[49] Ordinarily, when an orator whips a crowd into a frenzy, Goodin speculates, the "listeners realize fully well what they are doing—they are self-consciously going on an emotional binge."[50] They have not come for an argument but for a carnival. This they know. There can be no manipulation where there is no pretense.[51]

Goodin regards as iconic of manipulation not the sound and fury of the spellbinder but the subtler tactics of the measured speaker who "misleads people who are sincerely trying to be rational."[52] He identifies rhetorical trickery of two kinds: *veiled speech* and the *debasement of political language*.[53] Veiled speech activates audience prejudices under the cover of apparently sound argumentation by way of hidden presuppositions or implications, or by using metaphor to make invidious comparisons or spurious analogies.[54] Think of how the phrase "war on crime" frames the task of law enforcement in violent terms to justify militarizing domestic police forces so that they can "wage" it successfully. Recall the State of the Union address in 2002, where George W. Bush's phrase "axis of evil" (penned by David Frum) lumped North Korea, Iran, and Iraq together as if they were not vastly different regimes, and cast them all outside the reach of diplomacy. Veiled language is more manipulative than lies or secrecy, but Goodin proposes that it may not be worrisome, at least when leaders use it on "people who are sincerely trying to be rational," because it can be disarmed by "simple exposure of the tricks involved."[55] He also emphasizes that the use of veiled and coded language by oppressed groups engaged in both covert resistance and outright counterattacks against entrenched elites is nothing to denounce.

The really troublesome forms of manipulation go "largely unnoticed," Goodin argues, because they tend to be "impersonal and self-perpetuating."[56] Goodin holds up as exemplary the debasement of language, as manifested both in the hyperbolic claims of radical politicians and in bureaucratic doublespeak.[57] Think of how often politicians use such words as "crisis," "Holocaust," "rape," and "lynching" to describe events that are anything but. Or imagine reading every word in a credit-card contract or tax code. Neither of these examples comes immediately to mind as manipulative because they do not strike us as deceptive. Who could have missed the intended effect when then–Supreme Court nominee Clarence Thomas referred to his confirmation hearings as a "high-tech lynching"? Who doubts that legal waivers or tax or election laws are deliberately written to confuse?

Goodin argues that such modes of speech are manipulatory because they work on a different level than speech aiming to influence beliefs about issues. They alienate individuals from politics, discouraging their political engagement by making them believe that no political speech is trustworthy, regardless of the speaker. This process of alienation is, in Schattschneider's terms, a *bias* that troubles Goodin because it loads the deck against the disempowered. Widespread cynicism toward political discourse and discourses of advocacy need not trouble elites who have wealth, influence, and other means of exercising power. For those members of the public whose power resides in mass organizing, the debasement of political speech—the vehicle of mobilization—robs them of what may be their most potent "political tool."[58] Debased language may inhibit popular organizing even more if doublespeak makes it difficult for disempowered people to look at a law, rule, or settlement and discover that it gives them cause for "grievance."[59]

Goodin gives us reason to count the Cambridge Analytica story as manipulative but not for its most sensational aspects—the psychological profiling and targeting of the especially vulnerable. The gross manipulation lay in Facebook's default data settings. Individuals who accepted a few dollars to take a personality survey or thought it would be fun to learn which *Game of Thrones* character they were shared masses of data with political operatives—their own plus that of unknowing friends. To sensationalize the story by focusing on targeting certainly beats the drum of fears about democratic competence. Makers of algorithms had actually found a way to target susceptible people! They managed to deceive conspiracists! Authoritarians! Paranoids! And then the algorithm makers turned their targets out in sufficient numbers to sway an election! The targeting story sells but there is as yet no rigorous evidence that the algorithm worked.[60]

People may or may not have been deceived. Facebook certainly acted deceptively. Working without opt-in consent but with the willing, joyous participation of its distracted, or whimsical, or bored-at-work users, it turned an anodyne pastime into a political weapon. Manipulation occurred without anyone lying to people about their interests. And it preyed on more than the low-education voter.[61] Questions of targeting are beside the point.

Manipulation in Empirical Research

Maybe Goodin's late-twentieth-century arguments no longer suit our twenty-first-century media environment. Or maybe his work was actually ahead of its time. Goodin aimed to decouple observations of manipulation from assumptions about interests. He attempted to redirect analysis of manipulatory politics away from the "activities of anyone in particular" and toward the "relentless workings of systemic bias."[62] And he argued that manipulation-as-deception can be disarmed, provided it is possible to counterframe or even "counter-lie" falsehoods and expose trickery. These various claims now stand validated by two distinct strands of empirical research, one on public-opinion formation and the other on persuasive messaging. This research suggests that the most common forms of manipulation escape the familiar opposition between education and coercion. They call for a critical framework that trains attention away from the epistemic quality of individual beliefs and toward the systemic conditions under which political opinions and judgments are formed.

Can Presidents Manipulate?

James N. Druckman and Lawrence Jacobs's innovative study of presidential polling looks for manipulation where most people would expect it: at the intersection between presidential opinion polling and political messaging.[63] They paired archival research into the communications-strategy memos of three different presidents with statistical analysis of those administrations' private polling data to observe what presidents want to know about voters' beliefs and how they try to sway voters based on that knowledge. The study made an unexpected finding: for the most part, polling helps enable "presidents and their aides" to evade issue-based politics altogether.[64] The presidents studied by Druckman and Jacobs used polling strategically. Rather than poll to "manufacture support for their policies," a practice that social science shows to be ineffective, they pursued "a more limited but realistic strategy" along two distinct lines.[65] First, the presidents polled for nonopinion, to identify "weakly held attitudes or gaps in public knowledge" that left open areas for the exercise of either influence or discretion.[66] Second, they used polling to support "image priming," a kind of discussion around issues that aims first and foremost to affect the characteristics people attribute to a president or politician, not to change where the public stands on a matter of policy.[67]

Polling for nonopinion allows presidents to "widen their latitude on policy" and to "avoid policy direction from voters."[68] Save for their enduring interest in the highly prized segment "of the electorate that [is] affluent, well organized, and/or politically valued," whose preferences politicians feel bound to serve, these administrations designed their private polling neither to track and respond to people's issue positions nor to influence them.[69] Nixon made an especially strategic use of private polling to "pinpoint openings of voter disinterest" where he could "stake out conservative positions that quieted his restless base" without alienating swing voters.[70]

Issue priming works deceptively. It seems like issue talk but isn't. It aims not to inform or influence public opinion about policy but rather to redirect voters away from making judgments about politicians on the basis of "government policy" and toward "concentrating on perceptions of [politicians'] personality."[71] Nixon, for example, did not seek to change (hostile) public opinion toward the Vietnam War; instead, he used "foreign affairs to remind the electorate that he had been a competent, strong leader abroad" who could "achieve results."[72] Reagan emphasized his tax cuts "to bolster perceptions of his strength."[73] This is not to say that politicians can cut their image to suit, any more than they can change voters' preferences at will. Image priming is constrained by voters' preconceptions. In Nixon's case, all the priming in the world would not have made him seem likable; his advisors wisely counseled him not to waste resources trying.[74] Nixon's polling, and his messaging, focused on soliciting "grudging respect for his character in seeking a workable path" out of Vietnam, not on changing perceptions of his warmth or trustworthiness.[75]

This research is significant because it challenges one of democrats' great hopes—that leaders use polling to track and respond to people's issue positions—even as it mitigates one of our great fears: that polling gives leaders a tool to change those positions. It also demystifies the myth of the so-called bully pulpit, the (misplaced) hope or fear that the White House affords presidents a platform from which to alter the content of public preferences. The pulpit image of presidential power leaves a central assumption about the representative relationship intact: that it is and should be based on issues even as it tries to impose issue preferences from above.

Polling assists presidents in practicing what I call *representation by misdirection*, a use of power that is both manipulative in Goodin's terms and worrisome. It is manipulative because it involves acting deceptively. Using issue priming to "distract attention from unpopular policies" and image priming to redirect the focus toward "advantageous issues and personality traits," presidents manipulate the electorate without withholding information from or misinforming them.[76] Disarming public opposition to specific political agendas while simulating issue talk and responsiveness, misdirection impoverishes individuals' political judgment. It also systematically redefines the "nature of representation." By using the White House polling apparatus "to telescope the president's relationship with voters into a relatively small subset of issues that are salient and to recast his link to citizens from government policy to the nonpolicy dimension of personal image," US presidents beginning with Nixon have subtly—and deceptively—shifted the metrics of democratic representation in ways that favor likable politicians who avoid inconvenient truths.[77]

Do Voters Make Judgments?

The second body of empirical research that vindicates Goodin reconsiders existing findings on persuasive messaging. These studies find that early work in the field exaggerated individuals' susceptibility to political messaging. In real time, framing meets resistance from people's existing views and faces competition from opposing messages.[78] Following decades of experiments that tested frames one at a time, researchers have begun to design framing experiments to model the "clash of political arguments" by modeling the dynamics of framing and counterframing.[79] This pioneering experimental work on "*competitive* political rhetoric" confirms what Goodin would expect: democrats' intuitive fears about manipulation are misplaced.[80]

When political communications have to contend against "competing messages . . . sent by opposing parties,"[81] the competition stimulates individuals to "more careful evaluation" of elite messaging.[82] Competition among frames not only "reduces the likelihood that individuals will base their opinions about an issue on a skewed subset of beliefs"; it also makes them "more apt to see through weak frames"[83] and "tend[s] to stimulate individuals to deliberate on the merits of alternative interpretations."[84] Competition provides voters a measure of critical distance from political messaging. It sparks people to exercise some discernment in choosing what to believe and makes them measurably more likely to be moved by the relative strength of a frame than by its frequency of repetition.[85]

It is reassuring to learn that competitive political rhetoric stimulates people to recognize alternate framings and to think more carefully about which framings strike them as plausible, pertinent, and "strong."[86] If competition supports some measure of political judgment in mass publics, it does not go so far as to deliver on the elusive deliberative ideal of decisions reached by the unforced force of the better argument. Battles among messages conclude with the emergence of a "strong" frame, which temporarily suspends the exchange of reasons. A strong *frame* rarely equates to a strong *argument*. It persuades more by virtue of "its source and the cultural values and symbols it evokes" than by its "validity or relation to evidence."[87] Strong frames typically sway people because they make "more intuitive sense," tapping readily available stereotypes, or appealing to "goals such as homeownership and open space that [hold] special meaning" in a particular context.[88]

Politicians use strong frames to create a sense of shared values with their audience, making metaphorical use of terms like *war* or *family*, invoking compelling ideals like *justice* or *choice*, or tapping aversions to "preferential" treatment or "special interests." Moving someone by invoking a value they hold is neither lying to them nor misinforming them, although such strategies may well involve "bypassing" reason, which would qualify as manipulation in Goodin's terms.[89] Even so, Goodin would likely not find them especially worrying. Either such rhetorical strategies can be exposed or—even if they stand uncorrected—they can be countered, wherever the power to move people with loaded terms is "equally accessible to all."[90]

Chong and Druckman's empirical research concludes in a position similar to Goodin's. Rather than worry about the truth value of frames, they concern themselves with the robustness of competition among those frames—because competition provides "citizens with the freedom to choose."[91] Their work demonstrates that the "quality of the electorate's judgments" depends not primarily on competence but "on the nature of political competition and, more generally, on political institutions, such as the party system and the media that shape political debate."[92] Chong and Druckman confidently approach frames "from a political perspective" rather than an epistemic one, affirming that strategies such as framing and priming aim above all to "move people in the intended direction."[93] Regardless of how educative the dynamic of framing and counterframing proves to be, they value it for making people less likely to be moved by the first thing they hear, or to adopt uncritically the position of their political party or friends.

Justifying the Iraq War: Deception or Manipulation?

This chapter has argued that the public furor over targeted messaging and scholars' preoccupation with deception miss their mark. I have also drawn from research suggesting that mass political judgment relies more heavily on discursive competition, an "external force" on opinion-shaping, than it does on the veracity of political messaging.[94] These arguments prove their worth when applied to an episode from the lead-up to the Iraq war. The justification for that war became notorious as an instance of political manipulation. It won this notoriety, one journalist has argued, for the wrong reasons. I enlist Goodin to help correct the record.

The story of the machinations that preceded the 2003 invasion of Iraq by a US-led coalition received two different tellings. Most people will remember a version conforming to a manipulation template that is relatively straightforward: elites rallied support for the war with a theatrical lie regarding Iraq's possession of weapons of mass destruction (WMDs). This version, which I will call the *deception* story, was widely told and was taken to exemplify manipulation in all of the conventional senses that Goodin finds mostly unthreatening. The *manipulation* story was something else. It had a harder time finding an audience (or even a publisher) in the US because it lacked drama and theatrics. It involved leaders acting deceptively rather than deceiving.

In June 2005, the *New York Review of Books* published the manipulation story in a riveting narrative titled "The Secret Way to War," American journalist Mark Danner's urgent recounting of the significance of the Downing Street memo.[95] The memo reported a July 2002 secret meeting among high-level British government officials who discussed the justification for and likely pathways into the Iraq war. The memo had been released in the UK by the *Sunday Times* one month before Danner's account came out. Its publication immediately prior to the parliamentary elections in May 2005 contributed to a shattering loss for Prime Minister Tony Blair's Labour Party. In the US, editors of the major newspapers dismissed it for bringing to light "nothing new."[96]

Danner's account is important for asking why this memo, which caused an electoral cataclysm in Great Britain, initially received little coverage or commentary in mainstream US newspapers. To the US public and its daily news editors, UN chief weapons inspector David Kay had told all there was to tell back in January 2004, when he revealed that there never had been any WMDs in Iraq. The deception had been unveiled over a year before the Downing Street memo's release. What more could remain?

Danner is adamant: the Downing Street memo was revelatory—not for verifying that the US went to war in Iraq on a bogus premise, but for confirming "for the first time . . . that President Bush had decided, no later than July 2002, to 'remove Saddam, though military action,' that war with Iraq was 'inevitable'—and that what remained was simply to establish and develop the modalities of justification."[97] The memo details the collusion between the British and US governments to work those "modalities of justification," to establish—or better, *stage*—a "pretext" for the war.[98] In Goodin's terms, it reveals world leaders plotting to act deceptively.

Back in 2002, British heads of government pressed US leadership to court public opinion by simulating a fact-based pathway to a justified war. The Bush administration agreed. In an October address to Congress, George W. Bush issued an "ultimatum" to Saddam Hussein: declare and destroy all remaining weapons of mass destruction or "the United States would 'go into battle, as a last resort.'"[99] If the search yielded nothing, no matter. The administration planned to defy what a Bush advisor called the "reality-based community," prosecuting the war via an act of power propped up by propaganda and patriotism.[100] In the post-9/11 climate, US leadership imagined the reality-based community to be small and the mainstream media disposed to play along.

Danner's riveting account makes a bid to reframe what many people took to be the most serious offense of the Iraq war. He weighs Bush's orchestrated ultimatum more heavily than he does Colin Powell's lie to the UN and counts the memo as significant for having revealed it. This point is so important to Danner that he repeats it. "Though 'the UN route' would be styled as an attempt to avoid war, its essence, as the Downing Street memo makes clear, was a strategy to make the war possible, partly by making it politically palatable."[101] Danner clearly believes that staging the process of justification offended standards of democratic legitimacy more egregiously than did lying about the weapons themselves. But he does not fully articulate why this should be so. Goodin can help him.

The Downing Street memo catches George W. Bush ginning up public support for the war by simulating a decision process for those who sincerely wanted to be moved by "reasons rather than rationalizations."[102] This pretense counts as manipulation not in the textbook sense but in the sense that Goodin believes worthy of concern. Bush "deceiv[ed] others in pretending to play according to rules which [he] then proceed[ed] to violate."[103] The administration concealed that it was "doing something" to a reason-seeking public that such a public would otherwise resist.[104] Even leaking the memo was not quite enough to counter the manipulation because Bush's *acting deceptively* could not register as sharply as the vivid spectacle of Colin Powell's multimedia lie.

Conclusion

Take this lesson from Goodin's work and the empirical scholarship that bears it out. Deception, secrecy, and targeted communication fund their political impact primarily from discursive environments where they stand unchallenged, rather than from the gullibility of mass publics (or subsections thereof). Also, rumors and misinformation of other kinds are most effectively refuted by "statements from an unlikely source—a person who makes proclamations that run contrary to their personal and political interests"—rather than by a partisan opponent or someone who is perceived to have an ax to grind.[105] The tactics that many take to constitute the threat of misinformation are not, as Goodin shows, devastating in themselves; they become devastating only when competing messages are drowned out or neutralized.

If critics and even friends of mass democracy would take this lesson, they must focus on the systemic conditions for public-opinion and judgment formation, rather than on the truth or falsehood of individual beliefs. They must set aside the problem of competence for a new question: How well do current institutional and political conditions foster the potential of competitive political rhetoric to support political judgment in the ways that experimental research suggests it can—by exposing individuals to multiple communications and stimulating them to take rival messaging into account? They would also set manipulation, as the textbooks define it, to one side. This story from the Iraq War gives one example of an instance where the preoccupation with *deception* made it difficult to get a hearing for information shared to unmask manipulation in what Goodin considers its more threatening form: that of acting *deceptively*.

This chapter also brings back the claims I made earlier in this work about sorting and the value of plurality. I have noted that scholars provide rival explanations for sorting. One prominent and influential line of argument presents sorting as something that voters do and explains it as the expression of a psychological propensity that drives group identification. I take my lead from a constructivist alternative that explains sorting as a picture or representation with political effects. Elites represent the public to itself as divided from the outset into opposing, socially homogeneous teams. This division, a political act posing as a prepolitical condition, overrides the values and issue preferences that cut across both sides. Over time, it opens an epistemic gulf: what counts as fact-based reasoning to you sounds like partisan dogma to me.

The more the public pictures itself as prepolitically divided, the less competitive the discursive environment is likely to be.[106] The less competitive the discursive environment, the less open individuals will likely be to the correctives Goodin identifies for garden-variety manipulations.

Journalists and opposition politicians may hunt down lies and root out secrets, but their work goes to little effect if publics cannot or do not read their accounts. Or read but do not credit them. Wherever people "don't just *hold* opinions [but] those opinions [are] the sum of their personality," the dynamic interaction between frames and counterframes shuts down; take issue with one of them and you risk being "shunned."[107]

I turn now to focus on a corrective: *plurality*. I use this term as radical democrats define it, to name the "radical unfixity" of social relations that allows political actors and movements to draw new cleavages and craft unprecedented solidarities.[108] Absent plurality, it is difficult for mobilization to do its work of constituency-making. I develop this argument over these next two chapters, where readers will encounter a shift in tone and methodology. Up to now, I have made a point of engaging in dialogue with empirical research and examples from politics; the next two chapters are primarily interpretive, aiming to build an argument from works of political theory that set plurality's value to democracy into bold relief.

CHAPTER SIX

Debating Constructivism and Democracy in 1970s France

L ate twentieth-century debates in French political theory about the meaning and significance of the French Revolution broached fears and questions over manipulation that Anglo-American political scholars and public intellectuals still debate today. In the 1970s, prominent French polit-ical theorists divided over one of the central questions of this book, which is whether political representation follows from social relations or whether it creates social groups and positions them in relations of enmity and alli-ance. I have defined political representation as constituency-making and suggested that plurality, the "radical unfixity" of social relations, supplies the enabling condition for that work.[1] It allows political actors and move-ments to sculpt conflict in potentially world-transforming ways.

This chapter reaches back to late 1970s Paris, to the period that has been called the "antitotalitarian moment," to justify this link between radical un-fixity and democratic politics.[2] In the lead-up to the French bicentennial, prominent French intellectuals debated the "proper relationship between 'the political' and 'the social'" to determine the political legacy of the French Revolution: democracy or totalitarianism?[3] That Cold War question may seem remote from the concerns of this book. Yet the debates of the antito-talitarian moment in France bear on the central concerns of this book.

Lefort and Furet agreed that the French Revolution had set politi-cal representation loose from its moorings in what had been regarded as prepolitical social hierarchies.[4] I suggest that this interpretation cast the Revolution as materializing the constructivist turn. The revolutionaries transformed this notion that political constituencies are (and always have been) politically made from an abstract premise to a guiding principle for the design of the National Assembly, the Revolution's foremost democratic institution. Lefort and Furet concurred in recognizing modern democracy's revolutionary origins; they parted over the question of whether that origin made modern democracy a vehicle for values of liberty and equality or a threat to those values.

Lefort courageously held this question open. Furet's influential reading of the French Revolution settled the matter for a generation of French scholars. In the 1980s and 1990s, such prominent intellectual architects of French liberalism as Marcel Gauchet and Pierre Rosanvallon followed Furet's dictum that liberals should be against the Revolution, which he taught them to regard as "a founding pathological moment whose legacy democracy in France has had to overcome."[5]

This chapter stages a debate that never quite occurred because Lefort and Furet traded opposing arguments without making their rivalry explicit. As Samuel Moyn has demonstrated, Furet derived the basic architecture of his own argument from a "brilliantly vulgarized" rendering of Lefort's.[6] Lefort answered Furet in a review of *Interpreting the French Revolution* that is a masterpiece of indirection. Without a hint at their points of disagreement, let alone at Furet's hostile takeover of his work, Lefort deftly turns Furet's tactics against him. He interprets Furet's project as Furet did Lefort's—to align it with his own. I return to their (non) exchange to offer a different interpretation of its outcome. In my rendition, Lefort—not Furet—gets the final word.

The debates of the antitotalitarian moment have the potential to change the distribution of power in today's contest between proponents of a constructive approach to political representation and their critics. In the story as I tell it, Lefort's account of democracy gives the constructivist position the upper hand. His concept of *the political* changes the terms of a conversation that many critics of mass democracy have focused on the threat of manipulation. Lefort proposes *the political* to make the problem of ordering the social visible to democratic political theory and to elevate openness to reordering ("indeterminacy") as a primary democratic value.[7]

The "Antitotalitarian Moment" in France

In the 1970s, antitotalitarians tutored by intellectual historian François Furet saw the risk of totalitarianism in a modern democracy that lacked robust social bonds and social associations with which to counter "the political," which they identified with abstract individualism and political voluntarism.[8] Furet's widely read text *Interpreting the French Revolution* traced this threat to the Jacobins, whom he denounced for engaging a radical remaking of the social guided by the brutal fantasy of a self-legitimating politics.[9] Overthrowing the monarchy and reinventing everything from Catholicism to the calendar, the Jacobins believed they could uproot people from their traditional social ties and implant new ones by reason—or by terror. Furet and the antitotalitarians identified the political remaking of society as totalitarian and rendered the Revolution as trading the absolutist monarch for an equally arbitrary force, the "unconditional triumph of rule by opinion."[10]

Claude Lefort provided the constructivist counterpoint to Furet's claims. Lefort praised the Revolution for opening a path to democratic politics by exposing the "naturalist fiction" that mistakes social groups and social divisions for empirical givens.[11] The Revolution turned this primordialist notion around to reveal that social relations are "instituted" symbolically, by the "work of division" that Lefort termed the political (*le politique*).[12] By laying bare the political, the Revolution changed the way that the modern individual experienced social order. From a necessity of nature or a divine ordination, the order of society—class-hierarchal, apartheid-driven, interest-based—became recognizable as a human imposition and thereby open to democratic struggle. Lefort—who credited the Revolution for that shift—held *the political* to be modern democracy's signature advance over monarchal politics: it laid bare the irreducibility of political divisions to putatively given social differences and opened social order to democratic struggle. Whether that politicization of social order would spark a politics of new freedoms or set the "totalitarian adventure" on its way depended on how modern human beings chose to live with all that premodern society had foreclosed—the freedom, responsibility, and uncertainty of making social order.[13]

More than making a constructivist interpretation of the French Revolution, Lefort interpreted that Revolution as a constructivist *event*, a political transformation of philosophy and institutions that freed political representation to remap social relations rather than reflect them. This transformation prompted him to an unusual definition of democracy, which Antoon Braeckman aptly renders as the "moment in history when one realizes that societies are the work of *human beings*: that they are instituted and that this institution is basically contingent."[14] That moment presented "political philosophy" with a new task (which Lefort took up):

to "conceptualize the principle of the institution of the social"—in all its ambiguity—as both democracy's signature advance over monarchal politics and, potentially, also its conduit to totalitarianism.[15] Where Lefort saw ambiguity, Furet saw only the terrifying spectacle of a society integrated not organically, by means of robust social associations, but artificially: by the "incomparable" power of ideology.[16]

Moyn and Duong argue that the "antitotalitarian moment" of the 1970s marked a return to and reversal of themes that had first emerged in the 1950s, when postwar French intellectuals had cast totalitarianism not as an "outcome" of democracy's "claim to represent the popular will," but as democracy's "capture" by bureaucracy.[17] They "'discovered' [its] democratic origins" only later, in the 1970s, at a pivotal moment for the elaboration of a uniquely French liberalism that saw in democracy's promise of equality before the law a fatal contradiction.[18] That contradiction, framed for them by Lefort, held that it is impossible to create citizens, which is to say individuals of equal standing before the law, without abstracting each one "from the networks in which [their] social life develops"; democracy, then, makes each individual "a mere statistic."[19] That very abstraction undoes the robust "social cohesion" that secures "the possibility of a common good."[20] Furet would appropriate this logic, link it to the example of the Terror, and conclude that democracy is doomed to destroy itself.

Lefort's work initially put him out of step with his time. He advanced a critique of socialism immediately after World War II, well before anticommunism came into fashion among Left intellectuals in France. When the Left's critique of totalitarianism took hold in the mid-1970s, French intellectuals—most notably Furet—rediscovered Lefort's writings. Furet's attention and patronage, which secured an appointment for Lefort at the École des Hautes Études, gave Lefort a centrality in French intellectual life that he had not previously enjoyed.[21] This good fortune was no small irony because as Furet brought Lefort's work into the spotlight he stripped away its ambiguity. What Furet cast as democracy's fatal contradiction, Lefort had presented as its "paradox": "at the very moment when popular sovereignty is assumed to manifest itself [in the universal franchise], when the people is assumed to actualize itself by expressing its will, . . . social interdependence breaks down."[22] Using Lefort's constructivist concepts to trace an inexorable path from Revolution to demagogy and total domination, Furet made Lefort into a man for his (Furet's) time: the "central theorist of the antitotalitarian moment."[23]

Lefort on His Own Terms—
A "Negative" Conception of Democracy

Lefort defines democracy by two features that mark its "political original-ity."[24] First, that power, "no longer embodied in the person or persons who exercise it," constantly searches "for a basis."[25] Second, in his oft-quoted phrase, that "democracy is instituted and sustained by the *dissolution of the markers of certainty*."[26] Put simply, democratic society "welcomes and preserves indeterminacy" as to the foundation of political power—the criterion by which it can be judged legitimate—and as to democracy's own historical trajectory.[27] Premodern regimes sought to endow power with an "unassailable legitimacy" by representing it as transcendently au-thorized or incarnated in a particular group or person.[28] Lefort singles out democracy as the sole regime to "revea[l] that power belongs to no one" and to be uniquely transparent about its *symbolic* practice.[29]

Division: The Symbolic Work of Power

Lefort's notion of power as symbolic practice reverses commonsense as-sumptions about the relationship between social difference and political hierarchy. Take feudal or apartheid regimes. Rather than rest on preexist-ing differences of class or race, Lefort maintains that the exercise of class-power (feudalism) or race-power (apartheid) constitutes its own social ground. Political power orders a heterogeneous social field in relation to a symbolic "reference point" that endows certain characteristics with the capacity to differentiate, thereby representing a society "to itself" as di-vided by distinctions particular to its kind—race for an apartheid regime or class for a feudal one.[30] As Geenens writes, power can "be said to be 'symbolic'" by virtue of this work of social ordering that unifies a com-munity "not by mere force," but by force backed by this representation of fundamental, prepolitical divisions.[31]

Representation in Lefort's work "does not mean passively mirroring reality"; it "means the *activity* of making symbolic principles work so that an entire society acquires meaning and legitimacy."[32] A society defined by apartheid or class struggle or pluralist competition will give meaning and legitimacy to those principles by way of institutions that purport to derive from and reflect differences of race, class, and interest. Such differences are, in Lefort's terms, not differences but *orderings*, which makes them political in Lefort's sense of the term: they take form by the "primal division" between society and its symbolic representation, which stages "a model of social organization" to orient its members in relation to authority and each other.[33]

Social relations, then, never precede politics; they are "instituted" by the "work of division" that Lefort calls *the political*.[34] To hold that division "institutes" unity may seem contradictory.[35] But think of the way that a mirror or portrait offers the individual an image of a corporeal whole that is not available to one's own sensory experience except as an image. The image integrates as a body what is available to perception only as an aggregate of parts. As it constitutes the individual as a unity, it simultaneously alienates that individual, for such unity comes from outside, and stands at a distance.[36] Lefort theorizes the political to make it clear that representation is indispensable to sense-making. As he emphasizes, "social actors" do not understand "their behavior as being strictly determined" by material conditions or social relations; rather, they "*decipher* their condition and relationships*" in terms of an image of power.[37]

In feudal societies this image is the body of the king, a totality embodying hierarchy and, as Abraham Bosse's famous frontispiece to Thomas Hobbes' 1651 book *The Leviathan* demonstrates, representing multitudes as a unified agent. The king is in such renderings both person and figurehead. He can move through the realm inspiring his subjects to love and loyalty, yet stand apart from them as spectacle, a threat and promise of absolute power. The symbolic practice of premodern society gives power presence in the body of the king and in the distinctions of dress and habits of deference that mark off the nobility from the laboring classes. This practice, in attaching symbols to power, paradoxically denies that power *itself* is symbolic: to make power present is to make power literal. The king's body provides the legend that enables social relations to be "deciphered" as differences of class.[38] Representing society to itself as an organic hierarchy, that legend actively "institutes" the social order while disavowing its own symbolic practice like a living trompe l'oeil.[39]

The body of the king perpetuates the "naturalist fiction" that Lefort grasps analytically by way of his influential distinction between politics (*la politique*) and the political (*le politique*).[40] *Politics* names what we ordinarily think of as such: the "activity" of interest-group conflict, elections, legislative processes, and the relations among governments, courts, and civil society.[41] *The political* names the symbolic activity that makes these phenomena recognizable. It marks the moment where the social is "given a form" by power, which "order[s] and unif[ies it] across its divisions," and the moment where power retreats to disavow that activity of ordering.[42] *The political* both orders and "obscure[s]" the activity of ordering.[43] This "double movement" makes differences of race, sex, and class while perpetuating the primordial fiction that they inhere in nature, that political differences and interests arise from a social terrain that need not be given form.[44] In every regime prior to democracy, political representation involved both this activity of giving form and the subsequent work of obscuring that activity.

Ordering: The Activity of Representation

It is tempting to deduce social order "from empirical, 'positive' facts,"[45] as if slave societies came to be because "race" preceded them, or gender hierarchy sat "on anatomical sex like the beret on the head of the legendary Frenchman."[46] It is also normal for those subject to a particular order (and for those studying political behavior positivistically) to imagine class distinctions, groups, group interests, and the separations among various domains (e.g., economy versus politics) as social givens. Yet to take such distinctions literally in this way occludes the work of power in division, which is its symbolic practice.

Lefort names *the political* to take political theory (and political science) on a "reflexive turn."[47] That concept trains the analyst to recognize that such phenomena are politically—which is to say, symbolically—instituted. It also tutors political subjects to "grasp" the everyday "experience" of being "ordered" as an encounter with symbolic power, which imbues people with "an *implicit* conception" of their relations with one another and "with the world."[48] Think of the catchphrase "the personal is political," which Second Wave feminists used to make sexual difference visible as a political ordering and to solicit resistance to gender hierarchy. Recall that James Baldwin needed few words to capture what it feels like to be "ordered" and to call it out as political. He observed that "Negroes in this country—*and Negroes do not, strictly or legally speaking, exist in any other*—are taught really to despise themselves from the moment their eyes open on the world."[49] Baldwin's aside recasts race from a primordial difference to a representation that effects Lefort's "primal division," the symbolic act that makes whiteness the normative pillar of a social ordering that legitimates white people's domination over everything they construct as "colored."

Lefort presses this point against what he terms Marx's "positivism" by seizing on Marx's infamous claim that the division of labor under capitalism originated in the "division of labour in the sexual act."[50] Lefort criticizes Marx for assuming "a division of the sexes" that brings the "partners [to] naturally identify themselves as different," to "reflect upon this difference and to *represent themselves* as man and woman."[51] Surprisingly echoing the critique of gender made famous by materialist feminist Christine Delphy,[52] Lefort objects that Marx's analogy "presupposes" in the case of the sexual division exactly what needs to be "explained" in the case of *both* sex and class: how an "empirical distribution of individuals" comes to be seen as a division into groups and to be cast in political terms as a relation of cooperation, complementarity, oppression, or something else.[53] Like Delphy (whom he does not cite and probably had not read), Lefort insists that sex is not a marker of group difference by the sheer fact of procreation; it must be charged with significance by the mediation of a "symbolic order, the idea of a system of oppositions" that represents sex as a "model of co-operation and social division."[54]

The groups *men* and *women* are no more "positive terms" (or facts) than *workers* and *capitalists* are.[55] They do not exist in some "objective space that supposedly preexisted" *the political* but emerge by the symbolic "division" that "enunciates the order of the world."[56] This position does not mean that material reality is scripted, nor that representation takes "primacy" over the real. It states merely that "kinship or class"—or sex—are symbolic categories, not demographic ones.[57]

The "Empty Place" of Power

When Lefort names "modern democracy" he means that it is the only known regime to represent and actively own that "power is an *empty place*."[58] Lefort does not claim that democracy is literally empty of power, as it realizes neither the anarchist utopia of a regime without rule nor the liberal ideal that "no arbitrary power is exercised."[59] He means that modern democracy pictures the social order as relatively fluid or "without any positive determination."[60] Lefort reserves the term *democracy* for societies that "openly embrace" contestation over power and over claims regarding the basis of legitimacy.[61] This openness alone poses a revolutionary alternative to premodern society.

Monarchy figures power as embodied, and hence fixed, certain, and literal. If democracy constitutes a revolutionary break with absolutism, it cannot simply install the people in the place of the king. Lefort counts as democratic only those societies that neither stage power as emanating from a transcendent authority (such as God) nor succumb to the opposite temptation, which is to "make the law immanent within the order of the world" either by vesting it in the people or by conflating the "rule of law with the rule of power."[62] Democracy *disincorporates* sovereignty altogether. It initiates "a society without a body."[63] It thereby inaugurates "a history in which people experience a fundamental indeterminacy as to the basis of power, law and knowledge, and as to the basis of relations between *self* and *other*, at every level of social life."[64]

David Ingram has pointed out the "obvious yet seldom noted characteristic" of this striking theoretical move: "it is almost entirely *negative.*"[65] Lefort defines democracy as a regime that "does *not* . . . fill the symbolic place of power" as totalitarianism attempts to do.[66] Ingram notes that this definition creates "ambiguity" about the political implications of Lefort's political philosophy, but one thing is clear: Lefort refuses to equate democracy with "popular sovereignty."[67] Even elections, in Lefort's view, serve to stage the "fragmentation, division and conflictuality of society," rather than to deliver up the "will of the people in its unmediated emanation."[68]

Lefort uses this notion of power as an empty place to draw a bright line between democracy and populism. This move any liberal would like — right up to the point where Lefort flaunts the notion of extrapolitical legitimacy that liberals cherish. In a startling passage, Lefort asserts that "modern democracy" "invites us to *replace* the notion of a regime governed by laws, of a legitimate power, by the notion of a regime founded upon *the legitimacy of a debate as to what is legitimate and what is illegitimate*—a debate which is necessarily without any guarantor and without any end."[69] Lefort's "democratic debate" is no deliberative exchange oriented toward a consensus whose legitimacy supposedly rests on the "unforced force of the better argument."[70] Lefort renders legitimacy political in his unique sense of the term: it is specific to a social order whose rightness it cannot guarantee. In his words, the "division between legitimate and illegitimate is not materialized within the social space [but] is simply removed from the realm of certainty," which means that democratic societies hold any claim to sovereignty open to question.[71]

Lefort made the indeterminacy of social relations—and the "institutionalization of conflict"—the signature of modern democracy.[72] The democratic impulse as Lefort describes it is to ensure that any claim to speak for a people, nation, or group is always open to "change and historicity, and therefore again to conflict and struggle."[73] Yet Lefort holds only that democracies *necessarily* build their institutions around this indeterminacy, not that indeterminacy leads necessarily to democratic regimes. Indeterminacy can work expansively, extending political equality to ever more groups. It can also provoke the temptation to escape into seeming absolutes like "people, state and nation" and to indulge new, organicist fantasies of a social body without division, a "People-as-One" again "welded to its head."[74] As Lefort prominently acknowledges, when mixed with insecurities due to economic crisis or war, extreme polarization, or cynicism about politics, indeterminacy can supply the "conditions for the formation of totalitarianism."[75]

Lefort's concession, which gave Furet a foothold for his polemic, set this question as the focal point of their disagreement: Does indeterminacy lead inevitably to authoritarian terror? In that contest, Furet would not only claim the last word but (shamelessly) borrow it from Lefort. I stage a rematch that gives Lefort the final say.

Furet Appropriates Lefort

Samuel Moyn has shown that Lefort's "philosophy provided Furet with the critical intellectual tools" for rethinking the French Revolution as the event "in which democracy was born."[76] Furet does not welcome this birth. Rather, he claims that it brought about the advent of "democratic politics as a national ideology."[77] In a patent allusion to Lefort, Furet contends that this ideology took over the "vacant sphere of power."[78] Rather than preserve that vacancy, national ideology made the "people the supreme source of legitimacy," gave rise to a violent and suspicious mode of politics that was obsessed "with treason and plot," and categorically opposed representation.[79] This same national ideology also posed an "insoluble problem": how to determine "which group, which assembly, which meeting, which consensus was the trustee of the people's word."[80]

So far, Furet's argument may seem to have little to do with Lefort's. He describes democracy possessing an organicist theory of power that it invests in the body of the people and couples to righteous and violent action—a theory that is a far cry from one in which democracy stages uncertainty. But as Moyn has argued, and Lefort himself would underscore, Furet built this attack on a framework he appropriated from Lefort's work, beginning with his "naked allusions" to Lefort's notion of the empty place of power.[81] In Furet's rendering, that vacancy leads necessarily—not "potentially," as Lefort argued—to a "vertiginous descent into totalitarian dictatorship."[82] Most audaciously, Furet makes "a move that, in retrospect, thanks to him [Furet], seems so obvious" to us today.[83] He applies and "condense[s]" Lefort's account, thereby recasting from possible to inevitable the passage from "democracy's beginnings" to "its much later totalitarian potentiality."[84]

Furet pulls off this heist through his concept of *democratic sociability*, which he introduces to analyze the "new social and political fabric" that the philosophical societies and revolutionary clubs had created—a sociability that was distinctive for being "based on individuals, and no longer on the institutional groups to which they belonged."[85] The Revolution swept away the hierarchy of orders with their distinct, sometimes competing, interests to leave behind individuals—unanchored by membership in social institutions—who were ripe for demagogic appeals to the "nation" and the "people." Furet's concern is that this unfixing of politics from social structure did away with the "corporate bodies" that organized social interests, differentiated society into groups, and provided a counterpoint to and check on the sovereign in the Old Regime.[86] The "old mode of political sociability" was anchored in this differentiated society.[87] Being "centered on the King of France at the summit of the social order," and organized through the Estates General, it reflected status differences, interests, and responsibilities that were both established socially and codified in law.[88] Democratic sociability has no such anchor. When power acts on individuals who have no specifiable corporate interests, claims to democratic legitimacy are just that—assertions ungrounded by socially determined entitlements, privileges, or obligations.[89]

Furet premises this contrast between the new sociability and the old on an ontological and normative distinction between "actual power" and its "symbolic representation"—a distinction that contradicts the constructivist core of Lefort's argument.[90] If Lefort insisted that politics does not rest on a society of this or that kind but, rather, that *the political* defines society and gives it unity, Furet's position is almost diametrically opposed. As historian Lynn Hunt puts it, Furet holds that "[w]hen politics come first, the situation is by definition abnormal."[91]

Furet describes the Revolution as "usher[ing] in a world" where political power, cut loose from its proper social moorings, became entirely symbolic: "*mental representations* of power governed all actions, and . . . a network of signs completely dominated political life."[92] As Lynn Hunt argues, Furet identifies this "linguisticality" as the French Revolution's defining and most dangerous feature because it meant that politicians would no longer "represent social interest in the normal or expected fashion."[93] For Furet (as for Hanna Pitkin), the "normal or expected" mode was for representation to be rooted in society, with politics *following* from social divisions and interests, *not* constituting them. The Revolution gave rise to "a world where mental representations of power governed all actions, and where a network of signs completely dominated political life."[94] In that world, power would no longer be rooted in interest, but would become purely voluntarist—dynamically, oratorically constituted by elite manipulation of the "ordinarily soft and pliable thing we call opinion."[95]

Furet dates to revolutionary France the birth of punditry, which critics of mass democracy identify as one of the most manipulative features of today's politics. Men of letters, who had neither a prescribed constituency nor any practical access to power, promoted themselves to popular spokespersons. Clubs, societies, and other contestants for power had merely to invoke the "people" to legitimate their right to speak in the people's name.[96] Not a "datum or a concept that reflected existing society," this "people" was a purely rhetorical construct.[97] It furnished the catalyst for a political "alchemy" that turned mere words into an unquestionable authority, so that the "very fact that a philosophical society or club claimed to be speaking for the nation, or for the people, was sufficient to transform individual opinions into plain 'opinion' and opinion into *imaginary* absolute power."[98]

Furet's central thesis is just this: that the overthrow of the king traded an embodied sovereign for one that was unlimited by virtue of being unlocatable. The idea of "the people" intensified the concentration of power in the sovereign (now, nominally, popular) and lent to its arbitrary exercise an unprecedented legitimacy.[99] Contrary to its pretension to being the "advent of a new age," the Revolution destroyed the social foundation of the Old Regime only "*to appropriate, albeit at a different level, the absolutist tradition.*"[100] Furet does indeed side with Lefort to affirm democracy as the truth of the Revolution; contrary to Lefort, however, Furet holds democracy "in its chemically pure form" to have "engendered the Terror."[101]

Lefort Strikes Back

In 1977, François Furet appropriated Claude Lefort's nuanced argument in service of his own polemic. As Moyn has shown, Furet interpreted the

French Revolution as the advent of democracy, took up Lefort's conceptualization of democracy by way of the "empty" place of power, and judged
that vacancy to lead inexorably to Terror and then totalitarianism—all
without so much as citing Lefort's work.[102] In effect, Furet had made Lefort a silent partisan in a one-sided rendering of his own argument.

This story has another side: Lefort's resistance to Furet's reading. That
story is critical to my project because Lefort reaffirms the relationship
between the constructivist position on constituency-making and democratic politics that I have championed throughout this book. Lefort's resistance emerges in a 1980 review of Furet's book that is a rhetorical tour de
force.[103] Lefort takes Furet's argument neither as an appropriation of nor
an attack on his ideas but, rather, interprets Furet's project so as to align
it with his own. When Christofferson writes that Lefort's review "tried
to save Furet from himself and the innovations of the Revolution from
Furet's critique of its political illusions," he skates over Furet's borrowings
from Lefort's work.[104] Foregrounding those borrowings makes it plain to
see that by "saving Furet" Lefort advocates for himself.

Lefort interpolates his own claims into his account of Furet's text so
seamlessly that readers may fail to catch on to the many points where,
while seeming to affirm a position of Furet's, Lefort reasserts an argument of his own. The review begins with Lefort affirming what he and
Furet have in common: a desire to "redirect" crude materialist historical
analysis of "modes of production" towards a "reflection on politics."[105]
From that shared starting point, Lefort proceeds to represent Furet as
endorsing a constructivist premise that I have shown Furet in fact to resist:
that the "position and representation of power, and the figuration of its
locus are . . . *constitutive* of the social space."[106] Lefort attributes to Furet
an account of power's symbolic practice—as if Furet had not denounced
as pathology the confusion of "actual power" with its "symbolic representation."[107] Here and elsewhere in the text, Lefort's skillful ventriloquism
makes Furet's voice nearly indistinguishable from his own.

At points where their disagreements are too profound for this merging
of voice to be sustained, Lefort works even more deftly to align their views.
Take Furet's judgment that the disincorporation of power creates a new
"opacity" about accountability. Lefort writes, as if to correct what Furet
himself would regard as an error, that "this opacity is, *[Furet] should point
out,* an effect of the dissimulation of something that has entered the register
of the thinkable for the first time."[108] The "dissimulation" to which Lefort
refers is power's symbolic practice, whose entrance into the "register of

the thinkable" *troubles* Furet as much as it excites Lefort. Lefort positions himself as a privileged reader of Furet's text who presumes to know what Furet really believes and, hence, "*should* point out": not that the Revolution reduced "actual" politics to a "symbolic" contest, but—as Lefort has argued—that it put an end to the "dissimulation" that represented symbolic practices as passively expressing an underlying social reality. Lefort writes as if "democracy" designated the same thing for Furet as it does for Lefort, not an unmediated and ill-defined popular force but a regime that puts ordering (the representational aspect of power) on display.

As a final strategy, Lefort simply pulls his punches. Under cover of a round of applause for Furet's Left-affiliated critical reflection on the Revolution's legacy ("One could not hope for a more eloquent description of how the relationships we establish with the past are implicated in those we establish with the present"), Lefort launches a withering critique: "This certainly does not mean that we have to invert our identifications, rediscover totalitarianism in the ideal of Jacobinism or confuse the system of the Terror with that of the Gulag, *and I do not think that this is what Furet is saying.*"[109] Really? Is this not exactly what Furet is saying when he characterizes his own work as "deducing the Terror from revolutionary discourse," and calls for a "history of the French Left in relation to the Soviet Revolution . . . [that] would show that Stalinism took root in a modified Jacobin tradition"?[110] Rather than denounce Furet's polemicism, Lefort chalks it up as regrettable that Furet "merely mentions the invention of a 'democratic culture' or a 'democratic politics'" without either providing any evidence of them or "specifying" what makes them distinct from the "fantasmagoria of popular power."[111]

Lefort is too good a reader to have overlooked that in Furet's lexicon *democratic politics* is not a happy term. Recall Furet's "sociability" thesis, that democracy as enacted by the French Revolution is not a politics—"a set of rules or procedures" that tie political authority to elections—but a culture of terror and denunciation.[112] Far from merely failing to specify what *separates* democratic politics from the "fantasmagoria of popular power," Furet stops just short of *conflating* the two.

Conclusion

The dispute between Furet and Lefort poses a sharp question to theorists of the constructivist turn in democratic representation: the French

Revolution may have been constructivist in making it explicit that so-called social differences are politically made, but is this liberation of political conflict from its roots in the social democratic? Democratic theorists pursue that question in France today. Jainchill and Moyn document the legacy of the Furet–Lefort dispute in the work of Pierre Rosanvallon, who "hoped to avoid the reduction of democracy to terror and to find a way to think about institutionalizing it in some new form."[113] They characterize Rosanvallon as being "hobbled in the pursuit of his most cherished ends" by his fidelity to Furet's one-sided reading of Lefort.[114]

Critics who argue that constructivist accounts are "non-normative" and indifferent to manipulation assume the self-evidence of their own commitments to democracy while putting constructivists in the position of having to justify theirs. Giving rein to the ambiguity in Lefort's thought alters the default setting of that contemporary debate. Furet believed that individuals unmoored from their social-group attachments were easy prey for totalitarian ideologues. Thus, he maintained unequivocally, freeing political representation from its proper social base put modern democracy on the path to realizing its totalitarian potential. Lefort insisted on the indeterminacy of the relationship between the political and the social to emphasize the openness of social relations to remaking. Rather than an outright democratic victory, he counted this openness as an ambivalent bequest of the democratic revolutions. This ambivalence requires critics of mass democracy to justify their starting premise: namely, that when we acknowledge that acts of political representation create the social order that they are commonly understood to express, we do not inaugurate modernity's fragile experiment in representative democracy—we threaten it.

I continue this line of argument into the next chapter by way of reinterpreting a classic of radical democratic theory, Ernesto Laclau and Chantal Mouffe's *Hegemony and Socialist Strategy*. Taking inspiration from their passing references to Furet and Lefort, I situate that text in the context of the debates to which the antitotalitarian moment gave rise. I argue that Laclau and Mouffe succeed where Pierre Rosanvallon failed: they manage to extricate themselves from Furetian pessimism to elaborate both the optimism and the ambivalence that emerged from what they, echoing Claude Lefort, term the Revolution's "new mode of institution of the social."[115]

CHAPTER SEVEN

Radical Democracy and the Value of Plurality

*H*egemony and Socialist Strategy (*HSS*), Ernesto Laclau and Chantal Mouffe's classic work of radical democratic political theory, stakes out a distinctive position in the debates of the "antitotalitarian moment," a period that was consumed in no small part by debating whether Sieyes or Tocqueville (and Burke) got the French Revolution right.[1] Taking Tocqueville's side, François Furet damned the Revolution by means of a one-sided appropriation of the work of his colleague Claude Lefort. Laclau and Mouffe intervened in that debate from a unique vantage point. Intellectual historian Warren Breckman calls them "cultural *brokers*, standing at the point of exchange between [British and French] intellectual and political traditions."[2] Having made their academic careers in the "British context, where the crisis of Marxism was not accompanied by an 'antitotalitarian moment,' public rituals of self-abasement, and the manic-depressive tone of so much French thought of the period," Laclau and Mouffe escaped the "postmodern melancholia" that characterized the work of so many French intellectuals in that time.[3] They took a position antithetical to Furet's regarding the "continuity between the Jacobin and Marxist political imaginary" by claiming as the Revolution's democratic promise the "indeterminacy" that Lefort cautiously celebrated and Furet furiously denounced.[4] They gave that indeterminacy a new name: *plurality*.[5]

Neither a synonym for diversity nor a catchphrase for interest-group conflict, *plurality* designates the "radical unfixity" of political conflict from "*given* and relatively stable social identities"—an unfixity that opens the social to being radically remade.[6] Laclau and Mouffe use the term to mark the break between modern (post-eighteenth-century) democracies and premodern politics that they, like Lefort, frame as a break with primordialism. Plurality announces the displacement of a politics seemingly fixed to a God-given, hierarchal social substrate for another kind of politics, one in which group formation and social hierarchy could be politically remade. It becomes the enabling condition for a radical democratic politics as Laclau and Mouffe define it: building "unsuspected" links among struggles and thereby altering "the social and political identities that are permissible and even thinkable."[7]

It is possible to go too far in situating Laclau and Mouffe in relation to Lefort and Furet. Granted, Laclau and Mouffe take inspiration (as their very language bears witness) from Lefort's basic premise that the French Revolution initiated "a new mode of *institution of the social*" that lays bare the political work of ordering society.[8] But merely accepting this premise does not make them Lefortians. Although they welcome Lefort's thesis that the Revolution revealed the "site of power [to be] an empty space," they assimilate that thesis to their own radical democratic project.[9] Rather than hold open the "empty" place of power as Lefort would do, they aim to fill it in the manner of Gramsci: with a politically constituted agent whose position as representative of emancipatory struggle is consensual, contingent, and contestable—i.e., hegemonic.[10]

Taking inspiration from Breckman, I attempt in this chapter to place *HSS* in the "intellectual history of France after 1968," so as to reclaim the passionate constructivist defense of democracy that got lost in the controversy over post-Marxism, which defined the book's initial interpretive context.[11] I argue that, by virtue of being theorists of hegemony, Laclau and Mouffe count as theorists of political representation as well. I agree with Lasse Thomassen that the "hegemonic relation is essentially a relation of representation, where the representation is not the representation of an original presence but what brings about the represented—in short, it is a relation of articulation."[12] Laclau and Mouffe did not understand their text in this way at the time they wrote it. They presented *HSS* as "replac[ing] the principle of representation with that of *articulation*," defining representation on the authoritarian, positivist model of the communist party.[13]

I interpret *HSS* in light of the trajectory of their later work, particularly Laclau's, as a constructivist account of political representation that advances the mobilization conception in two ways. First, Laclau and Mouffe coin a vocabulary of terms—*democratic antagonism, articulation, equivalence*—that describe the work of what I term mobilization.

Second, they link that work both theoretically and historically to modern democracy, which they (like Lefort and Furet) consider unique for explicitly refusing social determinism. I draw upon that uniquely constructivist account of democracy to affirm that sorting poses a threat to mass democracy that rivals, and perhaps even exceeds, that of manipulation. Its refixing of political conflict to social determinants constrains modern democratic politics (like its premodern predecessor) merely to play out antagonisms that are "constituted beyond" it.[14] Sorting halts that radical democratic practice of building "unsuspected" links that bring unlikely social and political actors within the realm of the "thinkable."[15]

The French Revolution and the Dawn of Hegemonic Practice

Both the structure and the argument of *HSS* pivot on Laclau and Mouffe's reading of the democratic significance of the French Revolution. With Lefort, they interpreted that event as revolutionary for opening social relations to political construction in ways that remained impossible so long as "power was incorporated in the person of the prince."[16] With Furet, they located the uniqueness of the French Revolution in its invention of popular sovereignty, being the "first [regime] to found itself on no other legitimacy than the people."[17] Laclau and Mouffe applauded this invention—as Furet did not—and defended it, in Lefort's terms, for laying bare the "openness and indeterminacy of the social."[18] Endorsing indeterminacy was their key constructivist move, in its insistence on what Critchley terms the "political logic of the social," the notion that social relations of hierarchy and equity, enmity and alliance are politically made.[19]

Furet drove a wedge between constructivism and democratic politics. Laclau and Mouffe joined pieces of Furet's argument to pieces from that of his rival Lefort to make a constructivist turn in democracy's name. They celebrated the Revolution as democratic for making the constructivist turn a political event, in that it effected a tectonic shift from a feudal mode of representation based on "topographic [social] categories" to modern politics in its hegemonic form as a competition much like E. E. Schattschneider's "conflict of conflicts."[20] Laclau and Mouffe do not use the concept of *hegemony* as it is typically understood: as a term that reduces politics to a struggle for domination between opposing political forces.[21] Instead, it names the battle whereby political representatives (elected and not) compete to activate new social divisions, provoke unaccustomed conflicts, and engage disaffected people in unexpected alliances—all with the aim of taking power.

The feudal mode of topographic politics makes no provision for such competition because there is no need for it. Exemplified by the Estates General, it assumes a prepolitical hierarchy of social categories—the clergy, nobility, and Third Estate—that "fix permanently" people's group identities to social roles that political representation would simply reflect.[22] Echoing Lefort, Laclau and Mouffe credited the Revolution with redefining the "problem of the political [as] the problem of the *institution* of the social, that is, of the definition and articulation of social relations in a field crisscrossed with antagonisms."[23] If, as Lefort argued, the French Revolution opened to political construction relations of alliance and enmity that could not be politicized under the primordial order of the *ancien régime*, then Laclau and Mouffe maintained that from that event onward there could be "no politics without hegemony": the "*political construction* from dissimilar elements" of a collective social actor.[24]

Laclau and Mouffe's readers typically regard their hegemonic politics as an expression of their poststructuralist theoretical commitments; I emphasize that *HSS* also makes an argument from history. They present hegemonic practice as a "form of politics" that "becomes dominant at the beginning of modern times," that is, following the French Revolution, an event they counted as democratic because it rendered power visible—hence, contestable—as a dynamic force in setting the terms and defining the agents of political conflict.[25] In their final, crucial chapter, which bears the burden of redeeming the subtitle's promise to defend a "radical *democratic* politics," Laclau and Mouffe participate in interpreting the French Revolution, siding primarily with Lefort. They credit the Revolution with sweeping away the feudal imaginary wherein every element has its group and every group its place, and they describe it disincorporating the space of power. They applaud it for giving rise to plurality, thereby making it possible for relations of enmity and alliance to be constructed politically through calls to action.

The "Third Estate" as (Failed) Hegemonic Bid

In January 1789, a French clergyman made a bid to divide French society along a new line of conflict. He published a revolutionary pamphlet opposing the bourgeoisie's demands for fairer representation for the Third

Estate. He supported reform but he recognized that even if the king and the privileged orders were to give the bourgeoisie what they asked for—representatives drawn from their own ranks, equal in numbers to those allocated to the clergy and aristocracy combined, and voting by head rather than by order (or class)—the Third Estate would never acquire political influence commensurate with its share of the French population. One had only to look at the numbers. The existing arrangement allocated twice the number of deputies to represent the "200,000 privileged individuals of the first two orders" as it provided to the "25 or 26 million inhabitants" of the Third Estate.[26] By this calculation, the call for a "doubling of the Third"[27] is simply too modest: Why demand just half a share of seats in the representative body when you make up 97 percent of the French population?

That pamphlet, the Abbé de Sieyes's "What Is the Third Estate?," is known for its elegant protest against an allocation of seats in the Estates General that ensures disproportionate representation to the elite.[28] But it also calls for a new division of the social. Sieyes recognizes that the power of the privileged orders consists not merely in the force of numbers but in the desire of members of the Third Estate to join their ranks. The reformers who most ardently demanded equality in numbers were also, being the most accomplished members of the Third Estate, the same people who most urgently identified (and aspired) upward. Sieyes pictured the strivers to themselves with a striking metaphor: He cast them as servants standing by in "a sort of enormous ante-room; ceaselessly noting what its masters are doing or saying, [and] always ready to sacrifice everything to the fruits it anticipates from being lucky enough to find favor."[29]

What, in Sieyes's metaphor, were these members of the bourgeoisie waiting for? Simply this: to climb up and out of the Third Estate. As long as the nobility controlled territories, jobs, finances and security, Sieyes understood that the bourgeoisie would—in order to court aristocratic patronage—play the lapdog, thereby taming the proposed reform.

To the question "What is the Third Estate?," Sieyes voiced an aspiration that only revolution could realize: "The Nation."

That answer radically remapped the political geography of royal France. The "Third Estate" was not a group and even less a class. A collection of professionals, tradesmen, merchants, peasants, and the lowest menial workers, it lacked a collective sense, will, and agency. Sieyes proposed to shut down the "ante-room," unite this scattered collection of people against a common enemy, and install its formerly outnumbered deputies in a new National Assembly, where they would be promoted from "delegates of an inferior order in a hierarchal state into the sole and rightful bearers of the nation's sovereign will."[30]

Sieyes's French Revolution is not François Furet's. Furet saw only that this popular force, untempered by traditional class hierarchies, set French society on course that Edmund Burke foresaw ending with a "gallows" at the end of "every vista."[31] Save for the fact that the scaffold turned out to be a guillotine, Burke's words proved prescient. He identified the Revolution's iconic image, which Furet took to be its defining feature, years before the start of the Terror.

The revolutionaries sought to memorialize their event differently, or at least they did in 1790, when they commissioned Jacques-Louis David to paint the "Tennis Court Oath." That unfinished work nominated Sieyes's victory as the Revolution's iconic moment: the pledge of allegiance whereby the deputies for the Third Estate founded the National Assembly.[32] It captured what French historian Keith Baker calls the Revolution's "remarkable" feat.[33] In a context where established institutions and even new theories were concerned with "plac[ing] limits" on representation by securing it to social interests, that oath proclaimed "a revolution of the deputies against the conditions of their election."[34] Transforming the Estates General into the National Assembly required a "dramatic repudiation of the traditional notion of the binding mandate" that defined representatives as delegates, constraining them to "expressing the explicitly stated wills and needs" of their constituencies.[35] The deputies "liberated themselves" from that mandate to take up a dual role—as both sovereign representatives of the nation and makers of social order.[36]

Sieyes's text vividly testifies to Lefort's claim that the events of 1789 broke open a new mode of political representation. By overturning the Estates General and establishing the National Assembly, the revolutionaries threw off the political design that bound representatives to reflect and reproduce a hierarchal social order. They freed acts of representation— whether speeches, pamphlets, street protests or parliamentary bills—to rally a popular political force in pursuit of convention-challenging, liberty-expanding, equality-enhancing goals.

Sieyes aimed to persuade the most educated and upward-striving fraction of French society to disidentify with the privileged classes on whom they depended for patronage, and to align their sympathies downward. He hoped to forge common cause between the educated strivers and those less-educated countrymen with whom they did not identify but were nonetheless "united" by honest, underappreciated labor.[37] Social historian William

Sewell names this move Sieyes's "rhetoric of social revolution," a persuasive tactic involving the "identification and denunciation of a class enemy" with the aim of remapping existing relations of enmity and alliance.[38] Sewell credits Sieyes for his ingenuity in tapping "bourgeois resentment against aristocrats," thereby making "private social grievances" the motivating force for a program of "liberal political reform" that envisioned a radical equality among producers.[39]

Sewell describes Sieyes as making an exemplary "representative claim."[40] Sieyes aspired to speak for a Third Estate that he called into being by "represent[ing] the bourgeoisie to itself as a class of producers, whose useful private and public activities assured the prosperity of the country."[41] This act of picturing, of representing *as*, made a bold proposition: to differentiate the bourgeoisie from the idle aristocracy and unite it with the lower classes. In Laclau and Mouffe's terms, Sieyes launched a *hegemonic* bid. He solicited the most well-placed groups within the Third Estate to identify with the oppressed, to give up competing for status within the hierarchal ordering of French society, and to join manual laborers and shopkeepers in struggle against that ordering.

Plurality—or rather its lack—hindered Sieyes. Laclau and Mouffe describe the Revolution as the last premodern "moment" when opposition between the "people" and the "*ancien régime*" seemed "clear and empirically *given*."[42] Sieyes recognized that it was not, in fact, given; his pamphlet sought to unify the (denigrated) Third Estate and promote it as the (celebrated) nation of France. Within two years, the *sans-culottes* pressed his "anti-aristocratic rhetorical devices" into service to resuscitate a familiar cleavage.[43] Proposing that "only the poor people who worked with their hands to produce subsistence were members of the nation," they reactivated the familiar fault line dividing the upper and lower ranks of the Third Estate along the difference between rich and poor.[44] They counted the rich, whether members of the nobility or not, as "by definition aristocrats and idlers—and enemies of the nation."[45] Sieyes' radical vision fell prey to Jacobinism, which was, in Laclau and Mouffe's terms, a "popular struggle" whose dichotomous logic followed the feudal pattern that is so hostile to plurality: representing political conflict as if it arose out of a prepolitical social chasm.[46]

Democratic Antagonism

HSS makes a truly pivotal contribution to contemporary democratic political theory with a simple, monumentally optimistic gesture: to affirm the "*radical antagonistic* character of democratic struggles" against the presumption that truly radical conflict cleaves society in two.[47] By "democratic struggles," Laclau and Mouffe meant the particularistic, scattered struggles of the new social movements—struggles that "imply a plurality of political spaces"—as opposed to the "popular struggles" that "divide a single political space into two opposed fields."[48] They proposed the phrase "democratic antagonism" to refute the leftist prejudice that such struggles are "secondary" precisely because they do not divide "the political space into two camps."[49] The phrase names the potential for such scattered struggles to add up to consequential political transformation despite their failure to forge a united front, as Marx imagined the working class would do.

Acknowledging that potential enabled Laclau and Mouffe to cast the social movements of the New Left in a new light, as "*novel*" agents of social conflict operating in the context of "mature capitalism," which had established the wage labor contract as a source of opportunity, choice, and freedom rather than a site of exploitation.[50] Rather than dwell on how difficult late capitalism had made it for radicals to organize a "clearcut" frontier between exploiting and exploited classes, Laclau and Mouffe championed democratic antagonism.[51] They amplified the radical promise of opening up new "sites of antagonisms" in everyday life, taking up the forms of "subordination" that people simply accepted, actively desired, or patiently resigned themselves to and politicizing those forms of subordination as "relations[s] of oppression."[52] They saw that radical promise as manifesting in late-industrial societies in particular: in their capacity to disclose new sites of exploitation emerging not from labor but from "culture, free time, illness, education, sex and even death."[53]

Laclau and Mouffe took a distinctively political position on social-movement struggles, neither dismissing them "as marginal or peripheral with regard to the working class" nor counting on them to be "progressive."[54] When people organize to—for example—block a solid-waste facility, achieve same-sex marriage rights, or promote dismantling of single-family zoning, their efforts may either play into or challenge existing power relations. Such efforts may deepen environmental racism or foster sustainability, shore up traditional families or promote experimental households, accelerate capital accumulation or redistribute resources. Their political outcomes depend less on principle than on their framing ideologies, their political bedfellows, and the forces (market, state, courts, philanthropists, nongovernmental organizations) that latch onto them. Wherever plurality exists, this truth of politics holds: links take priority over elements.

Antagonism is not, as some readers have interpreted it, the opposite of engagement, generosity, or compromise.[55] Nor is it synonymous with disagreement, conflict or "interminable hostility," as others have claimed.[56] It names conflict of a particular kind, where a "confrontation between groups" provokes *resistance* in a social relationship that had previously reached an equilibrium.[57] It may be sparked by change that betrays the tacit compromises maintaining relations of exploitation, such as when a "fall in a [male] worker's wage" compromises his identity as a provider and head of household.[58] Or when white, college-educated married women in the 1960s woke up to their boredom as middle-class wives and began to demand (middle-class) careers. At such moments, habitual social relations stop being viable because one or more of the parties involved comes to realize that they can no longer go on pursuing what they had previously understood themselves to want or felt obligated and even born to be.

Moments of antagonism have a "revelatory function": to disclose imposition and ordering at work in relations that had previously seemed voluntary or necessary.[59] The opposite of antagonism is the "ideological," which Laclau defines as "those discursive forms through which a society tries to institute itself as such on the basis of closure, of the fixation of meaning, of the non-recognition of the infinite play of differences."[60] Democratic antagonisms make it plain that institutions exist in their present form by the exclusion of "historically available and politically articulated alternatives."[61] They are hegemonic all the way down.

Oliver Marchart has identified the "concept of antagonism" as Laclau and Mouffe's "main contribution to contemporary political thought."[62] I emphasize that *democratic* antagonism makes a striking departure from what, according to Marchart, *antagonism* "originally names in Laclauian theory": the classically radical division of a field of struggle "into two camps."[63] In *HSS*, Laclau and Mouffe assign dichotomous division specifically to "*popular* struggles."[64] They hold the plural, diffuse, and particularistic conflicts characteristic of *democratic* struggle to reflect the more "fundamental concept" in the following sense: They emphasize that wherever *popular* struggle manages to divide "the political space into two antagonistic fields," *democratic* struggle must already have occurred.[65] In *HSS*, dichotomous division moves from being the very definition of antagonism to being strategically subordinate to democratic antagonism. Rather than reflecting social fact, conflict that divides society in two is—like all forms of conflict—politically achieved; it depends on "the multiplication of equivalence effects" that links plural democratic struggles so that they constitute a single side.[66] *HSS* succeeded at the task that Laclau set for himself in 1977, which was to develop the "theoretical implications" of the "Gramscian concept" of hegemony in terms of the plurality of the social and the "non-class character of democratic ideology."[67]

Laclau and Mouffe describe a social field unlike the complex terrain of competing social groups that midcentury pluralists imagined and unlike the reduction to dichotomous class struggle that Marx hoped for. They argue that wherever terms such as "worker" or "women" or "rural people" mark seemingly self-evident differences among groups, political division has made them so, not demographic characteristics, and certainly not essential properties. Economic or historical logics do not create political actors. Class "unity" (or the unity of women, Black people, or any other social force) is "a precarious articulation" of heterogeneous elements.[68] Representatives do more than *stand for* the interests of groups populated by "Black," "white," "rural," "urban," "working class," and "male" or "female" people; they *constitute* those groups by cutting divisions into the "irreducible plurality of the social."[69] Laclau and Mouffe add that the "political meaning of a local community movement, of an ecological struggle, of a sexual minority movement . . . crucially depends upon its hegemonic articulation with other struggles and demands."[70] Whether a "workers'" or "women's" or "rural people's" politics proves emancipatory, opportunistic, atavistic, and so forth depends on its hegemonic articulation to other struggles.

To *articulate* as Laclau and Mouffe use the term is not, as in common parlance, to speak with noteworthy precision; it is to create an alliance in a specific way.[71] Rather than gather an array of groups whose "preconstituted" interests and identities coincide, an articulation makes a graft or link from one struggle to the next by asserting an "equivalence" that alters how they identify and what they fight for.[72] Think of how the objectives and course of midcentury feminism have differed with its articulation to ideologies ranging from biological essentialism and "separate spheres" to Marxism. Materialist feminism, which sought to overturn "patriarchy," forged an equivalence between wage exploitation and the exploitation of wives and daughters through the concept "family mode of production."[73] Versions of feminism that sought to "revalorize 'femininity'" articulated their claims through logics of "difference" that more and less radical proponents of patriarchy used to demand a family wage for white working-class men.[74] Feminists who demanded equal access to employment and education, equal pay, and equal political and civil rights articulated their movements toward both liberalism and capitalism as vehicles of liberation. A claim by any of these variants of feminism to be truly "feminist" cannot be warranted on the ground that it represents "women," their "will," or their "interests"—because none of those conceptualizations exists independently of the various articulations of feminist struggle. Nor can any claim to be genuinely emancipatory, as each faction has mobilized followers by equivalences that hailed some people as "women" and rebuffed—even repelled—others.

Laclau and Mouffe identify the "democratic discourse" of rights as an especially powerful engine of equivalences that makes it possible to "propose . . . different forms of inequality as illegitimate and anti-natural."[75] Laclau and Mouffe understand rights as Lefort does, as "political to the core."[76] They treat rights as claims, which is to say, as speech acts or public demands that solicit "at least tacit approval from a broad section of public opinion."[77] They concur with Lefort that whether claims hold depends as much or more on creating a "widespread conviction that [they] conform to the demand for freedom enshrined in existing rights" as it does on establishing that such claims follow from a Constitutional foundation.[78]

Claims about rights move like a contagion, with actors forging relations of equivalence on the "principle of analogy" and thereby displacing such claims away from one struggle and onto another of a different kind.[79] From the mid-twentieth century onward alone, such analogies led to a proliferation of struggles: from the movement for Black people's civil and political rights, to feminists' struggle for reproductive and economic rights, to struggle by gays and lesbians, transgender persons, fat people and the differently abled for rights of various kinds. Laclau and Mouffe emphasize these "irradiation effects" of rights discourse as the source of a "profound subversive power" that serves emancipatory and not-so-emancipatory ends alike.[80] In Laclau and Mouffe's contemporary context, the neoliberal Right had seized that subversive power to as-great or greater effect than had the radical democratic Left.[81]

Equivalence and the Struggle to Abolish Slavery

The theory of democratic antagonism makes the mobilizing activity of political representation visible. The terms *articulation* and *equivalence* describe its practice. Political representatives in democratic societies—elected officials, social movements, opinion shapers, and advocates of all kinds—do not represent in the typical substitutionist, mimetic understanding of the term. They engage in articulation, the stitching-together of collectivities or groups by way of a "metaphorical transposition" of one struggle to another.[82] Though metaphorical, equivalence is far from being merely symbolic; it "contributes to the moulding and constitution of social relations."[83]

Legal scholar Pamela Brandwein shows this contribution in her painstaking archival research into the rival articulations that battled *on the same side* to support the adoption of the Thirteenth Amendment to the US Constitution.[84] Brandwein demonstrates that the struggle over abolition marked an antagonism for wage labor as well. It took place at the culmination of a phase of industrialization that opened up an antagonism or "revelatory" moment in which activists entertained a question that is nearly inconceivable today: whether contract labor is the quintessence of freedom or its opposite.[85] Those debates culminated in a turn to the ideological that fused contract labor to autonomy. This fusion lent legitimacy to an ideological matrix that linked capitalism to freedom. Although that matrix would be dramatically and often successfully contested by labor militancy from the turn of the twentieth century to the New Deal, the articulation of contract and freedom tipped the field of public debate against collective bargaining to create an asymmetry that thwarts labor struggle today.

Brandwein's astute analysis makes it clear that this battle marked a failed democratic antagonism, a moment where the capitalist social became hegemonic by prevailing in a decisive choice between irreconcilable options: Is contract on the side of freedom or on the side of slavery? This question produced two discourses *within* the coalition that advocated for passing the Thirteenth Amendment. One side advocated for "free labor" republicanism and the other for "labor movement antislavery," a movement that Brandwein's archival research shows to have been more developed and long-lasting than other scholars have recognized.[86]

Free labor republicanism promoted contract as pivotal for the emancipation of workers, creating an equivalence between "self-ownership and the equal rights to contract" that rendered the struggle for the labor contract analogous to that for abolition.[87] Thanks to this analogy, many contemporary scholars have counted free labor republicanism as an anticapitalist demand, one linking the struggle against slavery and that against class hierarchy. Brandwein argues that this interpretation gets it wrong. To promote contracts as emancipating workers is to abet the assimilation of "wage labor to 'freedom'"—an assimilation on which capitalism depends for its legitimacy.[88]

Labor movement antislavery offered a radical critique of capitalism by proposing a rival equivalence: not between emancipation as freeing slaves and contract as freeing workers but between the *struggles* of wage laborers and those of slaves. It represented the "equal right to contract" as "a 'fraud'" that emancipated no one.[89] Rather, it brought slavery back in a new form. Free labor republicanism equated wage laborers with *freed* slaves by representing contract and abolition as emancipatory forces; labor movement antislavery equated slave labor with wage labor to disclose the coercion in contract.

It matters whether a critique of slavery proceeds by affirming that wage labor is equivalent to (i.e., no better than) slavery or by promoting the contract as equivalent to abolition in its emancipation of wage laborers. The triumph of the free labor position did not affect the passage of the Thirteenth Amendment. But it vindicated a discourse that helped institutionalize wage labor in the US as a prerequisite to personal and political independence. The triumph of free labor echoes today in the language of "right to work" that has so successfully devastated union membership. Free labor republicanism prevailed over labor movement antislavery hegemonically. Not because "self-ownership and the equal rights to contract" are a *legitimate* basis for liberal freedom, but because that notion won out at a particularly consequential moment in the development of capitalism, liberalism, and the relationship between them. Brandwein brings this antagonism and its hegemonic resolution to light by establishing labor movement antislavery as its excluded alternative.

Workers today who bargain collectively for better wages and benefits do not suffer from false consciousness. They act within the constraints of a failed democratic antagonism. Proponents of labor movement antislavery occupied, by virtue of the counterhegemonic critique whose durability and significance Brandwein establishes, an "external" position from which to regard the wage labor contract as "illegitimate."[90] They fought to make the labor contract a site of antagonism by transforming it from a mark of independence to a relation of subordination, and from there into a site of oppression. Free labor republicanism helped to depoliticize wage labor so that workers would regard it as a *vehicle* for democratic liberties. Its triumph marked an ideological closure that helped to set the stage for the theory of radical, plural democracy by promoting wage work as a source of opportunity rather than a site of "clear-cut" exploitation between opposing classes.[91]

Conclusion

In 1985, Laclau and Mouffe addressed *HSS* to a radical Left operating in the shadow of the ideological closure whose first dramatic instance Brand-

wein traces to what other scholars have represented as a victory for democratic struggle. Laclau and Mouffe witnessed new social movements press-
ing rights claims to awaken comfortable people to the oppressions of their
everyday lives. They called on the Left (meaning the socialist left) to solicit
these newly politicized actors to step beyond their own particular demands,
asking them to struggle as well against those of their material comforts
that constituted oppression in the lives of others. Exploiting the *radical antagonistic character* of democratic struggle means tapping the promise of
plurality.

Imagine moving feminists—who have awakened to gender oppression
in the home and family—to an awareness of the oppressions that are written into the family home, itself the material condition that sustains patriar-
chal domination together with a comfortable middle-class lifestyle. Imagine
articulating feminist struggle to the struggle against exclusionary lending
practices and zoning laws that have established home ownership as a privilege of race and, increasingly, generation.[92] Such an articulation would press
a democratic antagonism to its radical extreme by amplifying the feminist
demand for "women's" rights into a demand for system transformation.

HSS concludes with a chapter of great urgency that portrays the
playing-out of new social movements as a missed opportunity for hegemonic practice on the Left and a triumph of that same practice on the
Right. The Right capitalized on the antagonistic character of democratic
struggles to call forth new social identities and open up long-established
partisan allegiances to remaking. Boldly tapping "liberal-conservatism"
(i.e., "neoliberalism") as the basis for a "new historic bloc," the New Right
movements that supported politicians like Margaret Thatcher and Ron-
ald Reagan succeeded in realigning groups that had benefited from the
welfare state and from unions with a conservative crusade against both.[93]

What scholars call *sorting* today got started back then. The effect of
such movements over time has not only been to polarize the US electorate but to make it so that social differences once again appear to decide
the sides of a political struggle in advance and thus to effectively predeter-
mine its outcome. The trouble with sorting is not just its divisiveness but
that it restores a premodern representation of the society/politics relation. Put simply, sorting is a new feudalism in this sense: it refixes political
conflict to social identity and stands out as a particularly noxious mode of
political ordering. Epitomizing the "double movement" of Lefort's *political*, it represents political conflict as originating from a prepolitical division of the social field into opposing teams, thereby instituting an order
even as it covers over its own work.[94]

Laclau and Mouffe's theory affords a vantage point from which to think differently about the damage that sorting does to democracy. Their first concern would not be with its effects on citizen judgment but with its effects on plurality, the "openness of the social."[95] In the vernacular of political science, sorted partisans stop being cross-pressured.[96] In the language of radical democracy, sorting turns back the democratic legacy of plurality that makes mobilization possible.

The concept of *plurality* provides a pivot point for the mobilization conception of representation. I have argued that acts of representation define groups, produce interests, and forge identities. They change the bias of conflict to bring new democratic actors into being and open up long-established partisan allegiances to remaking. For acts of representation to be able to displace one cleavage for another, people, groups, and institutions must be moveable. Plurality "assures" that people can be moved, that their group affiliations can be realigned.[97]

Laclau and Mouffe's theory of democratic antagonism reframes plurality from a given of modern Western society to a political achievement. It is at once an effect of the new social logic that the French Revolution made possible and a condition for the success of articulatory practice — one that sorting puts in jeopardy. Plurality, the precondition for representation as mobilization, is always under threat when group identifications become "sedimented" as social fact.[98] In contrast to the midcentury US pluralists, who tended to presuppose both the multiplicity of points of conflict and their independence from social determinants, Laclau and Mouffe theorize plurality as both a condition of democracy and a fragile democratic achievement.

Conclusion

I wrote this book for democrats who cannot imagine democracy without citizens, even if citizen participation goes no deeper than voting. We democrats, scholars and citizens alike, do not understand representative democracy very well when we hold it to the measure of responsiveness. Responsiveness assumes that individuals know what they want. It also presupposes that representatives are and ought to be guided primarily by constituent preferences, and that when they vote otherwise, they will account for it. In a soundbite world where a dense foliage of election, ballot, and campaign-finance law couples with voting restrictions and partisan redistricting to protect incumbents from competition, democratic accountability works poorly. Without the threat of being voted out of office, few representatives feel compelled to give reasons for their actions.

Empirical research on public-opinion formation and political knowledge makes it clear that representation in mass democracies neither begins from the bedrock of individual preferences nor rests on a primordial terrain of social groups. Preferences form and group identifications take shape in response to cues and appeals from political parties, from opinion shapers, from advocacy organizations, from candidates and office holders—and more. These appeals make democratic representation a far more dynamic process than our most immediate normative intuitions and most widespread empirical models, with their unidirectional notion of responsiveness, imagine it to be.

Research findings that contest the unidirectional model feed the sense that the modern experiment with democracy is in crisis and that the ideal of responsiveness asks more of mass electorates than they are competent to provide. Take this book as a crusade against competence. Rather than leap to indict voters for what they cannot do, I ask critics of mass democracy to question their own convictions regarding what voters need to be able to do. New understandings about preference formation and political knowledge in mass electorates suggest that the norms and habits of thinking that sustain people's most basic intuitions about representative democracy are out of date, rather than suggesting that voters cannot live up to those norms.

Against the bedrock norm and the habit of commonsense primordial thinking about group identity, I have made a constructivist turn. I acknowledge that political representation makes constituencies, and I recognize social division as an effect of power rather than a foundation for it. From these constructivist premises, I have argued that political representation does not mirror people's "bedrock" preferences; it mobilizes them. I have also argued that acts of representation do not reflect social cleavages; they cut lines through a political field of competing antagonisms that could be differently divided. This line-drawing produces constituency effects that scholars in the fields of public policy, political institutions, and public opinion have documented with their stories of deserving (and undeserving) veterans, resentful rurals and oblivious urbanites, and more.

This might seem like the kind of argument a person would make to drive home the civic incompetence narrative rather than to rebut it. I contend that it *does* rebut that narrative, so long as the mobilization conception of representation stands as an expression of a realist perspective— and I mean a realism that has earned the term. It may seem "realistic" to take Brexit, the presidential election of Donald Trump, and the proliferation of democratically elected authoritarian leaders in the West as proof that democracy would be better off if fewer citizens exercised their right to vote. But to equate realism with the cultivation of lowered expectations is to reduce a rich concept to an ordinary attitude and to tap an all too available antidemocratic elitism.

Realism as I have defined it equates neither to pessimism nor to power politics. It holds that conflict involves people in politics; that political conflict is not reducible to social cleavages; that political institutions discriminate among conflicts; and that institutional bias solicits—and discourages— the formation of political agents. Realism so defined calls democrats to reckon with the constitutive effects of the institutions, policies, and discourses of contemporary mass democracy. It prompts empirical and normative scholars alike to ask different questions, to assess democratic institutions and actors not by their responsiveness to what is "out there" but by the way that they divide the social field, mount political conflict, and solicit political identification. It prompts activists to fight the bias in ballot, registration, districting, voting and other such laws, even when it means mounting ballot measures to secure reforms whose importance is difficult to convey in the "picture-writing" that works in mass politics.

I have drawn this realism from promiscuous reading of scholarly works from vastly different traditions. In these pages, the self-proclaimed "realist" E. E. Schattschneider became an ally of radical democrats Ernesto Laclau and Chantal Mouffe. All three thinkers characterize democratic politics as a struggle to substitute one cleavage for another so as to activate the marginalized. They all agree that political speech aims to move people rather than to educate them. They all recognize the contagiousness of conflict and urge political actors to exploit it by taking their fights public and universalizing their claims in the language of rights.

Laclau and Mouffe propose two terms of great value to realist analysis in this mode. The first, *antagonism* (like Schattschneider's *cleavage*), divides a social space, supplying the architecture of identity and alliance that brings some conflicts to the fore while rendering others inconceivable. Antagonism is *sharp* conflict—it forces decisions on fundamental, often zero-sum issues (like: slavery or not? segregation or not?) that our two-party pluralist democracy excels at keeping off the table. The second, *articulation*, puts a radical spin on the joining-together of or coalition-building among demands and struggles that is a characteristic feature of pluralism. To articulate is not simply to join different interests together as they are but to transform the terms on which people identify themselves. Black Power, the White Ally, the Common Man—these are just a few articulations in US politics that have given rise to new social and political actors.

Throughout this book I have maintained that manipulation poses a less significant threat to democracy than sorting. This claim, implausible as it must sound to those who remain preoccupied by citizen competence, makes sense from a radical democratic vantage point. Radical democracy counts plurality as the enabling condition of representative democracy, when representation is understood in constructivist terms as a constituency-making practice. *Plurality* gives a name to the democratic inheritance of the eighteenth-century French and American revolutions: the unfixing of social relations from traditional hierarchies that lets political actors and movements sculpt conflict in potentially world-transforming ways. Sorting brings back a premodern imaginary in which social position determines political allegiance. It works against plurality by locking in patterns of alliance and enmity and foreclosing movement.

To think of democracy means to think of it as plural in the precise sense I have developed here. This conception means that political constituencies ought not to be deducible or predictable or containable by given calculations of interest. Where plurality exists, acts of political representation articulate interests, make subjects, and create unprecedented alliances. In the US for almost a century, such acts have produced at least as many "Frankenstein" hybrids as beloved communities.[1] When such alliances vote for Brexit or put Donald Trump at the helm of the world's most dangerous nation, it is easy to take those outcomes as evidence that mass democracy cultivates political manipulation and mass electorates fall for it.

I wrote this book as a realist who has faith in mass democracy. My realism compels me to acknowledge the monstrous hybrids as real. They are not mangled versions of the American Dream but products of exclusions and entitlements that are built into its basic premises. My realism also counsels me that the democrat's job is not to denounce any of democracy's creatures but to take part in mobilizing counterforces against the ones I oppose. To believe in the power and possibility of countermobilization among sporadically inattentive people—people like myself, who follow more cues than we give—*that* comes down to faith.

Acknowledgments

I have been fortunate to enjoy the support of colleagues, institutions, editors, family, and friends over the long course of writing this book. Thanks first to my exceptional current and former political theory colleagues at the University of Michigan, Pam Brandwein, Don Herzog, Jennet Kirkpatrick, Mika LaVaque-Manty, Anne Manuel, Arlene Saxonhouse, David Temin, Elizabeth Wingrove, and Mariah Zeisberg, who have offered many insights that have improved and clarified this project. Most of all, they have welcomed and nurtured a political theory project that takes its bearings, in part, from problems that have emerged from empirical political science research. I am grateful to Michigan political science colleagues Ted Brader, John Jackson, Ken Kollman, Skip Lupia, Rob Mickey, Chuck Shipan, and Nick Valentino, who helped me find my way to and through some of those intersections.

I started this book almost two decades ago when the concept of political representation was beginning a renaissance among political theorists in the West. Two pathbreaking articles by Mary Hawkesworth and Jenny Mansbridge set me on the course of bringing questions from empirical political science research into dialogue with concepts from political theory. This focus on political representation has meant that, over the course of fifteen years, I enjoyed regular conversations about it with a rich and varied group of scholars including Dario Castiglione, Mark Devenney, Paula Diehl, Jean-Marie Donegani, Samuel Hayat, Jenny Mansbridge, Laura Montanaro, Mike Neblo, Andrew Rehfeld, Andy Sabl, Mark Sadoun, Mike Saward, Lasse Thomassen, and Mark Warren. Generous invitations to workshops in gorgeous settings—Vancouver, BC; Bern, Switzerland; Lake Como, Italy; Paris, France; and Cambridge, MA—made the book much more fun to write. I thank Mark Warren, Marc Bühlmann and Jan

Fivaz, Claudia Landwehr and Armin Schäfer, and Jenny Mansbridge, Dario Castiglione, and Johannes Pollak for organizing those events and doing me the honor of including me. Participating with a mixed group of political theorists and political scientists at "Responsiveness, Representation, Democracy," a conference held at Columbia University in March 2013, helped me to hone the connections I have tried to make across those scholarly literatures. Thank you to Jeffrey Lax, Justin Phillips, and Melissa Schwartzberg for inviting me to participate. "Power and Representation," a conference held at the KU Leuven Institute of Philosophy in June 2014, organized by Marta Resmini and Mathijs van de Sande, inspired me to think about the work of Claude Lefort and launched the collaboration among Mathijs, Nadia Urbinati, and me that brought those conference papers to publication in an edited volume.

I acknowledge the generosity of James Booth, Brooke Ackerly, and participants in the Political Theory Workshop at Vanderbilt; Gerry Mackie, Tracy Strong, and participants in the Political Theory Workshop at the University of California, San Diego; Keith Gaddie, Jonathan Havercroft, and participants in the Political Theory Workshop at the University of Oklahoma; Peter Enns, Jason Frank, Alex Livingston, Vijay Phulwani, and participants in the PSAC Workshop at Cornell University; Winfried Thaa, Marcus Linden, and participants in the Political Theory Workshop at the University of Trier; Dario Castiglione, Andy Schapp, Iain Hampsher-Monk, Sandra Kröger, Sarah Childs, and participants in the Political Theory Reading Group at Exeter University; Bob Brecher, Lars Cornelissen, Mark Devenney, Robin Dunford, Andy Knott, Ian Sinclair, Clare Woodford, and workshop participants at the Centre for Applied Philosophy, Politics and Ethics at the University of Brighton who gave an earlier version of the manuscript a full day of incisive comments; Benjamin Boudou, Astrid von Busekist Sadoun, Tom Theuns, and participants in the Political Theory Workshop at Sciences Po; Nadia Urbinati, Jean Cohen, Kevin Elliott, and participants in the Political Theory Workshop at Columbia University; Emilee Chapman, Alison McQueen, Bernardo Zacka, and participants in the Political Theory Workshop at Stanford University; Hélène Landemore, Karuna Mantena, Vatsal Naresh, Giulia Oskian, Naomi Scheinerman, Ian Shapiro, and participants in the Political Theory Workshop at Yale University; and Bernardo Zacka, Sally Haslanger, Devin Caughey, and participants in the Political Theory Workshop at MIT. I also thank the Working Group in Political Theory, organized (and fed) by Carlo Invernizzi Accetti, which has included Chris

Bickerton, Kevin Duong, Carlos De La Torre Espinosa, Samuel Hayat, Russell Muirhead, Alessandro Mulieri, Giulia Oskian, Nancy Rosenblum, Maria Paula Saffon, Yves Sintomer, and Nadia Urbinati.

I am especially grateful to a handful of people to whom I have turned multiple times to help me sort out my thinking, for advice on various scholarly literatures, and for periodic infusions of enthusiasm about the project. Thank you to Mark Brown, Sam Chambers, Jamie Druckman, Larry Jacobs, Samuel Hayat, and Joe Soss. Jamie, your well-tempered optimism about mass democracy sustained my belief in this project when world events put it to the test. Sam, you will find your eloquent phrases in these pages. Chapter 6 of this book benefited from comments from Sam Moyn, Greg Conti, and Will Selinger. Conversations with Jason Frank have shaped this project's course over the years, as did his engaged and insightful reading of the book manuscript for University of Chicago Press. I give special thanks to Chantal Mouffe for her long-standing support of my work, for confirming my enthusiasm for E. E. Schattschneider, and for providing thoughtful comments on several book chapters. I wish that Ernesto Laclau had lived to see the fruits of these labors that our conversations many years ago helped to launch.

I am privileged to work at one of the finest research universities in the US, where attention to graduate and undergraduate education is highly valued. The students who took graduate seminars with me on political representation here at the University of Michigan, at the University of Minnesota, and at Sciences Po in Paris participated with me in developing these ideas. Conversations with Chris Skovron and James Strickland helped me orient myself in debates over the "Big Sort" and interest-group politics. I have received considerable financial support for this project from the University of Michigan and its College of Literature, Science and the Arts. I am grateful for a yearlong Faculty Fellowship at the Institute for the Humanities (2010–2011), a release for duty off campus (fall 2014), and a Humanities Award that allowed me a full year's sabbatical (2019). The College of Liberal Arts and the Institute for Research on Women and Gender also funded a two-day Political Representation Institute (2010) that enabled me to bring together for a seminar-style discussion many of the scholars whose work appears in these pages. Thanks to Erin Baribeau for helping to compose the "syllabus" for that event and for her thoughtful participation in the discussions.

At the University of Chicago Press, I have been fortunate to work with two talented, compassionate, and extremely patient editors, John

Tryneski and Chuck Myers. Chuck has kept the project on track, welcomed every bit of progress, and forgiven many delays. I am grateful to him and to Jason Frank and three anonymous readers whose comments helped me reorganize and sharpen the arguments. Holly Smith managed the marketing and Tamara Ghattas supervised the copyediting, which Jessica Wilson performed on behalf of the press with thoughtfulness, care, and an acute sense for when evasive language attempted to provide cover for an argument that had not quite landed. Danielle LaVaque-Manty and Bonnie Washick also gave me invaluable editorial advice on the manuscript that helped bring the project into focus for me at different stages of its production. Thanks to Merisa Bahar Sahin and Janice Feng for their hours of painstaking work on the bibliography and endnotes.

I could not have finished this book without Arya, whose insatiable desire for fast walks liberated me from my desk. Nor would it have been possible without the support of the many friends with whom I have enjoyed improvisational conversation, storefront theater in Chicago, killer swim workouts, home-cooked gourmet dinners, Sunday brunches, bottles of champagne, baking Christmas stollen, summer weeks on Madeline Island, book groups, movie nights, and pandemic evenings huddled around fire pits or shivering on screened-in porches. Thank you, dear friends: Mika LaVaque-Manty, Danielle LaVaque-Manty, Sue Juster, and the Trollopistes; John Mowitt and Jeanine Ferguson; Gayle Rubin, David Halperin, and Rostom Mesli; Andy Buchsbaum and Cathy Fleischer; Kirsten Clark, Kerstin Barndt, Johannes von Moltke, Helmut Puff, Silke-Maria Weineck, Stefan Szymanski, Sophie Grillet, and Bipin Patel; and Ingrid Crause and Jamie Saville. And to Peter Handler, MaryBeth Sova, Francis Greene, Siobhan Moroney, and Paula Schriner, whose friendships have sustained me since elementary school, high school, or graduate school—can you believe how much we have seen together and how much more there is to come?

I close with family. My extended family, Elaine Disch and Barb, Linda, Robbin, and Dana Smith, believe in me no matter how long these books take to complete. The community of neighbors on Prospect Avenue in Evanston, Illinois, has watched over my mother for almost a decade now, which has made it possible for both of us to continue living independent lives. I wish I had the eloquence to thank my partner and husband, Andreas Gailus, as graciously as he has thanked me. I am grateful to him for building a life with me that allows each of us to follow our own interests, to throw ourselves into solitary pursuits, and to find each other again after periods of absence or distraction. I dedicate this book to him, with love.

Portions of the introduction and portions of chapter 2 of this work draw upon "The 'Constructivist Turn' in Democratic Representation: A Normative Dead-End?" *Constellations* 22, no. 4 (December 2015), 487–99, published by Wiley, and on two articles previously published by Cambridge University Press and used with permission here: "Toward a Mobilization Conception of Democratic Representation," *American Political Science Review* 105, no. 1 (February 2011), 100–114, and "Democratic Representation and the Constituency Paradox," *Perspectives on Politics* 10, no. 3 (September 2012), 599–616.

Notes

Introduction

1. I base this assertion on two different threads of empirical research: studies of heuristics or informational cues and studies of argumentative strategies such as framing and priming (see note 19, below). Although the studies of heuristics and argumentation constitute distinct lines of inquiry, the two phenomena overlap in practice both because people can learn from frames and because cues can be embedded in the frames proposed by political parties and interest groups. See James N. Druckman, Cari Lynn Hennessy, Kristi St. Charles, and Jonathan Webber, "Competing Rhetoric over Time: Frames versus Cues," *Journal of Politics* 72, no. 1 (2010): 136–48.

2. Lisa Disch, "Toward a Mobilization Conception of Democratic Representation," *American Political Science Review* 105, no. 1 (2011): 100–114. I take this distinction between the terms "conception" and "concept" from Schweber, who argues that political theorists are mistaken to think that they can propose a concept of "political representation"; the phrase "names a specific conception (or set of conceptions)" of the "larger concept" —representation. He also emphasizes that in contrast to concepts, which must be defined in universally valid terms, conceptions are "contestable," meaning that they serve to stimulate rather than settle debates about meaning and measurement. See Howard Schweber, "The Limits of Political Representation," *American Political Science Review* 110, no. 2 (2016): 382–96, at 384.

3. In 2016, survey research found the widest-ever gap between people who believed government was run for the benefit of a "few big interests" (81%) and those who had faith that it was run for the "benefit of all" (19%). See American National Election Studies, "Is the Government Run for the Benefit of All 1964–2016," Table 5A.2 in *The ANES Guide to Public Opinion and Electoral Behavior*, based on work supported by the National Science Foundation under grant numbers SES 1444721, 2014–2017, the University of Michigan, and Stanford University, accessed June 17, 2020, https://electionstudies.org/resources/anes-guide/top-tables/?id=59.

4. Martin Gilens, *Affluence and Influence: Economic Inequality and Political Power in America* (Princeton, NJ: Princeton University Press, 2012).

5. Christopher H. Achen and Larry M. Bartels, *Democracy for Realists: Why Elections Do Not Produce Responsive Government* (Princeton, NJ: Princeton University Press, 2016), 306.

6. James N. Druckman, "Pathologies of Studying Public Opinion, Political Communication, and Democratic Responsiveness," *Political Communication* 31, no. 3 (2014): 467–92.

7. Druckman, "Pathologies of Studying Public Opinion," 469.

8. A 2019 exhibition at the Grand Palais in Paris argued this point in objects and images. See Nicolas Liucci-Goutnikov, Galeries Nationales du Grand Palais (Paris), Établissement Public de la Réunion des Musées Nationaux et du Grand Palais des Champs-Élysées (France), and Centre National d'Art et de Culture Georges Pompidou (Paris), *Rouge: art et utopie au pays des Soviets* (Paris: Galeries Nationales du Grand Palais, 2019).

9. Drawing a distinction from Stanley Cavell's account of the political claim, Linda Zerilli observes that "feminists have not adequately articulated the difference between speaking about women as a demographic or social group and speaking about women as a political collectivity." See Zerilli, *Feminism and the Abyss of Freedom* (Chicago: University of Chicago Press, 2005), 171.

10. Nadia Urbinati, *Representative Democracy: Principles and Genealogy* (Chicago: University of Chicago Press, 2006), 5; emphasis in original.

11. Nancy L. Schwartz, *The Blue Guitar* (Chicago: University of Chicago Press, 1988), ch 2.

12. Iris Marion Young, *Inclusion and Democracy* (New York: Oxford University Press, 2002), 125.

13. Jacques Derrida, "Speech and Phenomena: Introduction to the Problem of Signs in Husserl's Phenomenology," in *Speech and Phenomena*, trans. David B. Allison (Evanston, IL: Northwestern University Press, 1973 [1967]): 1–104.

14. Urbinati, *Representative Democracy*, 46, 33.

15. Suzanne Mettler and Joe Soss, "The Consequences of Public Policy for Democratic Citizenship: Bridging Policy Studies and Mass Politics," *Perspectives on Politics* 2, no. 1 (March 2004): 55–73, at 58.

16. I find examples of constructivist empirical scholarship mostly in studies of heuristics and studies of framing and priming. For research on heuristics, see: Edward G. Carmines and James H. Kuklinski, "Incentives, Opportunities, and the Logic of Public Opinion in American Political Representation," in *Information and Democratic Processes*, ed. John A. Ferejohn and James H. Kuklinski (Urbana: University of Illinois Press, 1990): 240–68; Arthur Lupia, "Busy Voters, Agenda Control, and the Power of Information," *American Political Science Review* 86, no. 2 (June 1992): 390–403; "Shortcuts versus Encyclopedias: Information and Voting Behavior in California Insurance Reform Elections," *American Political Science*

Review 88, no. 1 (March 1994): 63–76; Arthur Lupia and Mathew D. McCubbins, *The Democratic Dilemma: Can Citizens Learn What They Need To Know?* (Cambridge, UK: Cambridge University Press, 1998); Samuel Popkin, *The Reasoning Voter* (Chicago: University of Chicago Press, 1991); Paul M. Sniderman, "Taking Sides: A Fixed Choice Theory of Political Reasoning," in *Elements of Reason: Cognition, Choice, and the Bounds of Rationality*, eds. Arthur Lupia, Mathew D. McCubbins, and Samuel L. Popkin (New York: Cambridge University Press, 2000): 67–84; Paul M. Sniderman, Richard A. Brody, and Philip E. Tetlock, *Reasoning and Choice: Explorations in Political Psychology* (Cambridge, UK: Cambridge University Press, 1991). For studies of framing and priming, see: Dennis Chong and James N. Druckman, "Framing Public Opinion in Competitive Democracies," *American Political Science Review* 101, no. 4 (November 2007): 637–55; James N. Druckman, "Political Preference Formation: Competition, Deliberation, and the (Ir)relevance of Framing Effects," *American Political Science Review* 98, no. 4 (November 2004): 671–86; James N. Druckman, "The Implications of Framing Effects for Citizen Competence," *Political Behavior* 23, no. 3 (September 2001): 225–56; William A. Gamson and Andre Modigliani, "Media Discourse and Public Opinion on Nuclear Power: A Constructionist Approach," *American Journal of Sociology* 95, no. 1 (July 1989): 1–37; Donald R. Kinder and Thomas E. Nelson, "Democratic Debate and Real Opinions," in *Framing American Politics*, ed. Karen Callaghan and Frauke Schnell (Pittsburgh: University of Pittsburgh Press, 2005): 103–22; Paul M. Sniderman and Sean M. Theriault, "The Structure of Political Argument and the Logic of Issue Framing," in *Studies in Public Opinion: Attitudes, Nonattitudes, Measurement Error, and Change*, eds. Willem E. Saris and Paul M. Sniderman (Princeton, NJ: Princeton University Press, 2004): 133–65; John Zaller, *The Nature and Origins of Mass Opinion* (Cambridge, UK: Cambridge University Press, 1992). See also Elisabeth R. Gerber and John E. Jackson, "Endogenous Preferences and the Study of Institutions," *American Political Science Review* 87, no. 3 (September 1993): 639–56.

17. I follow Zaller (*The Nature and Origins of Mass Opinion*, 6) in defining elites as "politicians, higher-level government officials, journalists, some activists, and many kinds of experts and policy specialists," as well as corporate elites. They influence preference formation primarily by means of the mass media, and secondarily through such organizations as lobbies, churches, and labor unions. Social movements afford one example of an important non-elite source of cues. Social media provides a platform for both elite and non-elite cue-giving. See David Karpf, *Analytic Activism: Digital Listening and the New Political Strategy* (New York: Oxford University Press, 2016) and Betsy Sinclair, *The Social Citizen: Peer Networks and Political Behavior* (Chicago: University of Chicago Press, 2012).

18. James N. Druckman, "The Implications of Framing Effects for Citizen Competence," 239.

19. Elmer Eric Schattschneider, *The Semisovereign People*, reprinted ed., intro. by David Adamany (Fort Worth: Harcourt Brace Jovanovich, 1975).

20. Some scholars understand competence to mean the simple capacity to make informed choices in one's own interests. Others demand more. They want citizens, both ordinary and elite, to be able to weigh various policy initiatives, consider their own interests, and land on an outcome that promotes "democratic values" and furthers "a common good." See Richard Krouse and George Marcus, "Electoral Studies and Democratic Theory Reconsidered," *Political Behavior* 6, no. 1 (1984): 23–39, at 31; and George Marcus, "Democratic Theories and the Study of Public Opinion," *Polity* 21, no. 1 (September 1988): 25–44, at 43, cited in Stephen Earl Bennett, "Democratic Competence, Before Converse and After," *Critical Review* 18, no. 1–3 (January 2006): 105–41, at 107.

21. Achen and Bartels, *Democracy for Realists*, 325.

22. Jason Brennan, *Against Democracy* (Princeton, NJ: Princeton University Press, 2016), 210–14.

23. Bennett, "Democratic Competence, Before Converse and After," 109.

24. Walter Lippmann, *The Phantom Public* (New York: Harcourt, Brace, 1925), 67. John Dewey, *The Public and its Problems* (Denver, Swallow, 1927).

25. Lippmann, *The Phantom Public*, 67, 55.

26. Dewey, *The Public and Its Problems*, 131, 146.

27. Druckman, "Pathologies of Studying Public Opinion," 478.

28. Druckman, "Pathologies of Studying Public Opinion," 478.

29. Druckman, "Pathologies of Studying Public Opinion," 481.

30. Schattschneider posed the problem well but he romanticized political parties, which he counted foremost among the forms of organizing that socialized conflict, as the solution. He also trusted too much that such concepts as "equality, consistency, equal protection of the laws, justice, liberty, freedom of movement, freedom of speech and association, and civil rights" would always serve emancipatory causes (*The Semisovereign People*, 7).

31. Joseph Uscinski, "The 5 Most Dangerous Conspiracy Theories of 2016," *Politico*, August 22, 2016, https://www.politico.com/magazine/story/2016/08/conspiracy-theories-2016-donald-trump-hillary-clinton-214183.

32. Druckman, "Pathologies of Studying Public Opinion," 478.

33. Druckman, "Pathologies of Studying Public Opinion," 468.

34. Lupia and McCubbins, *The Democratic Dilemma*, 37.

35. Druckman, "Pathologies of Studying Public Opinion," 478.

36. Lupia and McCubbins, *The Democratic Dilemma*, 21.

37. Druckman, "Pathologies of Studying Public Opinion," 478; Schattschneider, *The Semisovereign People*, 126.

38. Schattschneider, 66.

39. Schattschneider, 11, 34–35.

40. Schattschneider, 66.

41. Schattschneider, 100.

42. Schattschneider, 111.

43. Schattschneider, 100.

44. Ernesto Laclau and Chantal Mouffe, *Hegemony and Socialist Strategy: Towards a Radical Democratic Politics* (New York: Verso Books, 1985), hereafter *HSS*, 85.

45. Ernesto Laclau, *New Reflections on the Revolution of Our Time* (New York: Verso, 1990), 35.

46. Eric Schickler's account of this transformation emphasizes that President Lyndon Johnson's efforts to "mov[e] his party to embrace racial liberalism" did not originate this transformation; the national partisan realignment began in the mid-1930s with a political remaking of the social orchestrated by the CIO, civil rights advocacy groups, and state-level elected officials who linked together "concerns about class and race" in a relation of interdependence that went beyond mere coalition. Schickler describes issues of the *CIO News* dating to 1938 that proclaimed "the right to strike as a 'civil right'" and cast anti-Black terrorism as an indispensable tool in a system of forced labor so as to frame a democratic struggle that neither Black nor white workers could truly win without advancing each other's cause. See *Racial Realignment: The Transformation of American Liberalism, 1932–1965* (Princeton, NJ: Princeton University Press, 2016), 285, 4, 59.

47. Cristina Beltrán, *The Trouble with Unity: Latino Politics and the Creation of Identity* (New York: Oxford University Press, 2010), 9.

48. Laclau and Mouffe, *HSS*, 153.

49. Laclau and Mouffe, *HSS*, 60.

50. Morris P. Fiorina, with Samuel J. Abrams and Jeremy C. Pope, *Culture War? The Myth of a Polarized America* (New York: Longman, 2005).

51. Fiorina writes that "at the highest levels the parties are more polarized, but . . . this *partisan* polarization has only a faint reflection in *popular* polarization, so the latter certainly is not a cause of the former" (See Fiorina, *Culture War?*, 5–6).

52. For an early sounding of sorting through the popular theme of "red" America versus "blue" America that does not exaggerate the "chasm" between them, see David Brooks, "One Nation, Slightly Divisible," *Atlantic Monthly*, December 2001: 53–65, https://www.theatlantic.com/magazine/archive/2001/12/one-nation-slightly-divisible/376441/.

53. Fiorina, *Culture War?*, ix.

54. James N. Druckman, Samara Klar, Yanna Krupnikov, Matthew Levendusky, and John Barry Ryan, "(Mis)estimating Affective Polarization" (unpublished working paper, Northwestern University, Institute for Policy Research, last modified November 16, 2020, 2). https://www.ipr.northwestern.edu/documents/working-papers/2019/wp-19-25rev.pdf.

55. Bill Bishop, with Robert G. Cushing, *The Big Sort: Why the Clustering of Like-Minded America Is Tearing Us Apart* (Boston: Houghton Mifflin, 2008).

56. Bishop, 13.

57. Samuel Abrams and Morris P. Fiorina, "'The Big Sort' That Wasn't: A Skeptical Reexamination," *PS: Political Science and Politics* 45, no. 2 (2012): 203–10, at 204.

58. Abrams and Fiorina, 204.

59. Abrams and Fiorina, 203.

60. Shanto Iyengar, Gaurav Sood, and Yphtach Lelkes, "Affect, Not Ideology: A Social Identity Perspective on Polarization," *Public Opinion Quarterly* 76, no. 3 (Fall 2012): 405–31, at 407.

61. Matthew Levendusky, *The Partisan Sort: How Liberals Became Democrats and Conservatives Became Republicans* (Chicago: University of Chicago Press, 2009), 3.

62. Iyengar, Sood, and Lelkes, "Affect, Not Ideology: A Social Identity Perspective on Polarization," 407.

63. Shanto Iyengar, Yphtach Lelkes, Matthew Levendusky, Neil Mahotra, and Sean Westwood, "The Origins and Consequences of Affective Polarization in the United States," *Annual Review of Political Science* 22 (2019): 129–46, at 130.

64. Iyengar, Sood, and Lelkes, "Affect, Not Ideology: A Social Identity Perspective on Polarization," 407.

65. Iyengar, Sood, and Lelkes, 407.

66. Iyengar, Sood, and Lelkes, 405, 407.

67. Lilliana Mason, *Uncivil Agreement: How Politics Became Our Identity* (Chicago: University of Chicago Press, 2018), 6.

68. Mason, 23.

69. Mason, 14; emphasis in original.

70. Mason, 4; emphasis added.

71. Iyengar, Sood, and Lelkes, "Affect, Not Ideology: A Social Identity Perspective on Polarization," 417.

72. Iyengar, Sood, and Lelkes, 420.

73. Samara Klar, Yanna Krupnikov, and John Barry Ryan, "Affective Polarization or Partisan Disdain: Untangling a Dislike for the Opposing Party from a Dislike of Partisanship," *Public Opinion Quarterly* 82, no. 2 (2018): 379–90, at 379.

74. Druckman, Klar, Krupnikov, Levendusky, and Ryan, "(Mis)estimating Affective Polarization," 2.

75. Klar, Krupnikov, and Ryan, "Affective Polarization or Partisan Disdain," 379.

76. When researchers provided "context about how important partisan politics is to the hypothetical in-law," they found not only that people "appear willing to spend time with individuals with whom they disagree as long as they do not talk about politics," but that they are reluctant to spend time with those whose partisanship they *share* if those people are inclined toward political debate (Klar, Krupnikov, and Ryan, 380, 389, 383).

77. Levendusky, *The Partisan Sort*, 1.

78. Using a combination of cross-sectional studies and panel data studies from the National Election Study, Levendusky found that in 1972, "just 28 percent of the electorate was sorted" (*The Partisan Sort*, 45). Major political events of the 1990s—such as Newt Gingrich's "Contract with America," the Clinton administration's health reform initiative, and the impeachment of President Clinton—dramatically clarified elite political polarization. By 2004, sorting had increased to 46 percent of the electorate, with Levendusky noting that since "many Americans . . . cannot be sorted by definition"—either because they identify as moderates or because they do not position themselves in terms of ideology at all—"these trends [are] even more impressive" (45). For the subset of the US population that is politically engaged, it appears that sorting has become the norm.

79. Levendusky, 4.

80. Levendusky, 2.

81. Levendusky, 128–29.

82. Bernard Manin, *The Principles of Representative Government* (New York: Cambridge University Press, 1997), 227; emphasis in original.

83. Abrams and Fiorina, " 'The Big Sort' That Wasn't: A Skeptical Reexamination," 204.

84. Fiorina, *Culture War?*, 5.

Chapter One

1. David R. Cameron, "Toward a Theory of Political Mobilization," *Journal of Politics* 36, no. 1 (February 1974): 138–71, at 139.

2. Christopher H. Achen and Larry M. Bartels, *Democracy for Realists: Why Elections Do Not Produce Responsive Government* (Princeton, NJ: Princeton University Press, 2016), 311.

3. Patrick J. Egan, "Group Cohesion without Group Mobilization: The Case of Lesbians, Gays and Bisexuals," *British Journal of Political Science* 42, no. 3 (2012): 597–616, at 598; emphasis added. See also Bernard R. Berelson, Paul F. Lazarsfeld, and William N. McPhee, *Voting: A Study of Opinion Formation in a Presidential Campaign* (Chicago: University of Chicago Press, 1954).

4. Put differently, acts of political representation are "performative" in the sense that Judith Butler has used this concept, as a speaking and acting that bring realities into being while seeming merely to follow from an existing state of affairs (See Judith Butler, "For a Careful Reading," in *Feminist Contentions: A Philosophical Exchange*, by Seyla Benhabib, Judith Butler, Drucilla Cornell, and Nancy Fraser, with an introduction by Linda Nicholson (New York: Routledge, 1995): 127–44, at 134.)

5. Michael Saward, "The Representative Claim," *Contemporary Political Theory* 5, no. 3 (2006): 297–318. Howard Schweber objects that Saward's and other

constructivist understandings of political representation stretch the term beyond all meaning. Rather than counter constructivist argumentation, however, he fights such approaches by stipulation, asserting that "a claim that a relationship can be described as 'representative' requires not only authorization by a constituency but also a valid 'political constituency,'" which he defines as commonly "affected" individuals who have not yet *formed* as "a collective political actor." See Howard Schweber, "The Limits of Political Representation," *American Political Science Review* 110, no. 2 (2016): 382–96, at 390.

6. Laura Montanaro, "The Democratic Legitimacy of Self-Appointed Representatives," *Journal of Politics* 74, no. 4 (October 2012): 1094–1107.

7. Deva Woodly, *The Politics of Common Sense: How Social Movements Use Public Discourse to Change Politics and Win Acceptance* (Oxford: Oxford University Press, 2015).

8. Rogers Brubaker, *Ethnicity without Groups* (Cambridge, MA: Harvard University Press, 2004), 8.

9. Brubaker, *Ethnicity without Groups*, 8.

10. Paul Pierson, "When Effect Becomes Cause: Policy Feedback and Political Change," *World Politics* 45, no. 4 (July 1993): 595–628, at 595.

11. Jane McAlevey, *No Shortcuts: Organizing for Power in the New Gilded Age* (New York: Oxford University Press, 2016).

12. Hahrie Han, *How Organizations Develop Activists: Civic Associations and Leadership in the 21st Century* (New York: Oxford University Press, 2014), 8.

13. McAlevey, *No Shortcuts*, 10.

14. McAlevey, 2.

15. Bert Klandermans, "Mobilization and Participation: Social-Psychological Expansions of Resource Mobilization Theory," *American Sociological Review* 49, no. 5 (October 1984): 583–600.

16. Klandermans, 596.

17. Klandermans, 589.

18. Klandermans, 586. Consensus mobilization and action mobilization may not map exactly onto the opposition that Han and McAlevey set up between organizing and mobilizing. Klandermans can be faulted for leaving out the peer-to-peer cultivation of leadership on the shop floor that McAlevey centers in her account. But neither is Klandermans's "action mobilization" reducible to McAlevey's "shallow" corporate campaign.

19. Brubaker, *Ethnicity without Groups*, 8.

20. Brubaker, 10.

21. Brubaker, 3.

22. Brubaker, 9.

23. Brubaker, 17; emphasis in original.

24. Brubaker, 11.

25. Cameron, "Toward a Theory of Political Mobilization," 139.

26. Cameron, 139.

27. Cameron, 145.

28. Cameron, 139–40.

29. Cameron, 166.

30. Cameron, 167.

31. Cameron, 153.

32. Cameron, 153.

33. Cameron, 161; emphasis added.

34. Ernesto Laclau and Chantal Mouffe, *Hegemony and Socialist Strategy: Towards a Radical Democratic Politics* (New York: Verso Books, 1985), 153.

35. See Lisa Disch, *The Tyranny of the Two-Party System* (New York: Columbia University Press, 2002).

36. I discuss these examples further in the next chapter.

37. Pierson, "When Effect Becomes Cause," 595.

38. Andrea Campbell, "Policy Makes Mass Politics," *Annual Review of Political Science* 15 (2012): 333–51, at 334.

39. Pierson, "When Effect Becomes Cause," 595.

40. Campbell, "Policy Makes Mass Politics," 336.

41. Pierson, "When Effect Becomes Cause," 599.

42. Suzanne Mettler and Joe Soss, "The Consequences of Public Policy for Democratic Citizenship: Bridging Policy Studies and Mass Politics," *Perspectives on Politics* 2, no. 1 (March 2004): 55–73, at 58.

43. Mettler and Soss, 59.

44. Campbell, "Policy Makes Mass Politics," 333.

45. Jacob S. Hacker, *The Divided Welfare State: The Battle over Public and Private Social Benefits in the United States* (Cambridge, UK: Cambridge University Press, 2002), 42.

46. Hacker, 16. Hacker further points out that total spending for the US system's various modes of social provision—its comparatively low taxation of public benefits plus its "tax expenditures" (relief provided in the form of foregone tax revenues on both individuals and corporations), combined with transfer payments—is not "markedly smaller" than social spending in "other affluent democracies" (16).

47. Hacker, 94–5.

48. Hacker, 94.

49. Hacker, 113. An accounting detail played a role here too. The Federal government seemed to discourage this kind of pension—and workforce—stratification by requiring that pension plans be nondiscriminatory. But this requirement was defined in practice to mean only that pensions for higher-paid personnel should represent "no greater share of total pay" than those for lower-paid workers. Moreover, the 1942 Revenue Act provision for "integration" of private and public pension plans allowed employers to factor both what they *and their workers* paid in Social Security taxes into calculating those shares; consequently, private pension

plans "could continue to provide little or no benefits to most workers without running afoul of the nondiscrimination restrictions" (120).

50. Hacker, 303.

51. Hacker, 300; emphasis added.

52. Hacker, 23.

53. Hacker, xiii.

54. Hacker, 43, 42.

55. Hacker, 43.

56. Hacker, 43.

57. Iris Marion Young, *Justice and the Politics of Difference* (Princeton, NJ: Princeton University Press, 1990), 47.

58. Young, *Justice and the Politics of Difference*, 47–48.

59. William E. Connolly, *Identity/Difference: Democratic Negotiations of Political Paradox*, expanded ed. (Minneapolis: University of Minnesota Press, 2002), 64.

60. Laura S. Jensen, "Constructing and Entitling America's Original Veterans," in *Deserving and Entitled: Social Constructions and Public Policy*, eds. Anne L. Schneider and Helen M. Ingram (Albany: State University of New York Press, 2005): 35–62, at 35.

61. Jensen, 35–6.

62. Jensen, 35.

63. Jensen, 37.

64. Jensen, 38.

65. Jensen, 36; emphasis in original.

66. Jensen, 36.

67. Anne L. Schneider and Helen M. Ingram, *Policy Design for Democracy* (Lawrence: University of Kansas Press, 1997), 107.

68. Anne L. Schneider and Helen M. Ingram, "Introduction: Public Policy and the Social Construction of Deservedness," in Schneider and Ingram, eds., *Deserving and Entitled*: 1–33, at 3.

69. Schneider and Ingram, "Introduction," 3.

70. Deborah Stone, "Foreword," in Schneider and Ingram, eds., *Deserving and Entitled*: ix–xiii, at xi.

71. Joe Soss, "Making Clients and Citizens: Welfare Policy as a Source of Status, Belief, and Action," in Schneider and Ingram, eds., *Deserving and Entitled*: 291–328.

72. Soss, "Making Clients and Citizens," 313.

73. Soss, "Making Clients and Citizens," 313.

74. Soss, "Making Clients and Citizens," 317.

75. Suzanne Mettler, *Soldiers to Citizens: The G.I. Bill and the Making of the Greatest Generation* (Oxford: Oxford University Press, 2005), 17.

76. Mettler and Soss, "The Consequences of Public Policy for Democratic Citizenship," 61.

77. Soss, "Making Clients and Citizens," 312.

78. Joe Soss, panel comments delivered at the Annual Meeting of the Western Political Science Association, Los Angeles, CA, 2012, emphasis in original.

79. Joe Soss, "Comments."

80. Andrea Campbell, *How Policies Make Citizens: Senior Political Activism and the American Welfare State* (Princeton, NJ: Princeton University Press, 2003), 2, 77.

81. Campbell, *How Policies Make Citizens*, 138.

82. Campbell, *How Policies Make Citizens*, 40.

83. Campbell, *How Policies Make Citizens*, 2, 142.

84. Edwin Amenta, *When Movements Matter: The Townsend Plan and the Rise of Social Security* (Princeton, NJ: Princeton University Press, 2008), 1.

85. Amenta, 56.

86. Amenta, 56.

87. Ira Katznelson and Suzanne Mettler, "On Race and Policy History: A Dialogue about the G.I. Bill," in *Perspectives on Politics* 6, no. 3 (September 2008): 519–37.

88. Margot Canaday, *The Straight State: Sexuality and Citizenship in Twentieth-Century America* (Princeton, NJ: Princeton University Press, 2009): 147; emphasis in original.

89. Canaday, 138.

90. Canaday, 172.

91. Mettler and Soss, "The Consequences of Public Policy for Democratic Citizenship," 61.

92. Young, *Justice and the Politics of Difference*, 46, 43; William Connolly, *Identity/Difference*, 64.

Chapter Two

1. Nadia Urbinati, *Representative Democracy, Principles and Genealogy* (Chicago: University of Chicago Press, 2006), 24; emphasis added.

2. Lisa Disch, "Toward a Mobilization Conception of Political Representation," *American Political Science Review* 105, no. 1 (2011), 100.

3. Benjamin I. Page and Robert Y. Shapiro, *The Rational Public: Fifty Years of Trends in Americans' Policy Preferences* (Chicago: University of Chicago Press, 1992), 354; Christopher H. Achen, "Mass Political Attitudes and the Survey Response," *American Political Science Review* 69, no. 4 (1975): 1218–1231, at 1227; Larry Bartels, "Democracy with Attitudes," in *Electoral Democracy*, eds. Michael B. McKuen and George Rabinowitz (Ann Arbor: University of Michigan Press, 2003).

4. See Page and Shapiro, *The Rational Public*; and Stuart N. Soroka and Christopher Wlezien, *Degrees of Democracy: Politics, Public Opinion, and Policy* (Cambridge, UK: Cambridge University Press, 2010).

5. James N. Druckman, "Pathologies of Studying Public Opinion, Political Communication, and Democratic Responsiveness," *Political Communication* 31, no. 3 (2014): 467–92, at 468.

6. W. E. Miller and D. E. Stokes, "Constituency Influence in Congress," *American Political Science Review* 57, no. 1 (March 1963): 45–56.

7. Andrew Rehfeld, "Towards a General Theory of Representation," *Journal of Politics* 68, no. 1 (2006): 1–21, at 3.

8. Hanna Fenichel Pitkin, *The Concept of Representation* (Berkeley: University of California Press, 1967), 208.

9. Pitkin, *The Concept of Representation*, 140.

10. Christopher H. Achen and Larry M. Bartels, *Democracy for Realists: Why Elections Do Not Produce Responsive Government* (Princeton, NJ: Princeton University Press, 2016), 1.

11. John C. Wahlke, "Policy Demands and System Support: The Role of the Represented," *British Journal of Political Science* 1, no. 3 (1971): 271–90, at 272–3; Cass Sunstein, "Preferences and Politics," *Philosophy and Public Affairs* 20, no. 10 (1991): 3–34, at 6–7.

12. Pitkin, *The Concept of Representation*, 214, 220.

13. Pitkin, *The Concept of Representation*, 163.

14. Pitkin, *The Concept of Representation*, 221.

15. Pitkin, *The Concept of Representation*, 163.

16. Pitkin, *The Concept of Representation*, 163.

17. Pitkin, *The Concept of Representation*, 221–2.

18. Pitkin, *The Concept of Representation*, 224. Pitkin seems to retreat from this position in her later writings on representation, where she affirms the need for a "centralized, large-scale, necessarily abstract representative system [to be] based in a lively, participatory, concrete direct democracy at the local level." See Hanna Fenichel Pitkin, "Representation and Democracy: Uneasy Alliance," *Scandinavian Political Studies* 27, no. 3 (2004): 335–42, at 340.

19. Robert Weissberg, "Collective vs. Dyadic Representation in Congress," *American Political Science Review* 72, no. 2 (June 1978): 535–47, at 537; emphasis added.

20. James H. Kuklinski and John E. Stanga, "Political Participation and Government Responsiveness: The Behavior of California Superior Courts," *American Political Science Review* 73, no. 4 (1979): 1090–1099, at 1091.

21. Edward N. Muller, "The Representation of Citizens by Political Authorities," *American Political Science Review* 64, no. 4 (1970): 1149–66, at 1151.

22. Paul E. Peterson, "Forms of Representation: Participation of the Poor in the Community Action Program," *American Political Science Review* 64, no. 2 (1970): 491–507, at 493; emphasis added.

23. Heinz Eulau and Paul D. Karps, "The Puzzle of Representation: Specifying Components of Responsiveness," *Legislative Studies Quarterly* 2, no. 3 (1977): 233–54, at 249.

24. Pitkin, *The Concept of Representation*, 140; emphasis added.

25. Pitkin, *The Concept of Representation*, 232–3.

26. Pitkin, *The Concept of Representation*, 233.

27. Pitkin, *The Concept of Representation*, 215; emphasis added. Also see David Easton, *The Political System: An Inquiry into the State of Political Science* (New York: Knopf, 1953); David Truman, *The Governmental Process: Political Interests and Public Opinion* (New York: Knopf, 1951).

28. Pitkin, *The Concept of Representation*, 218; emphasis added. This made her a better pluralist than those who claimed the title, being truer than they were to the "anti-foundationalism" of Arthur Bentley's (1908) conception of groups. See Mika LaVaque-Manty, "Bentley, Truman, and the Study of Groups," *Annual Review of Political Science* 9 (2006): 1–18, at 10. LaVaque-Manty writes that Bentley "conceived of interest as a relationship that depended on the context in which similarly situated individuals might find themselves," so that groups do not precede politics but "come into existence" in response to that context. See Mika LaVaque-Manty, "Finding Theoretical Concepts in the Real World: The Case of the Precariat," in *New Waves in Political Philosophy*, eds. Boudewijn de Bruin and Christopher F. Zurn (Basingstoke: Palgrave Macmillan, 2009): 105–24, at 109.

29. Pitkin, *The Concept of Representation*, 218; emphasis added. As Hans Lindahl has put it, "unity is necessarily a *represented* unity." Hans Lindahl, "Acquiring a Community: The Acquis and the Institution of European Legal Order," *European Law Journal* 9, no. 4 (2003): 433–50, at 448.

30. Pitkin, *The Concept of Representation*, 233.

31. Pitkin, *The Concept of Representation*, 233; emphasis in original.

32. Pitkin, *The Concept of Representation*, 233.

33. This passage summarizes a conversation I had with Jason Frank about this book in November 2018. Mark Brown has patiently made a similar suggestion to me since I started working on this project over a decade ago.

34. For cites, see Introduction, note 16.

35. Jane J. Mansbridge, "Rethinking Representation," *American Political Science Review* 97, no. 4 (2003): 515–28, at 518; cf. Jeff Manza and Fay Lomax Cook, "A Democratic Polity? Three Views of Policy Responsiveness to Public Opinion in the United States," *American Politics Research* 30, no. 6 (2002): 630–67; Judith Squires, "The Constitutive Representation of Gender: Extra-Parliamentary Representations of Gender Relations," *Representation* 44, no. 2 (2008): 187–204; Melissa Williams, *Voice, Trust, and Memory: Marginalized Groups and the Failings of Liberal Representation* (Princeton, NJ: Princeton University Press, 1990).

36. Page and Shapiro, *The Rational Public*, 354.

37. Jane J. Mansbridge, "Rethinking Representation," 515. The other three—*anticipatory*, *gyroscopic*, and *surrogate*—conform to "normative criteria" that Mansbridge emphasizes are "systemic, in contrast to the dyadic criteria appropriate for promissory representation" (515).

38. Mansbridge, 518.

39. See Howard Schweber, "The Limits of Political Representation," *American Political Science Review* 110, no. 2 (2016): 382–96.

40. Mansbridge, "Rethinking Representation," 517. See also Morris P. Fiorina, *Retrospective Voting in American National Elections* (New Haven, CT: Yale University Press, 1981).

41. Mansbridge, "Rethinking Representation," 515.

42. Mansbridge, 515, 517; emphasis in original.

43. Mansbridge, 517.

44. Mansbridge, 519; emphasis added.

45. Mansbridge, 517.

46. Mansbridge, 517.

47. Mansbridge, 517; emphasis added.

48. Mansbridge, 519.

49. Mansbridge, 519.

50. Mansbridge, 519; emphasis added.

51. Mansbridge, 519–20.

52. Mansbridge, 520.

53. Dennis Chong and James N. Druckman, "Framing Public Opinion in Competitive Democracies," *American Political Science Review* 101, no. 4 (November 2007): 637–55; Dennis Chong and James Druckman, "Counterframing Effects," *Journal of Politics* 75, no. 1 (2013): 1–16.

54. Thomas E. Nelson, Rosalee A. Clawson, and Zoe M. Oxley, "Media Framing of a Civil Liberties Conflict and Its Effect on Tolerance," *American Political Science Review* 91, no. 3 (1997): 567–83, at 569.

55. Nelson et al., "Media Framing of a Civil Liberties Conflict," 575.

56. Nelson et al., 574.

57. Nelson et al., 578.

58. Nelson et al., 578–79. The experiment made two manipulations, first exposing participants to the competing frames and then subjecting them to a processing task that enabled researchers to differentiate between the accessibility of respondents' beliefs and the weight they attached to them (Ibid, 571).

59. Nelson et al., 578.

60. Nelson et al., 579.

61. Mansbridge, "Rethinking Representation," 520.

62. Nelson et al., "Media Framing of a Civil Liberties Conflict," 578; emphasis added.

63. Nelson et al., 571.

64. Michael Saward, *The Representative Claim* (Oxford: Oxford University Press, 2010), 18.

65. Michael Saward, "The Representative Claim," *Contemporary Political Theory* 5, no. 3 (2006): 297–318, at 306.

66. Saward, *The Representative Claim*, 38; emphasis in original.

67. Saward, *The Representative Claim*, 43–44; emphasis added. Various theorists of political representation have observed that the German language provides a specificity that not only makes it easier to differentiate the various uses of the term but to theorize the political effects of aesthetic representation together with the aesthetic aspects of political representation. German language speakers use *repraesentieren* for the work or "acting for" of elected officeholders and *darstellen* for the work or "standing for" of aesthetic objects and performances. See Alessandro Mulieri, "Exploring the Semantics of Constructivist Representation," in *The Constructivist Turn in Political Representation*, eds. Lisa Disch, Mathijs van de Sande and Nadia Urbinati (Edinburgh University Press, 2019): 205–23. See also Yves Sintomer, "Les sens de la representation politique: Usages et mésusages d'une notion," *Raisons Politiques* 50, no. 2 (2013): 13–34.

68. Saward, *The Representative Claim*, 66, 47.

69. Saward, *The Representative Claim*, 38, 73; emphasis in original.

70. Michael Saward, "Shape-Shifting Representation," *American Political Science Review* 108, no. 4 (2014): 723–36, at 726.

71. Saward, *The Representative Claim*, 51.

72. Saward, *The Representative Claim*, 47.

73. Saward, *The Representative Claim*, 75. See also Bernard Manin, *The Principles of Representative Government* (Cambridge, UK: Cambridge University Press, 1997).

74. Saward, *The Representative Claim*, 71; emphasis in original.

75. Saward, *The Representative Claim*, 47–48.

76. Saward, *The Representative Claim*, 157.

77. Eline Severs, "Substantive Representation through a Claims-Making Lens: A Strategy for the Identification and Analysis of Substantive Claims," *Representation* 48, no. 2 (2012): 169–81, at 172.

78. Eline Severs, "Representation as Claims-Making. Quid Responsiveness?," *Representation* 46, no. 4 (2010): 411–23, at 416.

79. Michael A. Neblo, *Deliberative Democracy between Theory and Practice* (Cambridge, UK: Cambridge University Press, 2015), 72.

80. Saward, *The Representative Claim*, 146.

81. Saward, *The Representative Claim*, 146-7.

82. Saward, "Shape-Shifting Representation," 734.

83. Saward, *The Representative Claim*, 42.

84. Saward, *The Representative Claim*, 49. Although early on in the book Saward conflates the terms *audience* and *constituency*, he later draws a bright line between them to emphasize their distinct roles (Saward, *The Representative Claim*, 37, 147–50).

85. Linda Zerilli pursues a similar line of argument by drawing a different distinction, that between political claims—identifiable by their "*anticipatory* structure"—

and "knowledge claims." Knowledge claims "can be adjudicated on the basis of giving proofs" but political claims involve claiming "commonalities" to others who "may well speak back, that is, say whether they find themselves spoken for." See Zerilli, *Feminism and the Abyss of Freedom* (Chicago: University of Chicago Press, 2005), 171–72.

86. Saward, *The Representative Claim*, 148, 145; emphasis in original.

87. Michael Saward, "Shape-Shifting Representation," 734.

88. Saward, *The Representative Claim*, 48.

89. Laura Montanaro, "The Democratic Legitimacy of Self-Appointed Representatives," *Journal of Politics* 74, no. 4 (2012), 1094–1107; *Who Elected Oxfam?* (Cambridge, UK: Cambridge University Press, 2017). For a critical response, see Jennifer Rubenstein, "Accountability in an Unequal World," *Journal of Politics* 69, no. 3 (2007), 616–32.

90. Saward, *The Representative Claim*, 145.

91. Saward, *The Representative Claim*, 148.

92. Saward, *The Representative Claim*, 149.

93. See Pieter de Wilde, "Representative Claims Analysis: Theory Meets Method," *Journal of European Public Policy* 20, no. 2 (2013): 278–94, for the criticism that the audience/constituency distinction lacks analytic purchase. See Laura Montanaro, "The Democratic Legitimacy of Self-Appointed Representatives," for a thoughtful development of that distinction into a frame for normative analysis.

94. Saward, *The Representative Claim*, 147.

95. Michael Levitin credits Occupy Wall Street with fueling the 2016 candidacy of Bernie Sanders and making that of Elizabeth Warren conceivable in 2020. In addition, he claims that the movement built momentum for a national minimum wage campaign, helped inspire and support students' calls for universities nationwide to divest from fossil fuels, emboldened President Obama to mandate new carbon emissions standards for power plants, and much more. Michael Levitin, "The Triumph of Occupy Wall Street," *Atlantic Monthly*, June 10, 2015, https://www.theatlantic.com/politics/archive/2015/06/the-triumph-of-occupy-wall-street/395408/.

96. Whether the group coordinated with the campaign or not, its ad extrapolated the narrative of a series of attack spots that were paid for and produced by the Bush campaign, featuring the Massachusetts furlough program but stopping just short of naming Horton. The initial inspiration for this line of attack came from Al Gore, who had used the program against Michael Dukakis during the Democratic primaries. Peter Baker, "Bush Made Willie Horton an Issue in 1988, and the Racial Scars Are Still Fresh," *New York Times*, December 3, 2018, https://www.nytimes.com/2018/12/03/us/politics/bush-willie-horton.html.

97. Associated Press, "Gravely Ill, Atwater Offers Apology," *New York Times*, January 13, 1991, section 1, p. 16, https://www.nytimes.com/1991/01/13/us/gravely-ill-atwater-offers-apology.html.

98. James Alan Fox, "The Facts on Furloughs," *Christian Science Monitor*, September 28, 1988, https://www.csmonitor.com/1988/0928/efur.html.

99. Michelle Alexander, "The Injustice of This Moment Is Not an 'Aberration,'" *New York Times*, January 17, 2020, https://www.nytimes.com/2020/01/17/opinion/sunday/michelle-alexander-new-jim-crow.html.

100. Vijay Phulwani, "The Poor Man's Machiavelli: Saul Alinsky and the Morality of Power." *American Political Science Review* 110, no. 4 (2016): 863–75.

101. Saul Alinsky, *Reveille for Radicals* (New York: Vintage Books, 1989 [1946]), 165; cited in Phulwani, "The Poor Man's Machiavelli," 873.

102. Alinsky, cited in Phulwani, "The Poor Man's Machiavelli," 873.

103. Phulwani, "The Poor Man's Machiavelli," 867.

104. Phulwani, "The Poor Man's Machiavelli," 874.

105. Nicholas von Hoffman, *Radical: A Portrait of Saul Alinsky* (New York: Nation Books, 2010), 53, cited in Phulwani, "The Poor Man's Machiavelli," 874.

106. Phulwani, "The Poor Man's Machiavelli," 874.

Chapter Three

1. Scholars define *democratic competence* as voters' capacity to make informed political judgments regarding, at a minimum, the best means to satisfy their own interests and, ideally, how to achieve ends that are best for society as a whole. Bennett offers a comprehensive review of both the empirical literature and of normative work that has objected to competence as an inherently elitist measure (Stephen Earl Bennett, "Democratic Competence, Before Converse and After," *Critical Review* 18, no. 1–3 [January 2006]: 105–41, at 107). *Critical Review* 18, no. 1–3 (January 2006) is devoted to debates on democratic competence, with special emphasis on how Philip E. Converse's classic 1964 article influenced and was misunderstood in these debates. See Philip E. Converse, "The Nature of Belief Systems in Mass Publics," *Critical Review* 18, no. 1–3 (2006 [1964]).

2. Morris P. Fiorina, "Identities for Realists," *Critical Review* 30, no. 1–2 (2018), 49. Fiorina recounts the debate that began when the "Michigan school" in the 1960s painted a disparaging portrait of voters based on the previous decade's survey research. (See Converse, "The Nature of Belief Systems in Mass Publics.") Beginning in the mid-1970s, empirical researchers inspired by the social movements and antiwar activism of the 1960s and early 1970s produced the first revisionist literature, which both criticized previous research for its civics-test ideal of informed citizenship and found evidence of voter rationality as defined by a variety of different models (see Jackson 1975).

3. Christopher H. Achen and Larry M. Bartels, *Democracy for Realists: Why Elections Do Not Produce Responsive Government* (Princeton, NJ: Princeton University Press, 2016), 306.

4. Achen and Bartels, *Democracy for Realists*, 325; emphasis in original.

5. See Richard Brownstein, "Federal Anti-poverty Programs Primarily Help the GOP's Base," *Atlantic Monthly*, February 16, 2017, https://www.theatlantic.com/politics/archive/2017/02/gop-base-poverty-snap-social-security/516861/ and Robert Porter, "Where Government Is a Dirty Word, but Its Checks Pay the Bills," *New York Times*, December 21, 2018, https://www.nytimes.com/2018/12/21/business/economy/harlan-county-republican-welfare.html. Multiple news stories drew on a study of census data by the liberal policy-analysis group Center on Budget and Policy Priorities. See Isaac Shapiro, Danilo Trisi, and Raheem Chaudhry, "Poverty Reduction Programs Help Adults Lacking College Degrees the Most," Center on Budget and Policy Priorities, Feb 16, 2017, https://www.cbpp.org/research/poverty-and-inequality/poverty-reduction-programs-help-adults-lacking-college-degrees-the.

6. Alex MacGillis, "Who Turned My Blue State Red?" *New York Times*, November 20, 2015, https://www.nytimes.com/2015/11/22/opinion/sunday/who-turned-my-blue-state-red.html.

7. Kristoffer Alhstrom-Vij, "Is Democracy an Option for the Realist?," *Critical Review: A Journal of Politics and Society* 30, no. 1–2 (2018): 1–12, at 9.

8. Alhstrom-Vij, 9.

9. Alhstrom-Vij, 11.

10. Jeffrey C. Isaac, *Power and Marxist Theory: A Realist View* (Ithaca, NY: Cornell University Press, 1987), 5.

11. James N. Druckman, "Pathologies of Studying Public Opinion, Political Communication, and Democratic Responsiveness," *Political Communication* 31, no. 3 (2014): 467–92, at 478.

12. Raymond Geuss, *Philosophy and Real Politics* (Princeton, NJ: Princeton University Press, 2008), 9, 11. Benjamin L. McKean argues that Geuss rejects ideal thinking to propose a critical project, not a purely descriptive one. (See Benjamin L. McKean, "What Makes a Utopia Inconvenient? On the Advantages and Disadvantages of a Realist Orientation to Politics," *American Political Science Review* 110, no. 4 [2016]: 876–88.)

13. Druckman, "Pathologies of Studying Public Opinion," 481.

14. Katherine J. Cramer, *The Politics of Resentment: Rural Consciousness in Wisconsin and the Rise of Scott Walker* (Chicago: University of Chicago Press, 2016). Suzanne Mettler, *The Submerged State: How Invisible Government Policies Undermine American Democracy* (Chicago: University of Chicago Press, 2011).

15. Matt Sleat, "Introduction: Politics Recovered—On the Revival of Realism in Contemporary Political Theory," in *Politics Recovered: Realist Thought in Theory and Practice*, ed. Matt Sleat (New York: Columbia University Press, 2018): 1–26, at 12.

16. Achen and Bartels, *Democracy for Realists*, 213.

17. Achen and Bartels, *Democracy for Realists*, 213.

18. Achen and Bartels, *Democracy for Realists*, 214.

19. For a summary of this literature, see Achen and Bartels, *Democracy for Realists*, 219–21.

20. Diana C. Mutz, "Status Threat Explains Trump," *Proceedings of the National Academy of Sciences* 115, no. 19 (May 2018): E4330-E4339; John Sides, Michael Tesler, and Lynn Vavreck, *Identity Crisis: The 2016 Presidential Campaign and the Battle for the Meaning of America* (Princeton, NJ: Princeton University Press, 2018).

21. Achen and Bartels, *Democracy for Realists*, 216, 215.

22. Achen and Bartels, *Democracy for Realists*, 215.

23. Achen and Bartels, *Democracy for Realists*, 219–21.

24. Henri Tajfel, "Experiments in Intergroup Discrimination," *Scientific American* 223, no. 5 (November 1970): 96–103.

25. Achen and Bartels, *Democracy for Realists*, 325. Achen and Bartels's critics object that evidence supports none of the following assumptions: that group "identities are affectively based and devoid of relevant political content" (Fiorina, "Identities for Realists," 50; Leonie Huddy, "The Group Foundations of Democratic Political Behavior," *Critical Review* 30, no. 1–2 [2018]: 71–86, at 73); that "solitary truth seekers" are better reasoners than people in groups (Simone Chambers, "Human Life Is Group Life: Deliberative Democracy for Realists," *Critical Review* 30, no. 1–2 [2018]: 36–48, at 37); that group identifications are "static" or demographically based (Huddy, "The Group Foundations of Democratic Political Behavior," 74; also Fiorina, "Identities for Realists," 54), and that they tend necessarily toward a "grudge-match style of politics" (Huddy, "The Group Foundations of Democratic Political Behavior," 82). Fowler and Hall argue that Achen and Bartels's sensationalist claim that voters assess politicians' performance because of shark attacks and other irrelevant information is especially "overblown" (1435). Not only is there "virtually no evidence that shark attacks influence elections," but this entire genre of research into the purportedly "irrelevant factors [that] supposedly influence behavior" likely inflates the evidence for incompetence, due to the disciplinary bias against publishing null findings (1424). For all the "published studies" that have claimed to identify a variety of irrelevant factors affecting the vote, "we have no way of knowing how many other irrelevant factors were examined and found to have no effect" (1436). See Anthony Fowler and Andrew B. Hall, "Do Shark Attacks Influence Presidential Elections? Reassessing a Prominent Finding on Voter Competence," *Journal of Politics* 80, no. 4 (2018), 1423–1437.

26. Jason Brennan, *Against Democracy* (Princeton, NJ: Princeton University Press, 2016).

27. Brennan, 6.

28. Brennan, 6.

29. Brennan, 37.

30. Brennan, 9.

31. Brennan, 214.

32. Brennan, 211.

33. Brennan, 211.

34. Brennan, 211–12. I doubt that Brennan's caveats would reassure anyone who is paying attention to redistricting in Texas, voter purges in Ohio, or voter identification laws and restrictions on early voting that other states have enacted in the wake of the Supreme Court's 2–13 decision in *Shelby County v. Holder* (2013). That decision lifted the preclearance provision of the 1965 Voting Rights Act that required nine southern states and scattered northern municipalities to get approval from a federal authority before making changes to their voting law that could dilute African-American voting strength, such as enacting restrictive election laws and redrawing district lines. See Vann R. Newkirk, "How *Shelby County v. Holder* Broke America," *Atlantic Monthly*, July 10, 2018, https://www.theatlantic.com/politics/archive/2018/07/how-shelby-county-broke-america/564707/.

35. Robert A. Dahl, *A Preface to Democratic Theory* (Chicago: University of Chicago Press, 1956), 128; emphasis in original. Achen and Bartels, *Democracy for Realists*, 325. Achen and Bartels neither use the term *minorities rule* nor acknowledge their debt to Dahl, who proposed it as an explicit retreat from *majority rule*, which he considered to be both an unrealistic expectation on the part of populists and an exaggerated fear on the part of populist critics like Madison. Dahl valued elections not for revealing the majority will but for vastly increasing the "size, number, and variety of minorities [i.e., organized interests] whose preferences must be taken into account by leaders in making policy choices." (See Dahl, *A Preface to Democratic Theory*, 132).

36. Achen and Bartels, *Democracy for Realists*, 321.

37. Achen and Bartels, *Democracy for Realists*, 322.

38. Harold Lasswell, *Propaganda Technique in the World War* (New York: Peter Smith, 1927). Cited in Brett Gary, *The Nervous Liberals: Propaganda Anxieties from World War I to the Cold War* (New York: Colombia University Press, 1999), 3.

39. Gary, *The Nervous Liberals*, 3.

40. Gary, *The Nervous Liberals*, 3, 5.

41. Gary, *The Nervous Liberals*, 13–14.

42. John Medearis, "Disenchantment versus Reconstruction: Lippmann, John Dewey, and Varieties of Democratic Realism," in *Politics Recovered*, ed. Matt Sleat (New York: Columbia University Press, 2018): 140–65, 143.

43. Medearis, 143.

44. Achen and Bartels, *Democracy for Realists*, 16; emphasis in original. Huddy notes that their "group model is not especially well developed" ("The Group Foundations of Democratic Political Behavior," 72).

45. Achen and Bartels, *Democracy for Realists*, 231. Achen and Bartels borrow this term without comment from political psychologist Karen Stenner, who coins it to argue that authoritarianism is rooted in *groupiness*, a general desire for "self and others to conform to *some* system, not a commitment to a specific

normative order" (*Democracy for Realists*, 18). Do Achen and Bartels mean to suggest that the "beliefs, preferences, and political behavior of democratic citizens" are driven by conformism? To suggest that all group attachments display authoritarian tendencies?

46. Achen and Bartels, *Democracy for Realists*, 222. Iris Marion Young distinguishes between methodologically individualist and relational approaches to understanding social groups and demonstrates how various kinds of group identifications and ways of identifying groups matter for democratic empowerment and political action. (See Iris Marion Young, *Justice and the Politics of Difference* (Princeton, NJ: Princeton University Press, 1990), 40–48; 168–73.)

47. Achen and Bartels, *Democracy for Realists*, 228.

48. Achen and Bartels, *Democracy for Realists*, 216.

49. Arthur F. Bentley, *The Process of Government: A Study of Social Pressures* (New Brunswick, NJ: Transaction Press, 2008 [1908]).

50. Mika LaVaque-Manty, "Bentley, Truman, and the Study of Groups," *Annual Review of Political Science* 9 (2006): 1–18, at 14.

51. LaVaque-Manty, "Bentley, Truman, and the Study of Groups," 8.

52. Wenman (61) is not wrong to charge mainstream political science research with assuming that "'interest groups' enter the arena of politics with fixed and essential identity," but it is imprecise to attribute this assumption to pluralism generally. Wenman, who mentions Bentley only in passing, generalizes about pluralism from select midcentury US work, Polsby's in particular (58). See Mark Anthony Wenman, "What Is Politics? The Approach of Radical Pluralism," *Politics* 23, no. 1 (2003): 57–75.

53. Achen and Bartels, *Democracy for Realists*, 16; emphasis in original.

54. William Graham Sumner, *What Social Classes Owe to Each Other* (Idaho: Caxton Press, 2003), 22. First published by Harper & Brothers, 1883.

55. See Porter, "Where Government Is a Dirty Word," for the story of Governor Matt Bevin of Kentucky, who won office by campaigning against government spending even though "Harlan County residents rely on government programs more than pretty much anybody else."

56. Arlie Hochschild's profile of Louisiana Tea Party members who turned their anger about corporate polluters against the EPA exemplifies this genre. See Arlie Russell Hochschild, *Strangers in Their Own Land: Anger and Mourning on the American Right* (New York: The New Press, 2016). George Packer stands out for his prescient account of the political, ideological, and economic homelessness that would make the "white working class" (a term he treats with skepticism) open to the appeal of a "crass strongman who tossed out fraudulent promises and gave institutions and élites the middle finger." See George Packer, "Hillary Clinton and the Populist Revolt," *New Yorker*, October 31, 2016, https://www.newyorker.com /magazine/2016/10/31/hillary-clinton-and-the-populist-revolt.

57. Hochschild, *Strangers in Their Own Land*, 16; ch. 9.

58. Thomas Frank, *What's the Matter with Kansas? How the Conservatives Won the Heart of America* (New York: Metropolitan Books, 2004).

59. Larry Bartels, "What's the Matter with What's the Matter with Kansas?," *Quarterly Journal of Political Science* 1, no. 2 (2006): 201–26.

60. Frank, *What's the Matter with Kansas*, 245.

61. Bartels, "What's the Matter with What's the Matter with Kansas?," 205.

62. Bartels, "What's the Matter with What's the Matter with Kansas?," 206.

63. Bartels, "What's the Matter with What's the Matter with Kansas?," 207.

64. Bartels, "What's the Matter with What's the Matter with Kansas?," 207; emphasis added.

65. Bartels, "What's the Matter with What's the Matter with Kansas?," 222.

66. Bartels, "What's the Matter with What's the Matter with Kansas?," 203.

67. Hochschild, *Strangers in Their Own Land*, 14, 21.

68. Hochschild, 25, 28–31.

69. Hochschild, 31.

70. Hochschild, 34, 135, 4; emphasis in original.

71. Hochschild, 135–36.

72. Hochschild, 135–38; ch. 5.

73. Hochschild, 135.

74. Hochschild, 4.

75. Hochschild, 227; emphasis in original.

76. Hochschild, 228.

77. Hochschild, 228.

78. Cramer, *The Politics of Resentment*, 4–5.

79. Cramer, 89.

80. Cramer, 14.

81. Cramer, 14.

82. The theme gained broad popularity after the presidential election of 2000, whose agonizing count intensified the divide between those parts of the country that David Brooks memorably described as doing "without motors" everything that "people in Red America do with motors." Brooks elaborated: "We sail; they powerboat. We cross-country ski; they snowmobile. We hike; they drive ATVs. We have vineyard tours; they have tractor pulls. When it comes to yard work, they have rider mowers; we have illegal aliens." David Brooks, "One Nation, Slightly Divisible," *Atlantic Monthly*, December 2001: 53–65, https://www.theatlantic.com /magazine/archive/2001/12/one-nation-slightly-divisible/376441/. In another influential twist on this theme, Richard Florida linked these cultural differences to an economic shift: the increasing centrality of creativity as an economic engine, specifically in cities. See Richard Florida, *The Rise of the Creative Class: And How It's Transforming Work, Leisure, Community, and Everyday Life* (New York: Basic Books, 2002).

83. Cramer, *The Politics of Resentment*, 15.

84. Cramer, 24.

85. Cramer, 83.

86. Cramer, 15.

87. Cramer, Appendix A, 227.

88. Cramer, 143–44.

89. Cramer, 143–44.

90. Cramer, 14.

91. Cramer, 5.

92. Cramer, 5–6.

93. Cramer, 9.

94. Cramer, 211.

95. Cramer, 9.

96. Cramer, 145.

97. Cramer, 141.

98. Cramer emphasizes that her interviewees had real economic grievances even if those grievances had little to do with their share of tax dollars (93–104). Cramer's subjects suffered from the global market in agriculture. Then as now, rural municipalities struggled to provide basic services like education and broadband to their sparse populations. People living in rural areas drive more and pay more for gas, electricity, food, health care premiums, and mortgages than do people who live in cities and suburbs. These distributional injustices, palpable enough as they are, intensify exponentially in tourist towns where the "locals know that it is not their year-round neighbors who are buying the $200 bottles of champagne in the grocery store" (104).

99. The (rare) appearance of researchers from UW-Madison and the regulatory presence of the DNR in rural areas reaffirmed to the people there how thoroughly the university-educated disregard local "knowledge and norms" (Cramer, 123; 127–30; 155–58).

100. Cramer describes Obama embodying everything these voters associated with being a "city person," not simply—or even primarily—as a Black man but by "his party affiliation, his past political experience, and his occupation (he had represented Chicago, been a professor, and been an urban community organizer)" (179). One interviewee predicted Obama would win because of his appeal to "all the young latte Democrat voters," invoking an urban identity that, far from coding Obama as Black, verges on stereotyping him as white (180).

101. Cramer, 209.

102. Cramer, 15.

103. Cramer, 219.

104. Cramer, 19.

105. Cramer, 219, 204–5.

106. Cramer, 205.

107. Cramer, 206.

108. Cramer, 206.

109. Cramer, ch. 8.

110. Cramer, 220.

111. Cramer, 219.

112. Cramer, 219.

113. Cramer, 205.

114. Porter, "Where Government Is a Dirty Word."

115. Mettler, *The Submerged State*, 10.

116. See previous chapter.

117. Mettler, *The Submerged State*, 10.

118. Mettler, *The Submerged State*, 21–22.

119. Mettler, *The Submerged State*, 16.

120. Mettler, *The Submerged State*, 11.

121. Mettler, *The Submerged State*, 16–17.

122. Mettler, *The Submerged State*, 27.

123. Mettler, *The Submerged State*, 26.

124. Mettler, *The Submerged State*, 27.

125. Mettler, *The Submerged State*, 26.

126. Elmer Eric Schattschneider, *The Semisovereign People: A Realist's View of Democracy in America*, reprinted ed., intro. by David Adamany (Fort Worth: Harcourt Brace Jovanovich, 1975), 69.

127. Mettler, *The Submerged State*, 28.

128. Mettler, *The Submerged State*, 28.

129. Mettler, *The Submerged State*, 23.

130. Cramer, *The Politics of Resentment*, 144.

131. Cramer, 101.

132. Cramer, 91.

133. Schattschneider, *The Semisovereign People*, 97.

Chapter Four

1. Arthur Lupia and Mathew D. McCubbins, *The Democratic Dilemma: Can Citizens Learn What They Need to Know?* (Cambridge, UK: Cambridge University Press, 1998), 10.

2. Elmer Eric Schattschneider, *The Semisovereign People: A Realist's View of Democracy in America*, reprinted ed., intro. by David Adamany (Fort Worth: Harcourt Brace Jovanovich, 1975).

3. Indeed, were he to address today's realists, there is no doubt as to what Schattschneider would say: "Only a pedagogue would suppose that the people must pass some kind of examination to qualify for participation in a democracy. Who, after all, are these self-appointed censors who assume that they are in a

position to flunk the whole human race? . . . Democracy is something for ordinary people, a political system designed to be sensitive to the needs of ordinary people regardless of whether or not the pedants approve of them" (132).

4. Schattschneider, 126.

5. Schattschneider, 69.

6. Schattschneider, 69.

7. Schattschneider, 70.

8. Schattschneider, 38; emphasis added.

9. Schattschneider, 60; emphasis in original. Schattschneider is no mere conflict theorist, a "facile" category that would lump him together with those who reduce politics to an amoral struggle for power. (David Adamany, introduction to E. E. Schattschneider, *The Semisovereign People: A Realist's View of Democracy in America*, reprinted ed., intro. by David Adamany (Fort Worth: Harcourt Brace Jovanovich, 1975), xiii.) Schattschneider theorizes conflict as a political force rather than a simple expression of competing interests and values.

10. Peter Mair, "E. E. Schattschneider's *The Semisovereign People*," *Political Studies* 45, no. 5 (1997): 947–54, at 949; emphasis added.

11. Mair, 949; emphasis in original.

12. Jason Frank, "Populism and Praxis: Between the Electorate and the Multitude," in *Means and Ends: Rethinking Political Realism*, ed. Karuna Mantena (New York: Cambridge University Press, forthcoming), quoted in Vijay Phulwani, "The Poor Man's Machiavelli: Saul Alinsky and the Morality of Power," *American Political Science Review* 110, no. 4 (2016): 863–75, at 864. See also Jason Frank, "Populism and Praxis," in *The Oxford Handbook of Populism*, eds. Cristobal Rovira Kaltwasser, Paul Taggart, Paulina Ochoa Espejo, and Pierre Ostiguy (New York: Oxford University Press, 2017): 629–43.

13. Schattschneider, *The Semisovereign People*, 135.

14. Jack L. Walker, *Mobilizing Interest Groups in America: Patrons, Professions, and Social Movements* (Ann Arbor: University of Michigan Press, 1991), 16.

15. New realism in political theory emerged slowly in the late twentieth century and picked up momentum in the first decades of the twenty-first, with the publication of Bernard Williams's "Realism and Moralism in Political Theory," in *In the Beginning Was the Deed: Realism and Moralism in Political Argument*, ed. Hawthorn Geoffrey (Princeton, NJ: Princeton University Press, 2005): 1–17 and Raymond Geuss's *Philosophy and Real Politics* (Princeton, NJ: Princeton University Press, 2008). William Galston, the first to characterize this "dissenting movement in political theory" as a new iteration of "realism," credits Bonnie Honig with originating it by attributing to "high liberalism" a desire to "evade, displace, or escape from politics." See William Galston, "Realism in Political Theory," *European Journal of Political Theory* 9, no. 4 (2010): 385–411, at 386, referencing Bonnie Honig, *Political Theory and the Displacement of Politics* (Ithaca, NY: Cornell University Press, 1993).

16. Christopher H. Achen and Larry M. Bartels, *Democracy for Realists: Why Elections Do Not Produce Responsive Government* (Princeton, NJ: Princeton University Press, 2016), 1, 18.

17. Matt Sleat, "Introduction: Politics Recovered—On the Revival of Realism in Contemporary Political Theory," in *Politics Recovered: Realist Thought in Theory and Practice*, ed. Matt Sleat (New York: Columbia University Press, 2018): 1–26, at 12.

18. Alison McQueen, "The Case for Kinship: Classical Realism and Political Realism," in *Politics Recovered: Realist Thought in Theory and Practice*, ed. Matt Sleat (New York: Columbia University Press, 2018): 243–69, at 246.

19. McQueen, 246; emphasis in original.

20. McQueen, 246. See Williams, "Realism and Moralism in Political Theory," 2, and Geuss, *Philosophy and Real Politics*, 7–9. A capacious category, political moralism encompasses utilitarianism together with Rawlsian and Habermasian neo-Kantianism, regardless of the differences among them.

21. Williams, "Realism and Moralism in Political Theory," 2.

22. Williams, "Realism and Moralism in Political Theory," 12–13.

23. Geuss, *Philosophy and Real Politics*, 7–9, 14.

24. Karuna Mantena, "Another Realism," *American Political Science Review* 106, no. 2 (2012): 455–70, at 465. Matt Sleat has aptly noted the "disciplinary insularity" of too much new realist scholarship. Despite claiming the mantle of new realism, this work gets so wrapped up in either debating the methodology of realism or interpreting the textual subtleties of the "work of Williams and Geuss" that it becomes "quite out of kilter" with its principal injunction, which is to practice theory on politics rather than theory on theory. See Sleat, "Introduction: Politics Recovered," 10.

25. Mantena, "Another Realism," 468.

26. Mantena, 460.

27. Mantena, 461.

28. Mantena, 465.

29. Marc Stears, *Demanding Democracy: American Radicals in Search of a New Politics* (Princeton, NJ: Princeton University Press, 2010), 154.

30. Stears, 155.

31. Benjamin McKean, "What Makes a Utopia Inconvenient? On the Advantages and Disadvantages of a Realist Orientation to Politics," *American Political Science Review* 110, no. 4 (November 2016): 876–88, at 884.

32. Mair, "E. E. Schattschneider's *The Semisovereign People*,", 950.

33. Schattschneider, *The Semisovereign People*, 130.

34. Mair, "E. E. Schattschneider's *The Semisovereign People*," 947.

35. McQueen, "The Case for Kinship," 243. McQueen points out that the canon-building lists of contemporary realist scholars include a panoply of thinkers (Thucydides, Paul, Augustine, Machiavelli, Hobbes, Hume, Nietzsche, Weber,

Schmitt) who did not identify as realists and exactly none of the midcentury political scientists who emphatically did.

36. Seymour Martin Lipset, introduction to Robert Michels, *Political Parties: A
Sociological Study of Oligarchical Tendencies of Modern Democracies*, trans. Eden
and Cedar Paul (New York: The Free Press, 1962), 33.

37. Jack L. Walker, who also omits the scare quotes, gave Lipset an especially
polemical reading. Quoting out of context, he claimed that Lipset "sees 'profoundly anti-democratic tendencies in lower class groups'" ("A Critique of the
Elitist Theory of Democracy," *American Political Science Review* 60, no. 2 (1966):
285–95, at 292). Lipset's full quotation reads: "Despite the profoundly antidemocratic tendencies in lower-class groups, workers' political organizations and
movements in the more industrialized democratic countries have supported *both*
economic and political liberalism," particularly when political freedoms are "necessary weapons" in workers' struggles (Seymour Martin Lipset, *Political Man: The
Social Bases of Politics* [Baltimore: Johns Hopkins University Press, 1981], 121,
123). The passage does not denounce "lower class groups" for their authoritarian propensities. Lipset argues, as do Laclau and Mouffe, that the connections
between economic and political liberalism have to be forged politically; there is no
guarantee that workers will support both, but they may if a skilled movement (like
Chartism) can sell them as being necessarily linked.

38. Robert Michels, *Political Parties: A Sociological Study of Oligarchical Tendencies of Modern Democracies*, trans. Eden and Cedar Paul (New York: The Free
Press, 1962).

39. Robert Dahl noted in response to Walker ("A Critique of the Elitist Theory
of Democracy") that Lipset "may have had his reasons" for using the occasion of
"writing a preface to the major work of Michels" to coin the expression "elitist
theory of democracy" and apply it to a diverse group of thinkers (Weber, Schumpeter, Parsons, Dahl, and Lipset himself) but he, Dahl, does not consider what
those reasons might have been (see Robert Dahl, "Further Reflections on 'The
Elitist Theory of Democracy,'" *American Political Science Review* 60, no. 2 [1966]:
296–305, at 297). Dahl is so anxious to distance himself from what he regards as a
"pejorative, even a polemical epithet" that he does not stop to consider that Lipset
had good reason to propose this term in an introduction to Michels: precisely to
draw the line between an elitism that a democrat like Dahl *could* approve and that
which he could not (Dahl, "Further Reflections on 'The Elitist Theory of Democracy,'" 297). Clearly Lipset miscalculated the power of scare quotes (which Dahl
omits) to take the sting out of the term.

40. Lipset, introduction to Robert Michels, *Political Parties*, 34; emphasis in
original.

41. Lipset, introduction to Robert Michels, *Political Parties*, 36. Lipset observed, "This image of democracy as conflict of organized groups and of access
by the ruled to their rulers may be far from the ideal of the Greek city state or

of small Swiss cantons, but in operation as a system it is far better than any other political system which has been devised to reduce the potential exploitation of man by man."

42. Lipset, introduction to Robert Michels, *Political Parties*, 33.

43. Robert Dahl, "Further Reflections on 'The Elitist Theory of Democracy,' " 301.

44. Schattschneider, *The Semisovereign People*, 136. Although Schattschneider emphasizes the indispensability of competition and choice in mass democracy, he is clearly no Schumpeterian elitist. Schumpeter's definition of democracy—as an "institutional arrangement for arriving at political decisions in which individuals acquire the power to decide by means of a competitive struggle for the people's vote"—gives representatives total discretion (Joseph A. Schumpeter, *Capitalism, Socialism, and Democracy* [Abingdon, UK: Routledge, 2010], 225). Compare Schattschneider's: "Democracy is a competitive political system in which competing leaders and organizations define the alternatives of public policy in such a way that *the public can participate* in the decision-making process" (*The Semisovereign People*, 138; entire sentence emphasized in original; my emphasis here).

45. Schattschneider, 135–36.

46. Schattschneider, 132, 136; emphasis added.

47. Schattschneider, 136.

48. Schattschneider, 126, 108. Schattschneider identifies two major conflict systems in US society. There is the *party system*, which promotes participation by staging it publicly for a broad audience and framing it in universal terms, and the *interest system*, which privatizes conflict and depresses participation. This dichotomy surely oversimplifies.

49. Schattschneider, 100.

50. Schattschneider, 126, 71–72.

51. Schattschneider, 61. Mair draws Schattschneider's work into a European context, linking it to "notions which were later to lie behind the pioneering work of Stein Rokkan and his various models of European political development," which detail how the "more or less simultaneous emergence and politicization of conflicts in the Norwegian case" facilitated a "multi-dimensional" structure in Norway, whereas the "more long-term and staged character of the politicization of conflicts in the British case" reinforced a unidimensional structure there ("E. E. Schattschneider's *The Semisovereign People*," 951–52). He credits Rokkan with illustrating the "practice of a conflict of conflicts in a much more evident and convincing fashion" that Schattschneider himself, whom Mair criticizes for giving little "empirical proof" for his ideas and providing "only very occasional and *ad hoc* illustrations" (Mair, 952, 949).

52. Schattschneider, *The Semisovereign People*, 126. Mair, one of the few political theorists to treat *Semisovereign People* to a close reading, rightly credits Schattschneider with proposing "a conception of politics in which the structure of

politics itself, and the structure of political competition or political conflict, in particular, helps determine the terms of reference for the development and processing of political ideas and demands" ("E. E. Schattschneider's *The Semisovereign
People*," 949). Mair goes on further with casting the conflict of conflicts as a war
of words, arguing that there is "a prevailing *language of* politics, which obliges
certain issues to be translated before they can even enter the debate" (Mair, 949).
As I read Schattschneider, he understands the structure of conflict to do even more
than provide a vocabulary for political claims in which agents are obliged to trans-
late their issues. It solicits—and discourages—those agents' very formation.

53. Schattschneider, 66.

54. Schattschneider, 2.

55. Schattschneider, 4.

56. Schattschneider, 2.

57. Schattschneider, 2–3.

58. Schattschneider, 3.

59. Peter Bachrach and Morton S. Baratz, "Two Faces of Power," *The American Political Science Review* 56, no. 4 (1962): 947–52.

60. William E. Connolly, ed., *The Bias of Pluralism* (New York: Atherton Press,
1969).

61. Peter Euben, "Political Science and Political Silence," in *Power and Community: Dissenting Essays in Political Science*, eds. Philip Green and Sanford
Levinson (New York: Random House, 1970).

62. Steven Lukes, *Power: A Radical View* (London: Macmillan, 1974).

63. Bachrach and Baratz, "Two Faces of Power," 949; emphasis in original.
Their work shifted political science analysis from the *first face* of power that is
manifest in conflict, to its *second face*, which can be observed in decisions that
suppress conflict, and to a *third face* that shapes individual preferences so as to
foreclose conflict entirely—altogether eliminating the need to either prevail over
or suppress one's opponents.

64. Jeffrey C. Isaac, "Beyond the Three Faces of Power: A Realist Critique,"
Polity 20, no. 1 (1987): 4–31, at 15.

65. Isaac, "Beyond the Three Faces of Power," 14–16.

66. Isaac, "Beyond the Three Faces of Power," 21–22. Isaac follows Bhaskar
to explain that realist philosophy of science is concerned "essentially with what
kinds of things there are and what they tend to do" and "only derivatively" with
prediction (Isaac, "Beyond the Three Faces of Power," 17; citing Roy Bhaskar, *A
Realist Theory of Science*, 2nd ed. (Atlantic Highlands, New Jersey: Humanities
Press, 1978), 51.

67. Isaac, "Beyond the Three Faces of Power," 21.

68. Isaac, "Beyond the Three Faces of Power," 23.

69. Isaac, "Beyond the Three Faces of Power," 17, 18, 25.

70. Isaac, "Beyond the Three Faces of Power," 24.

71. Isaac, "Beyond the Three Faces of Power," 24.

72. Isaac, "Beyond the Three Faces of Power," 24.

73. Schattschneider, *The Semisovereign People*, 69.

74. Schattschneider, 69.

75. Schattschneider, 64.

76. Schattschneider, 108.

77. Schattschneider, 100; emphasis added.

78. Schattschneider observes: "Nobody knows what American politics would be like if we had the institutions to facilitate the development of a wider span of political competition" (70).

79. Herbert Croly, quoted in Stears, *Demanding Democracy*, 33.

80. Schattschneider, *The Semisovereign People*, 60.

81. Schattschneider, 102; emphasis added.

82. Schattschneider, 99, 96.

83. Mair, "E. E. Schattschneider's *The Semisovereign People*," 953.

84. Schattschneider, *The Semisovereign People*, 102; emphasis in original.

85. Phulwani, "The Poor Man's Machiavelli," 863–4.

86. Phulwani, "The Poor Man's Machiavelli," 864.

87. Schattschneider, *The Semisovereign People*, 72.

88. Jack L. Walker, "The Origins and Maintenance of Interest Groups in America," *The American Political Science Review* 77, no. 2 (1983): 390–406, at 402.

89. Walker, "The Origins and Maintenance of Interest Groups in America," 390.

90. Walker, "The Origins and Maintenance of Interest Groups in America," 396, 390.

91. Walker, "The Origins and Maintenance of Interest Groups in America," 396.

92. Mançur Olson, *The Logic of Collective Action: Public Goods and the Theory of Groups* (Cambridge, MA: Harvard University Press, 1965).

93. Walker, "The Origins and Maintenance of Interest Groups in America," 396.

94. Walker, *Mobilizing Interest Groups in America*, 49.

95. Walker, *Mobilizing Interest Groups in America*, 49.

96. Walker began his career by writing one of the first political science analyses of the civil rights lunch counter sit-ins in a 1964 working paper for the Eagleton Institute of Politics at Rutgers University. See Jack L. Walker, *Sit-Ins in Atlanta* (New York: McGraw-Hill, 1964).

97. Walker, "A Critique of the Elitist Theory of Democracy."

98. Jeffrey C. Isaac, *Democracy in Dark Times* (Ithaca, NY: Cornell University Press, 1998), 29–31. Four years later, Carole Pateman launched the rival tradition of "participatory democracy" (*Participation and Democratic Theory* (Cambridge, UK: Cambridge University Press, 1970).

99. Robert A. Dahl, *A Preface to Democratic Theory* (Chicago: University of Chicago Press, 1956), 132.

100. Dahl, *A Preface to Democratic Theory*, 137. Dahl noted that in the "South, Negroes were not until recently an active group," without remarking on their legitimacy *(A Preface to Democratic Theory*, 138).

101. Walker, "A Critique of the Elitist Theory of Democracy," 289; emphasis added.

102. Walker, "A Critique of the Elitist Theory of Democracy," 291.

103. Walker, "A Critique of the Elitist Theory of Democracy," 291.

104. Walker, "A Critique of the Elitist Theory of Democracy," 291.

105. Walker, "A Critique of the Elitist Theory of Democracy," 292.

106. Walker, "A Critique of the Elitist Theory of Democracy," 292.

107. Walker, "A Critique of the Elitist Theory of Democracy," 293.

108. Walker, "A Critique of the Elitist Theory of Democracy," 293.

109. Walker, "A Critique of the Elitist Theory of Democracy," 293.

110. Dahl, "Further Reflections on 'The Elitist Theory of Democracy,'" 297.

111. Walker, "A Critique of the Elitist Theory of Democracy," 287.

112. Dahl, "Further Reflections on 'The Elitist Theory of Democracy,'" 297.

113. Dahl, "Further Reflections on 'The Elitist Theory of Democracy,'" 297.

114. Dahl, "Further Reflections on 'The Elitist Theory of Democracy,'" 297.

115. Dahl, "Further Reflections on 'The Elitist Theory of Democracy,'" 297.

116. Dahl, "Further Reflections on 'The Elitist Theory of Democracy,'" 297. Though I, like Dahl, may "appear to be nitpicking," I will note again that neither Dahl nor Walker picked up on Lipset's putting "elitist" in scare quotes.

117. Walker, "A Critique of the Elitist Theory of Democracy," 291.

118. Walker, "A Critique of the Elitist Theory of Democracy," 289–90.

119. Walker, "A Critique of the Elitist Theory of Democracy," 293; Dahl, *A Preface to Democratic Theory*, 132.

120. George Rudé, *The Crowd in History: A Study of Popular Disturbances in France and England, 1730–1848* (New York: John Wiley & Sons, 1964).

121. Eric Hobsbawm, *Primitive Rebels: Studies in Archaic Forms of Social Movement in the 19th and 20th Centuries* (Manchester: Manchester University Press, 1959).

122. Rudé, *The Crowd in History*, 9.

123. Hobsbawm, *Primitive Rebels*.

124. Rudé, *The Crowd in History*, 9.

125. Hobsbawm singles out "the mob" as the one among many "groupings of the poor" that can "rarely rouse" the historian's "sympathy" (*Primitive Rebels*, 125).

126. Hobsbawm, 3.

127. Rudé, *The Crowd in History*, 234.

128. Hobsbawm, *Primitive Rebels*, 116.

129. Hobsbawm, 124.

130. Hobsbawm, 2; emphasis in original.

131. Hobsbawm, 110.

132. Rudé, *The Crowd in History*, 34, 31.

133. Rudé, 122.

134. Schattschneider, *The Semisovereign People*, 72.

135. Walker, "A Critique of the Elitist Theory of Democracy," 293–4. Hobsbawm would not have counted the members of all of these movements as "primitive" rebels. The southern civil rights movement stands out in particular because it was organized, it had a well-articulated ideology, and it did call for a transformation of the segregationist governmental structure of the South.

136. Rudé, *The Crowd in History*, 268.

137. Rudé, 268.

138. Rudé, 269; emphasis added.

139. Schattschneider, *The Semisovereign People*, 60.

140. Walker, "A Critique of the Elitist Theory of Democracy," 294; emphasis added.

141. Walker, "A Critique of the Elitist Theory of Democracy," 293–4.

142. Schattschneider, *The Semisovereign People*, 102; emphasis in original.

143. In 1967, Walker partnered with Joel D. Aberbach to mount a groundbreaking survey of Detroiters' attitudes toward the slogan "Black Power," just months after the uprisings (See Joel D. Aberbach and Jack L. Walker 1970, "The Meanings of Black Power: A Comparison of White and Black Interpretations of a Political Slogan," *American Political Science Review* 64, no. 2 [June 1970]: 367–88). Aberbach and Walker set out explicitly to "lay to rest the so-called 'riffraff' theory," first put forth in a 1964 gubernatorial commission report on the uprisings in Watts, which held that "black power appeals strictly to the less privileged in the black community" (379). They found that the content of the slogan depended on who interpreted it. A broad range of Black Detroiters heard it favorably, "as another call for a fair share for blacks or as a rallying cry for black unity" (373). Middle-class Blacks gave voice to what scholars now study as "linked fate"; they expressed favorable views of Black Power not out of "personal dissatisfaction" but out of a shared "set of beliefs" and "mood of protest" regarding the slow pace of progress for the Black community as a whole (379). A majority of white respondents interpreted "black power" as a symbol of "a black desire to take over the country, or somehow deprive the white man," as if Blacks' racial solidarity and demands for things like fair wages and neighborhood and school desegregation mounted "an illegitimate, revengeful challenge" to white power (373, 386). White Detroiters made it clear that they inhabited whiteness, and the material privileges that came with it, as a racial status that had meaning and value only by virtue of the subordination of Black Americans. From this position of precarious privilege, Black Power cannot be heard as a simple call for a "fair share"; it is necessarily a bid for dominance in a zero-sum game where "blacks can gain something *only at*

the expense of whites and vice versa" (372; emphasis added). It is hard to imagine a more explicit defense of what Cheryl Harris would later call "whiteness as property." (See Cheryl Harris, "Whiteness as Property," *Harvard Law Review* 106, no. 8 [1993]: 1707–1791).

144. Schattschneider, *The Semisovereign People*, 63.

145. Frances Fox Piven and Richard A. Cloward, "Collective Protest: A Critique of Resource Mobilization Theory," *International Journal of Politics, Culture and Society* 4, no. 4 (Summer 1991): 435–58, at 436.

146. Piven and Cloward, 451.

147. Piven and Cloward, 454.

148. Schattschneider, *The Semisovereign People*, 63.

149. Mair, "E. E. Schattschneider's *The Semisovereign People*," 954.

150. Mair, 950.

Chapter Five

1. James N. Druckman, "The Implications of Framing Effects for Citizen Competence," *Political Behavior* 23, no. 3 (September 2001): 225–56; here, 226–31.

2. Robert E. Goodin, *Manipulatory Politics* (New Haven, CT: Yale University Press, 1980), 4.

3. Goodin, 3.

4. Goodin, 3.

5. Goodin, 3.

6. Goodin, 36.

7. Goodin, 36.

8. Goodin, 36, 238.

9. Goodin, 238.

10. Goodin, 238.

11. Goodin, 238.

12. Simone Chambers, "Deliberation and Mass Democracy," in *Deliberative Systems*, eds. Jane Mansbridge and John Parkinson (Cambridge, UK: Cambridge University Press, 2012): 52–71, at 65.

13. Goodin, *Manipulatory Politics*, 27.

14. Mark Scott, "Cambridge Analytica Did Work for Brexit Groups, Says Exstaffer." *Politico*, July 30, 2019, https://www.politico.eu/article/cambridge-analytica -leave-eu-ukip-brexit-facebook/.

15. The big-data company harvested data from the things that Americans watch, buy, "like" and "share" online to psychologically profile people for micro-targeted messaging that the company claimed could affect their participation in the 2016 election. Various media reports suggested that Cambridge Analytica had indeed done so (e.g., Alex Hern, "Cambridge Analytica: How Did It Turn Clicks into

Votes?," *Guardian*, May 6, 2018, https://www.theguardian.com/news/2018/may/06 /cambridge-analytica-how-turn-clicks-into-votes-christopher-wylie).

16. Paul M. Sniderman and Sean M. Theriault, "The Structure of Political Argument and the Logic of Issue Framing," in *Studies in Public Opinion: Attitudes, Nonattitudes, Measurement Error, and Change*, eds. Willem E. Saris and Paul M. Sniderman (Princeton, NJ: Princeton University Press, 2004): 133–65, at 158.

17. Sniderman and Theriault, 158.

18. Sniderman and Theriault, 139.

19. Dennis Chong, *Rational Lives: Norms and Values in Politics and Society* (Chicago: University of Chicago Press, 2000), 131.

20. Terence Ball, "Manipulation: As Old as Democracy Itself (and Sometimes Dangerous)," in *Manipulating Democracy: Democratic Theory, Political Psychology, and Mass Media*, eds. Wayne Le Cheminant and John M. Parrish (London: Routledge, 2011): 41–58, at 41.

21. Ball, 42.

22. Ball, 41.

23. James Bohman, "Emancipation and Rhetoric: The Perlocutions and Illocutions of the Social Critic," *Philosophy and Rhetoric* 21, no. 3 (1988): 185–204, at 198.

24. Bohman, "Emancipation and Rhetoric," 198.

25. Ball, "Manipulation: As Old as Democracy Itself," 43.

26. George Eliot, *Felix Holt: The Radical*, ed. Lynda Mugglestone (New York: Penguin Classics, 1995 [1866]), 354–5.

27. His actions indict both. Against the Tories, he supports liberalization of the franchise. Against the reformers whose political agenda he shares, he opposes the practice of buying workers' votes with rum—the very cause of the riot on Treby Manor where Holt, taking lead of the mob to steer it away from that property, was mistaken for its "leading spirit" (Eliot, 315).

28. Goodin, *Manipulatory Politics*, 6.

29. Jane J. Mansbridge, "Rethinking Representation," *American Political Science Review* 97, no. 4 (2003): 515–28, at 519.

30. James Fishkin, "Manipulation and Democratic Theory," in *Manipulating Democracy: Democratic Theory, Political Psychology, and Mass Media*, eds. Wayne Le Cheminant and John M. Parrish (New York: Routledge, 2011), 34.

31. Wayne Le Cheminant and John M. Parrish observe that "democratic theorists have tended to conceptualize manipulation as a subversion of the purely rational processes of individual choice, by means of the interference of emotion, misinformation, or similar, 'non-rational' intervening variables," while "cognitive science" challenges purely rationalist accounts of preferences and choice by teaching that "rational thought itself requires emotion." (See introduction to *Manipulating Democracy*, 11.)

32. Ball, "Manipulation: As Old as Democracy Itself," 42.

33. Ball, 42, 46; emphasis in original.

34. Goodin, *Manipulatory Politics*, 15.

35. Goodin, 15.

36. Goodin, 8.

37. Goodin, 31.

38. Goodin, 17.

39. Goodin, 13.

40. Goodin, 13, 21, 11. Goodin acknowledges that this definition keeps the problem of the counterfactual alive (to assert that someone has been manipulated implies that we could specify "what he would have done otherwise") but argues that this problem "seems so central to notions of 'power' and 'influence'" that it would be "suspicious" to propose an analysis that "fails even to acknowledge" it (18). If Goodin's definition of manipulation "does not evade any of these familiar problems," at least it does not complicate them still further by invoking notions of interest (18).

41. Goodin, 130, 138.

42. The first of these terms dates to the school desegregation battles of the 1970s (see Matthew F. Delmont, *Why Busing Failed: Race, Media, and the National Resistance to School Desegregation* [Oakland: University of California Press, 2016], 103). Donald Trump used the second in his Inaugural Address on January 20, 2017 ("Inaugural Address: Trump's Full Speech," CNN, Turner Broadcasting System, January 20, 2017, www.cnn.com/2017/01/20/politics/trump-inaugural-address /index.html).

43. Tali Mendelberg, "From the Folk Theory to Symbolic Politics: Toward a More Realistic Understanding of Voter Behavior," *Critical Review* 30, no. 1 (2018): 107–18.

44. Goodin, *Manipulatory Politics*, 52.

45. Goodin, 44–5.

46. Goodin, 45.

47. Propaganda, another common concern, Goodin dismisses as "only marginally manipulatory" because it is blatant and—the more crudely expressed, widely available, and obviously one-sided it is—the more likely it is to be discounted by the recipient (64). The *Washington Post* published a selection of the ads that Russian operatives created for Facebook between June 2015 and August 2017, together with information about the targeted population, number of impressions, and number of clicks they received. Many of the ads are so blatant and crudely produced—e.g., a picture of Jesus arm-wrestling Satan for the outcome of the election above the slogan: "Press 'like' to help Jesus win!"—that it hard to imagine them persuading anyone (the *Post* reports this one in particular receiving just 14 clicks). (Dan Keating, Kevin Schaul, and Leslie Shapiro, "The Facebook Ads Russians Targeted at Different Groups," *Washington Post*, November 1, 2017, https://www.washingtonpost.com/graphics/2017/business/russian-ads-facebook -targeting/?itid=lk_interstitial_manual_9.) There is no academic research yet verifying that online targeting of the kind that Russian operatives engaged in

or Cambridge Analytica sold to its clients can influence people's beliefs (Joshua A. Tucker, Andrew Guess, Pablo Barberá, Christian Vaccari, Alexandra Siegel, Sergey Sanovich, Denis Stukal, and Brendan Nyhan, "Social Media, Political Polarization, and Political Disinformation: A Review of the Scientific Literature," working paper prepared for the Hewlett Foundation, 2018, https://papers.ssrn.com/sol3/papers.cfm?abstract_id=3144139).

48. Goodin, *Manipulatory Politics*, 93.

49. Goodin, 93.

50. Goodin, 93.

51. Achen and Bartels regard this phenomenon as quintessentially manipulative because they subscribe to what Goodin terms the "more familiar psychological" model that, in its most "implausible" version, "pictures man as responding automatically to certain sorts of symbolic stimuli" and theorizes human behavior as driven by "causes" rather than motivated by "reasons" (Goodin, 28; see also Christopher H. Achen and Larry M. Bartels, *Democracy for Realists: Why Elections Do Not Produce Responsive Government* (Princeton, NJ: Princeton University Press, 2016). Goodin counters with a "rationalistic" model in which people are motivated by reasons that manipulation tricks them into "bypassing"—via lies, via rhetorical trickery, and even by playing on their psychological susceptibilities (Goodin, *Manipulatory Politics*, 28, 29). In Goodin's account, the tricks can be revealed and the manipulation disarmed; in that of Achen and Bartels, our group affiliations predispose us to fall for them.

52. Goodin, 108.

53. Goodin, 108.

54. Goodin, 95–108.

55. Goodin, 108.

56. Goodin, 36, 298.

57. Goodin attaches even more importance to what he terms the "rigging of the obvious" (196). He proposed this term to align himself with critics of political scientists' focus on Dahl's "first face" of power (Goodin, 30–31). Subsequent research has borne out his claim that manipulation is a different face of power, one that shows itself in "perceptions of 'obvious' obstacles" that decision-makers regard, and the public accepts, as constraining political action "in certain ways," or in the " 'obvious' solutions" to which decision-makers and publics are "unthinkingly" drawn (Goodin, 198). Although much of this work is prescient, I omit Goodin's account of the "rigging" of the obvious because it is derived so closely from the historical example of Watergate that I find it difficult to disentangle the general from the particular. Goodin argues that at the outset of the Watergate investigation, the concept of impeachment "lived at the conceptual fringes of constitutional law" (207). Impeachment needed "conceptual rehabilitation" to make it appear as the "obvious" solution to the nation's crisis, and elites achieved this rehabilitation by feeding "vague rumours of impeachment into the congressional grapevine" and

propagating anonymous information to the mass media to make it seem as though "everybody's talking about it" (Goodin, 208, 215, 214). Coming from a theorist who wants to redirect analysis of manipulation from the "activities of anyone in particular" to the "relentless workings of systematic bias," this account struck me as curiously conspiratorial (Goodin, 238).

58. Goodin, 116.

59. Goodin, 119.

60. Tucker et al., "Social Media, Political Polarization, and Political Disinformation: A Review of the Scientific Literature," 16.

61. This example provides one more highly visible reminder, akin to that brought about by the Snowden revelations, of just how accustomed we of the internet age have become to what Bernard Harcourt calls "exposure" (Bernard E. Harcourt, *Exposed: Desire and Disobedience in the Digital Age* (Cambridge, MA: Harvard University Press, 2015).

62. Goodin, *Manipulatory Politics*, 238.

63. James N. Druckman and Lawrence R. Jacobs, *Who Governs? Presidents, Public Opinion, and Manipulation* (Chicago: University of Chicago Press, 2015).

64. Druckman and Jacobs, 122.

65. Druckman and Jacobs, 14, 72.

66. Druckman and Jacobs, 15.

67. Druckman and Jacobs, 76.

68. Druckman and Jacobs, 122.

69. Druckman and Jacobs, 119. See Larry M. Bartels, *Unequal Democracy: The Political Economy of the Gilded Age* (New York and Princeton, NJ: Russell Sage Foundation and Princeton University Press, 2008); Lawrence R. Jacobs and Benjamin I. Page, "Who Influences US Foreign Policy?," *American Political Science Review* 99, no. 1 (February 2005): 107–23; Benjamin I. Page and Martin Gilens, *Democracy in America? What Has Gone Wrong and What We Can Do about It* (Chicago: University of Chicago Press, 2018); Jacob Hacker and Paul Pierson, *Winner-Take-All Politics: How Washington Made the Rich Richer—and Turned Its Back on the Middle Class* (New York: Simon and Schuster, 2010).

70. Druckman and Jacobs, *Who Governs?*, 59.

71. Druckman and Jacobs, 33.

72. Druckman and Jacobs, 88.

73. Druckman and Jacobs, 90.

74. Druckman and Jacobs, 81.

75. Druckman and Jacobs, 92.

76. Druckman and Jacobs, 74.

77. Druckman and Jacobs, 7.

78. Sniderman and Theriault, "The Structure of Political Argument and the Logic of Issue Framing," 139.

79. Sniderman and Theriault, 158.

80. Dennis Chong and James N. Druckman, "Framing Public Opinion in Competitive Democracies," *American Political Science Review* 101, no. 4 (November 2007): 637–55; also Dennis Chong and James N. Druckman, "Counterframing Effects," *Journal of Politics* 75, no. 1 (2013): 1–16.

81. Chong, *Rational Lives*, 130.

82. Chong and Druckman, "Framing Public Opinion in Competitive Democracies," 652.

83. Chong and Druckman, "Framing Public Opinion in Competitive Democracies," 652, 649.

84. Chong and Druckman, "Framing Public Opinion in Competitive Democracies," 651.

85. Chong and Druckman, "Framing Public Opinion in Competitive Democracies," 645.

86. Chong and Druckman, "Framing Public Opinion in Competitive Democracies," 652.

87. Chong and Druckman, "Framing Public Opinion in Competitive Democracies," 652.

88. Chong and Druckman, "Framing Public Opinion in Competitive Democracies," 652; cf. James N. Druckman, "What's It All About? Framing in Political Science," in *Perspectives on Framing*, ed. Gideon Keren (New York: Psychology Press/Taylor and Francis, 2010).

89. Goodin, *Manipulatory Politics*, 29.

90. Goodin, 116.

91. Chong and Druckman, "Framing Public Opinion in Competitive Democracies," 652.

92. Chong and Druckman, "Framing Public Opinion in Competitive Democracies," 652.

93. Chong and Druckman, "Framing Public Opinion in Competitive Democracies," 652.

94. Arthur Lupia and Mathew D. McCubbins, *The Democratic Dilemma: Can Citizens Learn What They Need to Know?* (Cambridge, UK: Cambridge University Press, 1998), ch. 2.

95. Mark Danner, "The Secret Way to War," *New York Review of Books*, June 9, 2005, https://www.nybooks.com/articles/2005/06/09/the-secret-way-to-war/.

96. John Walcott and Mark Danner, "'The Secret Way to War': An Exchange," *New York Review of Books*, July 14, 2005, https://www.nybooks.com/articles/2005/07/14/the-secret-way-to-war-an-exchange/.

97. Danner, "The Secret Way to War."

98. Danner, "The Secret Way to War." For those who may not recall the details, the British had committed to join forces with the US in Iraq. But because they—unlike the US—could be called to account for their actions by the International

Criminal Court, they were reluctant to do so without the appearance of a justified cause. At the July meeting, Britain's Prime Minister and senior intelligence officials scrambled to "'fix,' as it were, what Blair [would] later call 'the political context.'" They decided to persuade the Bush administration to secure a resolution from the United Nations Security Council to let UN inspectors back into Iraq to search for WMDs. The British fervently hoped Saddam Hussein would refuse, which would give them their cause. When he did not—because, as chief US weapons inspector David Kay confirmed in January 2004, there were no weapons to be found—the process led to a stalemate. Inspectors found nothing. Some world leaders called for more time. The US, impatient for conflict, set up a parallel process of its own and spun the null result as "undermining the credibility of the United Nations process itself" (Danner, "The Secret Way to War"). In February 2003, Colin Powell's "multimedia presentation to the UN Security Council" cut off what Vice President Dick Cheney derisively called the "UN route," clearing the way to war and leaving Blair "without the protection of international approval." British elections were held one week after the memo's publication, and voters reelected Blair but crippled his party in Parliament. "The Iraq war, and the damage it had done to [Blair's] reputation for probity, was widely believed to have been a principal cause." Evidently more discerning than US newspaper editors, the British public believed that they had learned something from the memo. It revealed Blair's authorship of a failed—and, more importantly, duplicitous—political strategy.

99. Danner, "The Secret Way to War."

100. Danner, "The Secret Way to War."

101. Danner, "The Secret Way to War."

102. Goodin, *Manipulatory Politics*, 108.

103. Goodin, 22.

104. Goodin, 31.

105. Adam J. Berinsky, "Rumors and Health Care Reform: Experiments in Political Misinformation," *British Journal of Political Science* 47, no. 2 (2017): 241–62, at 242.

106. To date, researchers have focused on the consequences of sorting for individuals' social relationships rather than for their political judgment. They have studied its effects on civil society and personal relations, looking for evidence of "affective polarization" in people's willingness to live near, marry, or have their children marry partisans of the opposite party. See Gregory Huber and Neil Malhotra, "Political Homophily in Social Relationships: Evidence from Online Dating Behaviour," *Journal of Politics* 79, no. 1 (January 2017): 269–83; Keith M. Chen and Ryne Rohla, "The Effect of Partisanship and Political Advertising on Close Family Ties," *Science* 360, no. 6392 (June 2018): 1020–4. For the effects of sorting on economic decisions about hypothetical job applicants and scholarship recipients, see Christopher McConnell, Yotam Margalit, Neil Malhotra, and Matthew Levendusky, "The Economic Consequences of Partisanship in a Polarized Era," *American Journal of*

Political Science 62, no. 1 (2018): 5–18. One study, which finds that "cross-party dialogue" (in small, face-to-face groups) fosters trust and opens up communication, suggests that sorting likely does the opposite. Insofar as it frustrates dialogue across political differences, sorting likely spreads distrust and shuts down communication. See Matthew Levendusky and Dominik Stecula, "Can We Talk: Does Cross-Party Dialogue Reduce Affective Polarization?" (unpublished manuscript).

107. This observation, made by Chude Jideonwo, a friend of the author Chimamanda Ngozi Adichie, reflects on his experience of political conversation with American liberals at Yale. See Larissa MacFarquhar, "Chimamanda Ngozi Adichie Comes to Terms with Global Fame," *New Yorker*, May 28, 2018, https://www.new yorker.com/magazine/2018/06/04/chimamanda-ngozi-adichie-comes-to-terms -with-global-fame.

108. Ernesto Laclau and Chantal Mouffe, *Hegemony and Socialist Strategy: Towards a Radical Democratic Politics* (New York: Verso Books, 1985), 85.

Chapter Six

1. Ernesto Laclau and Chantal Mouffe, *Hegemony and Socialist Strategy: Towards a Radical Democratic Politics* (New York: Verso Books, 1985), hereafter *HSS*, 85.

2. Michael Scott Christofferson, *French Intellectuals against the Left: The Antitotalitarian Moment of the 1970s.* (New York: Berghahn Books, 2004).

3. Kevin Duong, "'Does Democracy End in Terror?' Transformations of Antitotalitarianism in Postwar France," *Modern Intellectual History* 14, no. 2 (2017): 537–63, at 562.

4. François Furet, *Interpreting the French Revolution*, trans. Elborg Forster (Cambridge, UK: Cambridge University Press, 1977), 48; Claude Lefort, *Democracy and Political Theory*, trans. David Macey (Minneapolis: University of Minnesota Press, 1988), 18, 92; Claude Lefort, *The Political Forms of Modern Society*, ed. John B. Thompson (Cambridge, MA: MIT Press, 1986), 194.

5. Andrew Jainchill and Samuel Moyn, "French Democracy Between Totalitarianism and Solidarity: Pierre Rosanvallon and Revisionist Historiography," *Journal of Modern History* 76, no. 1 (2004): 107–54, at 114. Note that the term *liberal* in France is not synonymous with neoliberalism; it is also more capacious than its Anglo-American counterpart, encompassing left-wing critics of totalitarianism, neo-Tocquevillians, advocates of democratic pluralism, free marketeers, *and* critics of neoliberalism. See Emile Chabal, *A Divided Republic: Nation, State and Citizenship in Contemporary France* (Cambridge, UK: Cambridge University Press, 2015), ch. 6.

6. Samuel Moyn, "On the Intellectual Origins of François Furet's Masterpiece," *Tocqueville Review* 29, no. 2 (2008): 59–78, at 69.

7. Lefort, *Democracy and Political Theory*, 16.

8. Duong, 541.

9. Furet, *Interpreting the French Revolution*, 26.

10. Furet, *Interpreting the French Revolution*, 49.

11. Lefort, *The Political Forms of Modern Society*, 194.

12. Lefort, *Democracy and Political Theory*, 226–7.

13. Lefort, *The Political Forms of Modern Society*, 233.

14. Antoon Braeckman, "Neoliberalism and the Symbolic Institution of Society: Pitting Foucault against Lefort on the State and the 'Political,'" *Philosophy and Social Criticism* 41, no. 9 (2015): 945–62, at 948; emphasis in original.

15. Lefort, *Democracy and Political Theory*, 225.

16. Furet, *Interpreting the French Revolution*, 26.

17. Moyn, "On the Intellectual Origins of François Furet's Masterpiece," 67.

18. Duong, "'Does Democracy End in Terror?,'" 540, 551.

19. Lefort, *Democracy and Political Theory*, 19.

20. Duong, "'Does Democracy End in Terror?,'" 551.

21. Warren Breckman, *Adventures of the Symbolic: Postmarxism and Radical Democracy* (New York: Columbia University Press, 2013), 140–41.

22. Lefort, *Democracy and Political Theory*, 18–19.

23. Samuel Moyn, "Antitotalitarianism and After," introduction to Pierre Rosanvallon, *Democracy Past and Future*, ed. Samuel Moyn (New York: Columbia University Press, 2006): 1–30, at 8. It could be objected that those of us who read Lefort as a standard-bearer for the constructivist turn and return to representation today perpetuate Furet's model of opportunistic misreading. In the 1970s, Lefort tended to side with the antirepresentative politics of the "independent, libertarian left" that "sought to free itself from the authoritarian tendencies" it perceived in Left party politics. James Ingram suggests that recruiting Lefort as an intellectual ally of the constructivist turn may not do much interpretive violence after all. He notes that Lefort kept a distance from the politics of the time, and that he "rejected" the "anarchist as well as the liberal" alternatives, so that his own political position was "hard to discern" (James D. Ingram, "The Politics of Claude Lefort's Political: Between Liberalism and Radical Democracy," *Thesis Eleven* 87 [November 2006]: 33–50, at 38–39).

24. Lefort, *Democracy and Political Theory*, 34.

25. Lefort, *Democracy and Political Theory*, 34.

26. Lefort, *Democracy and Political Theory*, 19; emphasis in original.

27. Lefort, *Democracy and Political Theory*, 16.

28. Lefort, *Democracy and Political Theory*, 34.

29. Lefort, *Democracy and Political Theory*, 225.

30. Lefort, *Democracy and Political Theory*, 92; Lefort, *The Political Forms of Modern Society*, 194.

31. Raf Geenens, "Democracy, Human Rights and History: Reading Lefort," *European Journal of Political Theory* 7, no. 1 (2008): 269–86, at 271.

32. Wim Weymans, "Freedom through Political Representation? Lefort, Gauchet and Rosanvallon on the Relationship between State and Society," *European Journal of Political Theory* 4, no. 3 (2005): 263–82, at 266.

33. Lefort, *Democracy and Political Theory*, 225; Weymans, "Freedom through Political Representation?," 266, citing Claude Lefort, *Invention démocratique*, 2nd ed. (Paris: Fayard, 1994 [1981]).

34. Lefort, *Democracy and Political Theory*, 226.

35. Oliver Marchart, *Post-Foundational Political Thought: Political Difference in Nancy, Lefort, Badiou and Laclau* (Edinburgh: Edinburgh University Press, 2007), 93.

36. Lefort, *Democracy and Political Theory*, 225. Samuel Moyn explains that that Lefort proposes a "socialized version" of Lacan's mirror stage by a "deeply improvisational move" that takes over Merleau-Ponty's notion of the symbolic and "infus[es] it with some of the content of Lacan's 'imaginary'" (Moyn," Claude Lefort, Political Anthropology, and Symbolic Division" in *Claude Lefort: Thinker of the Political* 2013, ed. Martín Plot (Basingstoke: Palgrave Macmillan, 2013): 51–70, at 61). Just as Lacan holds that the self forms only by means (and at the price) of alienation from the image that constitutes it as a unity, so Lefort maintains that "division is . . . constitutive of the very unity of society" (*Democracy and Political Theory*, 18). Thus, "it is the *representation of the community's identity*, necessarily separated off from its real nature just as the mirror is outside the child, that nonetheless integrates the group" (Moyn, "Claude Lefort, Political Anthropology, and Symbolic Division," 62; emphasis in original).

37. Lefort, *Democracy and Political Theory*, 91; emphasis added.

38. Lefort, *Democracy and Political Theory*, 91.

39. Lefort, *The Political Forms of Modern Society*, 194.

40. Lefort *Democracy and Political Theory*, 227–28.

41. Lefort *Democracy and Political Theory*, 227–28.

42. Lefort *Democracy and Political Theory*, 18, 11.

43. Lefort *Democracy and Political Theory*, 11.

44. Lefort *Democracy and Political Theory*, 11.

45. Marchart, *Post-Foundational Political Thought*, 92.

46. Christine Delphy, "Introduction to the Collection," in *Close to Home*, trans. Diana Leonard (Amherst: University of Massachusetts Press, 1984): 5–27, at 24.

47. Ingram, "The Politics of Claude Lefort's Political," 36.

48. Lefort, *Democracy and Political Theory*, 12; emphasis added.

49. James Baldwin, *The Fire Next Time* (New York: Vintage International, 1993 [1963]), 25; emphasis added.

50. Lefort, *The Political Forms of Modern Society*, 193.

51. Lefort, *The Political Forms of Modern Society*, 193; emphasis added.

52. Christine Delphy, "Patriarchy, Feminism and Their Intellectuals," in *Close to Home*, trans. Diana Leonard: 138–53.

53. Lefort, *The Political Forms of Modern Society*, 193.

54. Lefort, *The Political Forms of Modern Society*, 194. For an account of Delphy's elaboration of this "constructivist materialist" argument, see Lisa Disch, "Christine Delphy's Constructivist Materialism," *South Atlantic Quarterly* 114, no.4 (2015): 827–49.

55. Lefort, *The Political Forms of Modern Society*, 194.

56. Lefort, *The Political Forms of Modern Society*, 194.

57. Lefort, *The Political Forms of Modern Society*, 194.

58. Lefort, *Democracy and Political Theory*, 225; emphasis in original.

59. Marchart, *Post-Foundational Political Thought*, 86.

60. Lefort, *Democracy and Political Theory*, 228, 226.

61. Geenens, "Democracy, Human Rights and History," 274.

62. Lefort, *Democracy and Political Theory*, 39.

63. Lefort, *Democracy and Political Theory*, 18.

64. Lefort, *Democracy and Political Theory*, 19; emphasis in original.

65. Ingram, "The Politics of Claude Lefort's Political," 42; emphasis in original.

66. Ingram, "The Politics of Claude Lefort's Political," 42; emphasis in original.

67. Ingram, "The Politics of Claude Lefort's Political," 42, 46.

68. Marchart, *Post-Foundational Political Thought*, 106.

69. Lefort, *Democracy and Political Theory*, 39; emphasis added on "replace"; all other emphasis in original.

70. Jürgen Habermas, *The Inclusion of the Other: Studies in Political Theory*, edited by Ciaran Cronin and Pablo De Greiff (Boston: MIT Press, 1998), 37.

71. Lefort, *Democracy and Political Theory*, 39.

72. Marchart, *Post-Foundational Political Thought*, 91.

73. Braeckman, "Neoliberalism and the Symbolic Institution of Society," 948.

74. Lefort, *Democracy and Political Theory*, 232, 20.

75. Lefort, *Democracy and Political Theory*, 19.

76. Moyn, "On the Intellectual Origins of François Furet's Masterpiece," 62.

77. Furet, *Interpreting the French Revolution*, 26.

78. Furet, *Interpreting the French Revolution*, 29.

79. Furet, *Interpreting the French Revolution*, 29, 27.

80. Furet, *Interpreting the French Revolution*, 29.

81. Moyn, "On the Intellectual Origins of François Furet's Masterpiece," 66.

82. Moyn, "On the Intellectual Origins of François Furet's Masterpiece," 65.

83. Moyn, "On the Intellectual Origins of François Furet's Masterpiece," 66.

84. Moyn, "On the Intellectual Origins of François Furet's Masterpiece," 66, 67.

85. Furet, *Interpreting the French Revolution*, 38. Furet's concept of *"democratic" sociability*, of which the Revolution is one incarnation, gives him a way of getting at the power of order that Lefort conceives through the notion of *the political*. Furet defines *democratic sociability* as the "mode of organizing the relations between citizens (or subjects) and power, as well as among citizens (or subjects) themselves in relation to power" (*Interpreting the French Revolution*, 37). To the extent that Furet recognizes, with Lefort, that politics is not simply grounded on

social relations but participates in constituting them, this approach may mark a constructivist thread in Furet's own work.

86. Furet, *Interpreting the French Revolution*, 38.

87. Furet, *Interpreting the French Revolution*, 45.

88. Furet, *Interpreting the French Revolution*, 45.

89. Furet, *Interpreting the French Revolution*, 38.

90. Furet, *Interpreting the French Revolution*, 78.

91. Lynn Hunt, *Politics, Culture, and Class in the French Revolution* (Berkeley: University of California Press, 1984), 12.

92. Furet, *Interpreting the French Revolution*, 48; emphasis added.

93. Hunt, *Politics, Culture, and Class in the French Revolution*, 320, 12.

94. Furet, *Interpreting the French Revolution*, 49, 48.

95. Furet, *Interpreting the French Revolution*, 48.

96. Furet, *Interpreting the French Revolution*, 51.

97. Furet, *Interpreting the French Revolution*, 51.

98. Furet, *Interpreting the French Revolution*, 38–39; emphasis added.

99. Furet, *Interpreting the French Revolution*, 13.

100. Furet, *Interpreting the French Revolution*, 78; emphasis added.

101. Furet, *Interpreting the French Revolution*, 79.

102. Moyn, "On the Intellectual Origins of François Furet's Masterpiece."

103. Lefort, *Democracy and Political Theory*, ch. 5.

104. Michael Scott Christofferson, "An Antitotalitarian History of the French Revolution: François Furet's 'Penser la Révolution française' in the Intellectual Politics of the Late 1970s," *French Historical Studies* 22, no. 4 (Autumn 1999): 557–611, at 604–5.

105. Lefort, *Democracy and Political Theory*, 99, 90.

106. Lefort, *Democracy and Political Theory*, 91; emphasis added.

107. Lefort, *Democracy and Political Theory*, 91; Furet, *Interpreting the French Revolution*, 78.

108. Lefort, *Democracy and Political Theory*, 93; emphasis added.

109. Lefort, *Democracy and Political Theory*, 95; emphasis added.

110. Furet, *Interpreting the French Revolution*, 61, 11.

111. Lefort, *Democracy and Political Theory*, 105.

112. Furet, *Interpreting the French Revolution*, 27.

113. Jainchill and Moyn, "French Democracy between Totalitarianism and Solidarity," 118.

114. Jainchill and Moyn, 153. Gregory Conti and William Selinger argue that Rosanvallon's democratic impulse is constrained by the fact that he is deeply torn between a) his "*pre-scholarly*" conviction that political (as opposed to ethnic) minorities who are disempowered are best served by "descriptive inclusiveness" in representation and b) his empirical commitment to a constructivist premise he takes from Lefort: that "in a democracy there is no objective underlying social reality that must determine representative arrangements." They argue that the

constructivism Rosanvallon inherits from Lefort frustrates his normative democratic objective to extend representation to "existing groups and categories within
contemporary society that do not possess an adequate presence in political life"
because that constructivism rules out the possibility of taking recourse to "an image" of patterns of social exclusion that would make it possible to judge how well
a representative arrangement had ameliorated those patterns ("The Other Side of
Representation: The History and Theory of Representative Government in Pierre
Rosanvallon," *Constellations* 23, no. 4 (2016): 548–62, at 2, 10, 8, and 11).

115. Ernesto Laclau and Chantal Mouffe, *HSS*, 155.

Chapter Seven

1. Michael Scott Christofferson, *French Intellectuals against the Left: The Antitotalitarian Moment of the 1970s* (New York: Berghahn Books, 2004).

2. Warren Breckman, *Adventures of the Symbolic: Postmarxism and Radical
Democracy* (New York: Columbia University Press, 2013), 191; emphasis in original.

3. Breckman, 202, 193; see also Andrew Jainchill and Samuel Moyn, "French
Democracy between Totalitarianism and Solidarity: Pierre Rosanvallon and Revisionist Historiography," *Journal of Modern History* 76, no. 1 (2004): 107–54.

4. Ernesto Laclau and Chantal Mouffe, *Hegemony and Socialist Strategy: To-
wards a Radical Democratic Politics* (New York: Verso Books, 1985), hereafter
HSS, 152; Claude Lefort, *Democracy and Political Theory*, trans. David Macey
(Minneapolis: University of Minnesota Press, 1988), 16.

5. Laclau and Mouffe, *HSS*, 11.

6. Laclau and Mouffe, *HSS*, 170–71; emphasis in original.

7. Laclau and Mouffe, *HSS*, 134.

8. Laclau and Mouffe, *HSS*, 155; emphasis added. Compare Claude Lefort, *Democracy and Political Theory*, 11.

9. Laclau and Mouffe, *HSS*, 186.

10. Jeremy Valentine argues that Laclau and Mouffe introduce Lefort's "theory
of democracy" to account for the democratic possibilities of their Gramscian politics. See "Lefort and the Fate of Radical Democracy," in *Claude Lefort: Thinker
of the Political*, ed. Martín Plot (Basingstoke: Palgrave Macmillan, 2013): 203–17,
at 207.

11. Breckman, *Adventures of the Symbolic*, 184. For that initial reception, see
Norman Geras, "Post-Marxism?" *New Left Review* 163, no. 1 (May/June 1987):
40–82; Ernesto Laclau and Chantal Mouffe, "Post-Marxism without Apologies,"
New Left Review 166, no. 1 (November/December 1987): 79–106.

12. Lasse Thomassen, "In/exclusions: Towards a Radical Democratic Approach
to Exclusion," in *Radical Democracy: Politics Between Abundance and Lack*, eds.
Lars Tønder and Lasse Thomassen, (Manchester: Manchester University Press,
2005): 103–22, at 106.

13. Laclau and Mouffe, *HSS*, 65.

14. Laclau and Mouffe, *HSS*, 65.

15. Laclau and Mouffe, *HSS*, 134.

16. Laclau and Mouffe, *HSS*, 186.

17. Laclau and Mouffe, *HSS*, 155.

18. Laclau and Mouffe, *HSS*, 155; 144–45.

19. Simon Critchley, "Is There a Normative Deficit in the Theory of Hegemony?," in *Laclau: A Critical Reader*, eds. Simon Critchley and Oliver Marchart (New York: Routledge, 2004): 113–22, at 114.

20. Laclau and Mouffe, *HSS*, 180, 138; Elmer Eric Schattschneider, *The Semisovereign People*, reprinted ed., intro. by David Adamany (Fort Worth: Harcourt Brace Jovanovich, 1975), 64.

21. David Howarth, "Hegemony, Political Subjectivity, and Radical Democracy," in *Laclau: A Critical Reader*, eds. Critchley and Marchart: 256–76, at 256.

22. Laclau and Mouffe, *HSS*, 180.

23. Laclau and Mouffe, *HSS*,153; emphasis added.

24. Laclau and Mouffe, *HSS*, 151, 85; emphasis original.

25. Laclau and Mouffe, *HSS*, 138.

26. Abbé Emmanuel Joseph Sieyes, *What Is the Third Estate?*, trans. M. Blondel; ed., with historical notes, by S. E. Finer (New York: Prager, 1964 [1789]), 83.

27. William Sewell, *A Rhetoric of Bourgeois Revolution: The Abbé Sieyes and "What Is the Third Estate?"* (Durham, NC: Duke University Press, 1994), 4.

28. For the spelling, I follow Sewell, who reports that whereas "Sieyes himself spelled the name in three different ways during the course of his lifetime," it appeared in "most of his published writings" as "Sieyes, without an accent" (*A Rhetoric of Bourgeois Revolution*, 2).

29. Sieyes, *What Is the Third Estate?*, 70.

30. Sewell, *A Rhetoric of Bourgeois Revolution*, 52.

31. Edmund Burke, *Reflections on the Revolution in France*, ed. Frank M. Turner (New Haven, CT: Yale University Press, 2003 [1790]), 66.

32. The revolutionaries initially followed Sieyes' model in the "constitutional order [they] elaborated between the summer of 1789 and the summer of 1791" (Sewell, *A Rhetoric of Bourgeois Revolution*, 187). Only later did the constitutional vision that Sieyes grounded in the principles of liberal political economy cede to republican values of virtue and sacrifice for nation (Sewell, 189–90).

33. Keith Michael Baker, *Inventing the French Revolution* (Cambridge, UK: Cambridge University Press, 1990), 244.

34. Baker, *Inventing the French Revolution*, 244.

35. Baker, *Inventing the French Revolution*, 244.

36. Baker, *Inventing the French Revolution*, 245.

37. Sewell, *A Rhetoric of Bourgeois Revolution*, 58.

38. Sewell, 54. Sewell recognizes that this rhetoric was only partially revolutionary. Sieyes's tactic, to unify the Third Estate by tapping the resentment of its

most privileged members, proved a better tool (quite literally) for "sever[ing] the nobility from the body of the nation" than for uniting France as a "collective of producers" (Sewell, 55, 58).

39. Sewell, 54.

40. Michael Saward, "The Representative Claim," *Contemporary Political Theory* 5, no. 3 (2006): 297–318.

41. Sewell, *A Rhetoric of Bourgeois Revolution*, 186.

42. Laclau and Mouffe, *HSS*, 151, emphasis in original.

43. Sewell, *A Rhetoric of Bourgeois Revolution*, 199.

44. Sewell, 200.

45. Sewell, 200.

46. Laclau and Mouffe, *HSS*, 137.

47. Laclau and Mouffe, *HSS*, 132, 133; emphasis added.

48. Laclau and Mouffe, *HSS*, 137, 152.

49. Laclau and Mouffe, *HSS*, 132.

50. Laclau and Mouffe, *HSS*, 159; emphasis in original.

51. Laclau and Mouffe, *HSS*, 133.

52. Laclau and Mouffe, *HSS*, 153–4.

53. Laclau and Mouffe, *HSS*, 133, 161.

54. Laclau and Mouffe, *HSS*, 87.

55. Romand Coles, "Liberty, Equality, Receptive Generosity: Neo-Nietzschean Reflections on the Ethics and Politics of Coalition," *American Political Science Review* 90, no. 2 (1996): 375–88.

56. Clive Barnett, "Deconstructing Radical Democracy: Articulation, Representation, and Being-with-Others," *Political Geography* 23, no. 5 (2004): 503–28, at 505.

57. Laclau, *New Reflections on the Revolution of Our Time*, 6.

58. Laclau, *New Reflections on the Revolution of Our Time*, 16.

59. Laclau, *New Reflections on the Revolution of Our Time*, 18.

60. Laclau, *New Reflections on the Revolution of Our Time*, 92.

61. Oliver Marchart, *Post-Foundational Political Thought: Political Difference in Nancy, Lefort, Badiou and Laclau* (Edinburgh: Edinburgh University Press, 2007), 148; Oliver Marchart, "Institution and Dislocation: Philosophical Roots of Laclau's Discourse Theory of Space and Antagonism," *Distinktion: Journal of Social Theory* 15, no. 3 (2014): 271–82, at 275.

62. Marchart, *Post-Foundational Political Thought*, 140.

63. Laclau and Mouffe, *HSS*, 132; Marchart, *Post-Foundational Political Thought*, 140.

64. Laclau and Mouffe, *HSS*, 137; emphasis in original.

65. Laclau and Mouffe, *HSS*, 137.

66. Laclau and Mouffe, *HSS*, 137.

67. Ernesto Laclau, *Politics and Ideology in Marxist Theory: Capitalism, Fascism, Populism* (New York: New Left Books, 1977), 142.

68. Laclau and Mouffe, *HSS*, 65, 58; Laclau, *New Reflections on the Revolution of Our Time*, 184.

69. Laclau and Mouffe, *HSS*, 139.

70. Laclau and Mouffe, *HSS*, 87.

71. Laclau and Mouffe emphasize that articulation "has a performative character," meaning that it exhibits the capacity Austin's speech act theory imputed to language: *enacting* states of being (as in "I bet" or "I promise") rather than merely *describing* them (*HSS*, 64). For a succinct account of the differences among performance studies, ethnomethodological, and speech act conceptions of the term *performative*, see Moya Lloyd, "Performativity and Performance," in *The Oxford Handbook of Feminist Theory*, eds. Lisa Disch and Mary Hawkesworth (Oxford: Oxford University Press, 2014): 572–92.

72. Laclau and Mouffe, *HSS*, 23, 63.

73. Christine Delphy, "The Main Enemy," in *Close to Home*, trans. Diana Leonard (Amherst: University of Massachusetts Press, 1984 [1981]): 65–77, at 67.

74. Laclau and Mouffe, *HSS*, 168. See Anna Clark, *Struggle for the Breeches: Gender and the Making of the British Working Class* (Berkeley: University of California Press, 1997).

75. Laclau and Mouffe, *HSS*, 155.

76. Samuel Moyn, "The Politics of Individual Rights: Marcel Gauchet and Claude Lefort," in *French Liberalism from Montesquieu to the Present Day*, eds. Raf Geenens and Helena Rosenblatt (Cambridge, UK: Cambridge University Press, 2012): 291–310, at 295.

77. Lefort, *Democracy and Political Theory*, 36. Samuel Chambers argues convincingly that Laclau understands rights as "empty signifiers that mediate the gap between universal and particular," providing a language in which a specific demand can invoke an ideal that affords a discursive framework for linking various demands in a broader struggle. Chambers insightfully concludes that the radical democratic understanding of rights not only dissociates rights-based struggle from liberal identity politics (the link that its critics have emphasized) but demonstrates that the "viability of hegemonic politics today depends on the discourse of rights" (Samuel Chambers, "Giving Up (on) Rights? The Future of Rights and the Project of Radical Democracy," *American Journal of Political Science* 48, no. 2 [2004]: 185–200, at 197 and 198).

78. Lefort, *Democracy and Political Theory*, 36.

79. Laclau and Mouffe, *HSS*, 110.

80. Laclau and Mouffe, *HSS*, 156, 155.

81. Laclau and Mouffe, *HSS*, 175–76.

82. Laclau and Mouffe, *HSS*, 110.

83. Laclau and Mouffe, *HSS*, 110.

84. Pamela Brandwein, "The 'Labor Vision' of the Thirteenth Amendment, Revisited," *Georgetown Journal of Law and Public Policy* 15 (2017): 13–57.

85. Brandwein draws on a body of new economic scholarship that charts the uneven development of industrialization across different sectors of the antebellum economy to emphasize that railroad workers, shoemakers, and tailors, among others, were by the 1820s and 1830s already experiencing an "intensification of the division of labor" and intensified extraction of surplus value (40). These transformations, which predated the arrival of "stereotypical big and mechanized factories" by decades, created forms of social dependence that made "Republican promises of social mobility . . . implausible for specific groups of wage laborers as early as the 1830s" (Brandwein, 39, 40). This work alters the valence of the term *free labor*, which workers were already using at this time not to affirm the emancipatory promise of the labor contract, but to contest it.

86. Brandwein, 32.

87. Brandwein, 16.

88. Brandwein, 16, 29.

89. Brandwein, 29, 32.

90. Laclau and Mouffe, *HSS*, 154.

91. Laclau and Mouffe, *HSS*, 133.

92. Nikole Hannah-Jones, *Living Apart: How the Government Betrayed a Landmark Civil Rights Law* (New York: ProPublica, 2012); Richard Rothstein, *The Color of Law: A Forgotten History of How Our Government Segregated America* (New York: Liveright, 2017).

93. Laclau and Mouffe, *HSS*, 176; Kevin Phillips, *Emerging Republican Majority* (New Rochelle, NY: Arlington House, 1969); Mary D. Edsall and Thomas B. Edsall, *Chain Reaction: The Impact of Race, Rights, and Taxes on American Politics* (New York: W. W. Norton & Company, 1992); Jacob Hacker and Paul Pierson, *Let Them Eat Tweets: How the Right Rules in an Age of Extreme Inequality* (New York: Liveright, 2020).

94. Lefort, *Democracy and Political Theory*, 11.

95. Laclau and Mouffe, *HSS*, 142.

96. Lilliana Mason, *Uncivil Agreement: How Politics Became Our Identity*. Chicago: University of Chicago Press, 2018, 7–8.

97. Laclau and Mouffe, *HSS*, 145.

98. Laclau, *New Reflections on the Revolution of Our Time*, 35. I perceived this connection thanks to Marchart's excellent interpretation of Laclau's later work (*Post-Foundational Political Thought*, ch. 6).

Conclusion

1. I resort to scare quotes here to bid forgiveness for invoking the popular-culture "Frankenstein," the literal monster who is an affront to the title creature of Mary Shelley's novel—himself a being not monstrous but tragically misunderstood.

Bibliography

Aberbach, Joel D., and Jack L. Walker. "The Meanings of Black Power: A Comparison of White and Black Interpretations of a Political Slogan." *American Political Science Review* 64, no. 2 (June 1970): 367–88.

Abrams, Samuel, and Morris P. Fiorina. "'The Big Sort' That Wasn't: A Skeptical Reexamination." *PS: Political Science and Politics* 45, no. 2 (2012): 203–10.

Achen, Christopher H. "Mass Political Attitudes and the Survey Response." *American Political Science Review* 69, no. 4 (1975): 1218–1231.

Achen, Christopher H., and Larry M. Bartels. *Democracy for Realists: Why Elections Do Not Produce Responsive Government*. Princeton, NJ: Princeton University Press, 2016.

Adamany, David. Introduction to E. E. Schattschneider, *The Semisovereign People: A Realist's View of Democracy in America*. Fort Worth: Harcourt Brace Jovanovich, 1975. First published by Holt, Rinehart and Winston, 1960. Page references are to the 1975 edition, ix–xxxi.

Alexander, Michelle. "The Injustice of This Moment Is Not an 'Aberration." *New York Times*, January 17, 2020. https://www.nytimes.com/2020/01/17/opinion/sunday/michelle-alexander-new-jim-crow.html.

Alhstrom-Vij, Kristoffer. "Is Democracy an Option for the Realist?" *Critical Review: A Journal of Politics and Society* 30, no. 1–2 (2018): 1–12.

Alinsky, Saul. *Reveille for Radicals*. New York: Vintage Books, 1989 (1946).

Amenta, Edwin. *When Movements Matter: The Townsend Plan and the Rise of Social Security*. Princeton, NJ: Princeton University Press, 2008 (2006). Page references are to the 2008 edition.

American National Election Studies, *The ANES Guide to Public Opinion and Electoral Behavior*, based on work supported by the National Science Foundation under grant numbers SES 1444721, 2014–2017, the University of Michigan, and Stanford University. https://electionstudies.org/resources/anes-guide/.

Associated Press. "Gravely Ill, Atwater Offers Apology." *New York Times*, January 13, 1991, section 1, p. 16. https://www.nytimes.com/1991/01/13/us/gravely-ill-atwater-offers-apology.html.

Bachrach, Peter, and Morton S. Baratz. "Two Faces of Power." *American Political Science Review* 56, no. 4 (1962): 947–52.

Baker, Keith Michael. *Inventing the French Revolution.* Cambridge, UK: Cambridge University Press, 1990.

Baker, Peter. "Bush Made Willie Horton an Issue in 1988, and the Racial Scars Are Still Fresh." *New York Times*, December 3, 2018. https://www.nytimes.com /2018/12/03/us/politics/bush-willie-horton.html.

Baldwin, James. *The Fire Next Time.* New York: Vintage International, 1993 (1963).

Ball, Terence. "Manipulation: As Old as Democracy Itself (and Sometimes Dangerous)." In *Manipulating Democracy: Democratic Theory, Political Psychology, and Mass Media*, edited by Wayne Le Cheminant and John M. Parrish, 41–58. London: Routledge, 2011.

Barnett, Clive. "Deconstructing Radical Democracy: Articulation, Representation, and Being-with-Others." *Political Geography* 23, no. 5 (2004): 503–28.

Bartels, Larry. "Beyond the Running Tally: Partisan Bias in Political Perceptions." *Political Behavior* 24, no. 2 (2002): 117–50.

Bartels, Larry. "Democracy with Attitudes." In *Electoral Democracy*, edited by Michael B. McKuen and George Rabinowitz, 48–82. Ann Arbor: University of Michigan Press, 2003.

Bartels, Larry. *Unequal Democracy: The Political Economy of the New Gilded Age.* New York and Princeton, NJ: Russell Sage Foundation and Princeton University Press, 2008.

Bartels, Larry. "What's the Matter with What's the Matter with Kansas?" *Quarterly Journal of Political Science* 1, no. 2 (2006): 201–26.

Bellamy, Richard, and Sandra Kröger. "Representation Deficits and Surpluses in EU Policy-Making." *Journal of European Integration* 35, no. 5 (2013): 477–97.

Beltrán, Cristina. *The Trouble with Unity: Latino Politics and the Creation of Identity.* New York: Oxford University Press, 2010.

Bennett, Stephen Earl. "Democratic Competence, Before Converse and After." *Critical Review* 18, no. 1–3 (January 2006): 105–41.

Bentley, Arthur F. *The Process of Government: A Study of Social Pressures.* New Brunswick, NJ: Transaction Press, 2008 (1908).

Berelson, Bernard R., Paul F. Lazarsfeld, and William N. McPhee. *Voting: A Study of Opinion Formation in a Presidential Campaign.* Chicago: University of Chicago Press, 1954.

Berinsky, Adam J. "Rumors and Health Care Reform: Experiments in Political Misinformation." *British Journal of Political Science* 47, no. 2 (2017): 241–62.

Bhaskar, Roy. *A Realist Theory of Science.* 2nd ed. Atlantic Highlands, New Jersey: Humanities Press, 1978.

Bishop, Bill, with Robert G. Cushing. *The Big Sort: Why the Clustering of Like-Minded America Is Tearing Us Apart.* Boston: Houghton Mifflin, 2008.

Block, Fred, and Frances Fox Piven. "Déjà Vu, All Over Again: A Comment on Jacob Hacker and Paul Pierson, 'Winner-Take-All Politics.'" *Politics & Society* 38, no. 2 (2010): 205–11.

Bohman, James. "Emancipation and Rhetoric: The Perlocutions and Illocutions of the Social Critic." *Philosophy and Rhetoric* 21, no. 3 (1988): 185–204.

Bohman, James. *Public Deliberation: Pluralism, Complexity, and Democracy*. Cambridge, MA: MIT Press, 1996.

Braeckman, Antoon. "Neoliberalism and the Symbolic Institution of Society: Pitting Foucault against Lefort on the State and the 'Political.'" *Philosophy and Social Criticism* 41, no. 9 (2015): 945–62.

Brandwein, Pamela. "The 'Labor Vision' of the Thirteenth Amendment, Revisited." *Georgetown Journal of Law and Public Policy* 15 (2017): 13–57.

Breckman, Warren. *Adventures of the Symbolic: Postmarxism and Radical Democracy*. New York: Columbia University Press, 2013.

Brennan, Jason. *Against Democracy*. Princeton, NJ: Princeton University Press, 2016.

Brooks, David. "One Nation, Slightly Divisible." *Atlantic Monthly*, December 2001: 53–65. https://www.theatlantic.com/magazine/archive/2001/12/one-nation-slightly-divisible/376441/.

Brownstein, Richard. "Federal Anti-poverty Programs Primarily Help the GOP's Base." *Atlantic Monthly*, February 16, 2017. https://www.theatlantic.com/politics/archive/2017/02/gop-base-poverty-snap-social-security/516861/.

Brubaker, Rogers. *Ethnicity without Groups*. Cambridge, MA: Harvard University Press, 2004.

Burke, Edmund. *Reflections on the Revolution in France*. Edited by Frank M. Turner. New Haven, CT: Yale University Press, 2003 (1790).

Butler, Judith. "For a Careful Reading." In *Feminist Contentions: A Philosophical Exchange*, by Seyla Benhabib, Judith Butler, Drucilla Cornell, and Nancy Fraser, with an introduction by Linda Nicholson, 127–44. New York: Routledge, 1995.

Cameron, David R. "Toward a Theory of Political Mobilization." *Journal of Politics* 36, no. 1 (February 1974): 138–71.

Campbell, Andrea. *How Policies Make Citizens: Senior Political Activism and the American Welfare State*. Princeton, NJ: Princeton University Press, 2003.

Campbell, Andrea. "Policy Makes Mass Politics." *Annual Review of Political Science* 15 (2012): 333–51.

Campbell, Andrea. "The Public's Role in Winner-Take-All Politics." *Politics and Society* 38, no. 2 (2010): 227–32.

Canaday, Margot. *The Straight State: Sexuality and Citizenship in Twentieth-Century America*. Princeton, NJ: Princeton University Press, 2009.

Carmines, Edward G., and James H. Kuklinski. "Incentives, Opportunities, and the Logic of Public Opinion in American Political Representation." In *Information and Democratic Processes*, edited by John A. Ferejohn and James H. Kuklinski, 240–68. Urbana: University of Illinois Press, 1990.

Carpini, Michael X. Delli, and Scott Keeter. *What Americans Know about Politics and Why It Matters*. New Haven, CT: Yale University Press, 1996.

Celis, Karen, Sarah Childs, and Johanna Kantola. "Constituting Women's Interests through Representative Claims." *Politics & Gender* 10, no. 2 (2014): 149–74.

Chabal, Emile. *A Divided Republic: Nation, State and Citizenship in Contemporary France*. Cambridge, UK: Cambridge University Press, 2015.

Chambers, Samuel A. "Giving Up (on) Rights? The Future of Rights and the Project of Radical Democracy." *American Journal of Political Science* 48, no. 2 (2004): 185–200.

Chambers, Samuel A. *The Lessons of Rancière*. Oxford: Oxford University Press, 2012.

Chambers, Samuel. "Walter White Is a Bad Teacher: Pedagogy, Partage, and Politics in Season 4 of *Breaking Bad*." *Theory & Event* 17, no. 1 (2014).

Chambers, Simone. "Human Life Is Group Life: Deliberative Democracy for Realists." *Critical Review* 30, no. 1–2 (2018): 36–48.

Chambers, Simone. "Deliberation and Mass Democracy." In *Deliberative Systems*, edited by Jane Mansbridge and John Parkinson, 52–71. Cambridge, UK: Cambridge University Press, 2012.

Chen, Keith M., and Ryne Rohla. "The Effect of Partisanship and Political Advertising on Close Family Ties." *Science* 360, no. 6392 (June 2018): 1020–4.

Chong, Dennis. "Creating Common Frames of Reference on Political Issues." In *Political Persuasion and Attitude Change*, edited by Diana C. Mutz, Richard A. Brody, and Paul M. Sniderman, 195–224. Ann Arbor: University of Michigan Press, 1996.

Chong, Dennis. *Rational Lives: Norms and Values in Politics and Society*. Chicago: University of Chicago Press, 2000.

Chong, Dennis, and James N. Druckman "Counterframing Effects." *Journal of Politics* 75, no. 1 (2013): 1–16.

Chong, Dennis, and James N. Druckman. "Framing Public Opinion in Competitive Democracies." *American Political Science Review* 101, no. 4 (November 2007): 637–55.

Chong, Dennis, and James N. Druckman. "Public-Elite Interactions: Puzzles in Search of Researchers." In *The Oxford Handbook of the American Public Opinion and the Media*, edited by Robert Y. Shapiro, Lawrence R. Jacobs, and George C. Edwards III, 170–88. Oxford: Oxford University Press, 2011.

Christofferson, Michael Scott. "An Antitotalitarian History of the French Revolution: François Furet's 'Penser la Révolution française' in the Intellectual Politics of the Late 1970s." *French Historical Studies* 22, no. 4 (Autumn 1999): 557–611.

Christofferson, Michael Scott. *French Intellectuals against the Left: The Antitotalitarian Moment of the 1970s*. New York: Berghahn Books, 2004.

Clark, Anna. *Struggle for the Breeches: Gender and the Making of the British Working Class*. Berkeley: University of California Press, 1997.

Coles, Romand. "Liberty, Equality, Receptive Generosity: Neo-Nietzschean Reflections on the Ethics and Politics of Coalition." *American Political Science Review* 90, no. 2 (1996), 375–88.

Connolly, William E., ed. *The Bias of Pluralism*. New York: Atherton Press, 1969.

Connolly, William E. *Identity/Difference: Democratic Negotiations of Political Paradox*. Expanded ed. Minneapolis: University of Minnesota Press, 2002.

Conti, Gregory, and William Selinger. "The Other Side of Representation: The History and Theory of Representative Government in Pierre Rosanvallon." *Constellations* 23, no. 4, (2016): 548–62.

Converse, Philip E. "The Nature of Belief Systems in Mass Publics," *Critical Review* 18, no. 1–3 (2006 [1964]): 1–74.

Cramer, Katherine J. *The Politics of Resentment: Rural Consciousness in Wisconsin and the Rise of Scott Walker*. Chicago: University of Chicago Press, 2016.

Critchley, Simon. "Is There a Normative Deficit in the Theory of Hegemony?" In *Laclau: A Critical Reader*, edited by Simon Critchley and Oliver Marchart, 113–22. New York: Routledge, 2004.

Dahl, Robert. "Further Reflections on 'The Elitist Theory of Democracy.'" *American Political Science Review* 60, no. 2 (1966): 296–305.

Dahl, Robert A. *A Preface to Democratic Theory*. Chicago: University of Chicago Press, 1956.

Danner, Mark. "The Secret Way to War." *New York Review of Books*, June 9, 2005. https://www.nybooks.com/articles/2005/06/09/the-secret-way-to-war/.

Delmont, Matthew F. *Why Busing Failed: Race, Media, and the National Resistance to School Desegregation*. Oakland: University of California Press, 2016.

Delphy, Christine. "Introduction to the Collection." In *Close to Home*, translated by Diana Leonard, 15–27. Amherst: University of Massachusetts Press, 1984.

Delphy, Christine. "The Main Enemy." In *Close to Home*, translated by Diana Leonard, 55–77. Amherst: University of Massachusetts Press, 1984.

Delphy, Christine. "Patriarchy, Feminism and Their Intellectuals." In *Close to Home*, translated by Diana Leonard, 138–53. Amherst: University of Massachusetts Press, 1984.

Derrida, Jacques. "Speech and Phenomena: Introduction to the Problem of Signs in Husserl's Phenomenology." In *Speech and Phenomena*, translated by David B. Allison, 17–104. Evanston: Northwestern University Press, 1973 (1967).

Dewey, John. *The Public and Its Problems*. Denver: Swallow, 1927.

de Wilde, Pieter. "Representative Claims Analysis: Theory Meets Method." *Journal of European Public Policy* 20, no. 2 (2013): 278–94.

Disch, Lisa. "Christine Delphy's Constructivist Materialism." *South Atlantic Quarterly* 114, no. 4 (2015): 827–49.

Disch, Lisa. "The 'Constructivist Turn' in Democratic Representation: A Normative Dead-End?" *Constellations* 22, no. 4 (2015): 487–99.

Disch, Lisa. "Publicity-Stunt Participation and Sound Bite Polemics: The Health
Care Debate 1993–94." *Journal of Health Politics, Policy and Law* 21, no. 1
(Spring 1996): 3–33.

Disch, Lisa. "The Tea Party: A 'White Citizenship' Movement?" In *Steep: The
Precipitous Rise of the Tea Party*, edited by Lawrence Rosenthal and Christine
Trost, 133–51. Berkeley: University of California Press, 2012.

Disch, Lisa. "Toward a Mobilization Conception of Democratic Representation."
American Political Science Review 105, no. 1 (2011): 100–114.

Disch, Lisa. *The Tyranny of the Two-Party System*. New York: Columbia University Press, 2002.

Druckman, James N. "The Implications of Framing Effects for Citizen Competence." *Political Behavior* 23, no. 3 (September 2001): 225–56.

Druckman, James N. "Pathologies of Studying Public Opinion, Political Communication, and Democratic Responsiveness." *Political Communication* 31, no. 3
(2014): 467–92.

Druckman, James N. "Political Preference Formation: Competition, Deliberation,
and the (Ir)relevance of Framing Effects." *American Political Science Review*
98, no. 4 (November 2004): 671–86.

Druckman, James N. "What's It All About? Framing in Political Science." In *Perspectives on Framing*, edited by Gideon Keren, 279–301. New York: Psychology
Press/Taylor and Francis, 2010.

Druckman, James N., Cari Lynn Hennessy, Kristi St. Charles, and Jonathan Webber. "Competing Rhetoric over Time: Frames versus Cues." *Journal of Politics*
72, no. 1 (2010): 136–48.

Druckman, James N., and Lawrence R. Jacobs. *Who Governs? Presidents, Public
Opinion, and Manipulation*. Chicago: University of Chicago Press, 2015.

Druckman, James N., Samara Klar, Yanna Krupnikov, Matthew Levendusky, and
John Barry Ryan. "(Mis)estimating Affective Polarization." Unpublished working paper, Northwestern University, Institute for Policy Research, last modified
November 16, 2020. https://www.ipr.northwestern.edu/documents/working-pa
pers/2019/wp-19-25rev.pdf.

Duong, Kevin. "'Does Democracy End in Terror?' Transformations of Antitotalitarianism in Postwar France." *Modern Intellectual History* 14, no. 2 (2017): 537–63.

Easton, David. *The Political System: An Inquiry into the State of Political Science*.
New York: Knopf, 1953.

Edsall, Mary D., and Thomas B. Edsall. *Chain Reaction: The Impact of Race, Rights,
and Taxes on American Politics*. New York: W. W. Norton & Company, 1992.

Egan, Patrick J. "Group Cohesion without Group Mobilization: The Case of Lesbians, Gays and Bisexuals." *British Journal of Political Science* 42, no. 3 (2012):
597–616.

Eliot, George. *Felix Holt: The Radical.* Edited by Lynda Mugglestone. New York: Penguin Classics, 1995 (1866).

Euben, Peter. "Political Science and Political Silence." In *Power and Community: Dissenting Essays in Political Science,* edited by Philip Green and Sanford Levinson, 3–58. New York: Random House, 1970.

Eulau, Heinz and Paul D. Karps. "The Puzzle of Representation: Specifying Components of Responsiveness." *Legislative Studies Quarterly* 2, no. 3 (1977): 233–54.

Fiorina, Morris P., with Samuel J. Abrams and Jeremy C. Pope. *Culture War? The Myth of a Polarized America.* New York: Longman, 2005.

Fiorina, Morris P. "Identities for Realists." *Critical Review* 30, no. 1–2 (2018): 49–56.

Fiorina, Morris P. *Retrospective Voting in American National Elections.* New Haven, CT: Yale University Press, 1981.

Fishkin, James. "Manipulation and Democratic Theory." In *Manipulating Democracy: Democratic Theory, Political Psychology, and Mass Media,* edited by Wayne Le Cheminant and John M. Parrish, 31–40. New York: Routledge, 2011.

Florida, Richard. *The Rise of the Creative Class: And How It's Transforming Work, Leisure, Community, and Everyday Life.* New York: Basic Books, 2002.

Fowler, Anthony, and Andrew B. Hall. "Do Shark Attacks Influence Presidential Elections? Reassessing a Prominent Finding on Voter Competence." *Journal of Politics* 80, no. 4 (2018): 1423–37.

Fox, James Alan. "The Facts on Furloughs." *Christian Science Monitor,* September 28, 1988. https://www.csmonitor.com/1988/0928/efur.html.

Frank, Jason. "Populism and Praxis." In *The Oxford Handbook of Populism,* edited by Cristobal Rovira Kaltwasser, Paul Taggart, Paulina Ochoa Espejo, and Pierre Ostiguy, 629–43. New York: Oxford University Press, 2017.

Frank, Thomas. *What's the Matter with Kansas? How the Conservatives Won the Heart of America.* New York: Metropolitan Books, 2004.

Friedman, Jeff, ed. "Democratic Competence," special issue. *Critical Review* 18, no. 1–3 (2006): 1–360.

Furet, François. *Interpreting the French Revolution.* Translated by Elborg Forster. Cambridge, UK: Cambridge University Press, 1977.

Furet, François. *Marx and the French Revolution.* Translated by Deborah Furet; edited by Lucien Calvié. Chicago: University of Chicago Press, 1988.

Gabbat, Adam. "Thousands of Americans Backed by Rightwing Donors Gear Up for Protests." *Guardian.* https://www.theguardian.com/us-news/2020/apr/18/coronavirus-americans-protest-stay-at-home.

Galston, William A. "Realism in Political Theory." *European Journal of Political Theory* 9, no. 4 (2010): 385–411.

Gamson, William A., and Andre Modigliani. "Media Discourse and Public Opinion on Nuclear Power: A Constructionist Approach." *American Journal of Sociology* 95, no. 1 (July 1989): 1–37.

Garsten, Bryan. "Representative Government and Popular Sovereignty." In *Political Representation*, edited by Ian Shapiro, Susan C. Stokes, Elisabeth Jean Wood, and Alexander S. Kirshner, 90–110. Cambridge, UK: Cambridge University Press, 2009.

Gary, Brett. *The Nervous Liberals: Propaganda Anxieties from World War I to the Cold War*. New York: Colombia University Press, 1999.

Geenens, Raf. "Democracy, Human Rights and History: Reading Lefort." *European Journal of Political Theory* 7, no. 1 (2008): 269–86.

Geras, Norman. "Post-Marxism?" *New Left Review* 163, no. 1 (May/June 1987): 40–82.

Gerber, Elisabeth R., and John E. Jackson. "Endogenous Preferences and the Study of Institutions." *American Political Science Review* 87, no. 3 (September 1993): 639–56.

Geuss, Raymond. *Philosophy and Real Politics*. Princeton, NJ: Princeton University Press, 2008.

Gilens, Martin. *Affluence and Influence: Economic Inequality and Political Power in America*. Princeton, NJ: Princeton University Press, 2012.

Goodin, Robert E. *Manipulatory Politics*. New Haven, CT: Yale University Press, 1980.

Gore, Al. *An Inconvenient Truth: The Planetary Emergency of Global Warming and What We Can Do About It*. New York: Rodale, 2006.

Grant, Judith. *Fundamental Feminism: Contesting the Core Concepts of Feminist Theory*. New York: Routledge, 1993.

Habermas, Jürgen. *The Inclusion of the Other: Studies in Political Theory*, edited by Ciaran Cronin and Pablo De Greiff. Boston: MIT Press, 1998.

Habermas, Jürgen. *Between Facts and Norms*. Translated by William Rehg. Cambridge, MA: MIT Press, 1996.

Hacker, Jacob S. *The Divided Welfare State: The Battle over Public and Private Social Benefits in the United States*. Cambridge, UK: Cambridge University Press, 2002.

Hacker, Jacob, and Paul Pierson. *Let Them Eat Tweets: How the Right Rules in an Age of Extreme Inequality*. New York: Liveright, 2020.

Hacker, Jacob S., and Paul Pierson. *Winner-Take-All Politics: How Washington Made the Rich Richer—and Turned Its Back on the Middle Class*. London: Simon & Schuster, 2010.

Han, Hahrie. *How Organizations Develop Activists: Civic Associations and Leadership in the 21st Century*. New York: Oxford University Press, 2014.

Hancock, Ange-Marie. *The Politics of Disgust: The Public Identity of the Welfare Queen*. New York: New York University Press, 2004.

Hannah-Jones, Nikole. *Living Apart: How the Government Betrayed a Landmark Civil Rights Law*. New York: ProPublica, 2012.

Harcourt, Bernard E. *Exposed: Desire and Disobedience in the Digital Age*. Cambridge, MA: Harvard University Press, 2015.

Harris, Cheryl. "Whiteness as Property." *Harvard Law Review* 106, no. 8 (1993), 1707–1791.

Hayat, Samuel. *Quand la République était révolutionnaire: citoyenneté et représentation*. Paris: Seuil, 2014.

Hern, Alex. "Cambridge Analytica: How Did It Turn Clicks into Votes?" *Guardian*, May 6, 2018. https://www.theguardian.com/news/2018/may/06/cambridge-analytica-how-turn-clicks-into-votes-christopher-wylie.

Hobsbawm, Eric. *Primitive Rebels: Studies in Archaic Forms of Social Movement in the 19th and 20th Centuries*. Manchester: Manchester University Press, 1959.

Hochschild, Arlie Russell. *Strangers in Their Own Land: Anger and Mourning on the American Right*. New York: The New Press, 2016.

Honig, Bonnie. *Political Theory and the Displacement of Politics*. Ithaca, NY: Cornell University Press, 1993.

Howarth, David. "Hegemony, Political Subjectivity, and Radical Democracy." In *Laclau: A Critical Reader*, edited by Simon Critchley and Oliver Marchart, 256–76. New York: Routledge, 2004.

Huber, Gregory A., and Neil Malhotra. "Political Homophily in Social Relationships: Evidence from Online Dating Behavior." *Journal of Politics* 79, no. 1 (January 2017): 269–83.

Huddy, Leonie. "The Group Foundations of Democratic Political Behavior." *Critical Review* 30, no. 1–2 (2018): 71–86.

Hunt, Lynn. *Politics, Culture, and Class in the French Revolution*. Berkeley: University of California Press, 1984.

Ingram, James D. "The Politics of Claude Lefort's Political: Between Liberalism and Radical Democracy." *Thesis Eleven* 87 (November 2006): 33–50.

Isaac, Jeffrey C. "Beyond the Three Faces of Power: A Realist Critique." *Polity* 20, no. 1 (1987): 4–31.

Isaac, Jeffrey C. *Democracy in Dark Times*. Ithaca, NY: Cornell University Press, 1998.

Isaac, Jeffrey C. *Power and Marxist Theory: A Realist View*. Ithaca, NY: Cornell University Press, 1987.

Iyengar, Shanto, Yphtach Lelkes, Matthew Levendusky, Neil Mahotra, and Sean Westwood. "The Origins and Consequences of Affective Polarization in the United States." *Annual Review of Political Science* 22 (2019): 129–46.

Iyengar, Shanto, Gaurav Sood, and Yphtach Lelkes. "Affect, Not Ideology: A Social Identity Perspective on Polarization." *Public Opinion Quarterly* 76, no. 3 (Fall 2012): 405–31.

Jackson, John. "Issues, Party Choices, and Presidential Votes." *American Journal of Political Science* 19, no. 2 (May 1975): 161–85.

Jacobs, Lawrence R., and Benjamin I. Page. "Who Influences US Foreign Policy?" *American Political Science Review* 99, no. 1 (February 2005): 107–23.

Jainchill, Andrew, and Samuel Moyn. "French Democracy between Totalitarianism and Solidarity: Pierre Rosanvallon and Revisionist Historiography." *Journal of Modern History* 76, no. 1 (2004): 107–54.

Jensen, Laura S. "Constructing and Entitling America's Original Veterans." In *De-
serving and Entitled: Social Constructions and Public Policy*, edited by Anne L.
Schneider and Helen M. Ingram, 35–62. Albany: State University of New York
Press, 2005.

Karpf, David. *Analytic Activism: Digital Listening and the New Political Strategy.*
New York: Oxford University Press, 2016.

Katznelson, Ira and Suzanne Mettler. "On Race and Policy History: A Dialogue
about the GI Bill." *Perspectives on Politics* 6, no. 3 (September 2008): 519–37.

Keating, Dan, Kevin Schaul, and Leslie Shapiro. "The Facebook Ads Russians Targeted at Different Groups." *Washington Post*, November 1, 2017. https://www
.washingtonpost.com/graphics/2017/business/russian-ads-facebook-targeting
/?itid=lk_interstitial_manual_9.

Kinder, Donald R., and Thomas E. Nelson. "Democratic Debate and Real Opinions." In *Framing American Politics*, edited by Karen Callaghan and Frauke
Schnell, 103–22. Pittsburgh: University of Pittsburgh Press, 2005.

Klandermans, Bert. "Mobilization and Participation: Social-Psychological Expansions of Resource Mobilization Theory." *American Sociological Review* 49,
no. 5 (October 1984): 583–600.

Klar, Samara, Yanna Krupnikov, and John Barry Ryan. "Affective Polarization or
Partisan Disdain: Untangling a Dislike for the Opposing Party from a Dislike
of Partisanship." *Public Opinion Quarterly* 82, no. 2 (2018): 379–90.

Kröger, Sandra and Dawid Friedrich. "The Representative Turn in European
Union Studies." *Journal of European Public Policy* 20, no. 2 (2013): 171–89.

Krouse, Richard, and George Marcus. "Electoral Studies and Democratic Theory
Reconsidered." *Political Behavior* 6, no. 1 (1984): 23–39.

Kuklinski, James H., and Gary M. Segura. "Endogeneity, Exogeneity, Time, and
Space in Political Representation." *Legislative Studies Quarterly* 20, no. 1
(1995): 3–21.

Kuklinski, James H., and John E. Stanga. "Political Participation and Government
Responsiveness: The Behavior of California Superior Courts." *American Political Science Review* 73, no. 4 (1979): 1090–99.

Laclau, Ernesto. *Emancipations*. New York: Verso, 1996.

Laclau, Ernesto. "Glimpsing the Future." In *Laclau: A Critical Reader*, edited by
Simon Critchley and Oliver Marchart, 279–328. New York: Routledge, 2004.

Laclau, Ernesto. *New Reflections on the Revolution of Our Time*. New York: Verso,
1990.

Laclau, Ernesto. *On Populist Reason*. New York: Verso, 2005.

Laclau, Ernesto. *Politics and Ideology in Marxist Theory: Capitalism, Fascism, Populism*. New York: New Left Books, 1977.

Laclau, Ernesto and Chantal Mouffe. *Hegemony and Socialist Strategy: Towards a Radical Democratic Politics*. New York: Verso Books, 1985.

Laclau, Ernesto and Chantal Mouffe. "Post-Marxism without Apologies." *New Left Review* 166, no. 1 (November/December 1987): 79–106.

Lasswell, Harold. *Propaganda Technique in the World War*. New York: Peter Smith, 1927.

LaVaque-Manty, Mika. "Bentley, Truman, and the Study of Groups." *Annual Review of Political Science* 9 (2006), 1–18.

LaVaque-Manty, Mika. "Finding Theoretical Concepts in the Real World: The Case of the Precariat." In *New Waves in Political Philosophy*, edited by Boudewijn de Bruin and Christopher F. Zurn, 105–24. Basingstoke: Palgrave Macmillan, 2009.

LaVaque-Manty, Mika. *The Playing Fields of Eton: Equality and Excellence in Modern Meritocracy*. Ann Arbor: University of Michigan Press, 2009.

Le Cheminant, Wayne, and John M. Parrish. Introduction to *Manipulating Democracy: Democratic Theory, Political Psychology, and Mass Media*, edited by Wayne Le Cheminant and John M. Parrish, 1–24. New York: Routledge, 2011.

Lefort, Claude. *Democracy and Political Theory*. Translated by David Macey. Minneapolis: University of Minnesota Press, 1988.

Lefort, Claude. "Democracy and Representation." Translated by Greg Conti. In *The Constructivist Turn in Political Representation*, edited by Lisa Disch, Mathijs van de Sande, and Nadia Urbinati, 104–17. Edinburgh: Edinburgh University Press, 2019 (1989).

Lefort, Claude. *Invention démocratique*. 2nd ed. Paris: Fayard, 1994 (1981).

Lefort, Claude. *The Political Forms of Modern Society*. Edited by John B. Thompson. Cambridge, MA: MIT Press, 1986.

Levy, Jacob, ed. *The Oxford Handbook of Classics in Contemporary Political Theory*. Oxford: Oxford University Press, 2015.

Levendusky, Matthew. *The Partisan Sort: How Liberals Became Democrats and Conservatives Became Republicans*. Chicago: University of Chicago Press, 2009.

Levendusky, Matthew, and Dominik Stecula. "Can We Talk: Does Cross-Party Dialogue Reduce Affective Polarization?" Unpublished manuscript, last modified September 2019.

Levitin, Michael. "The Triumph of Occupy Wall Street." *Atlantic Monthly*, June 10, 2015. https://www.theatlantic.com/politics/archive/2015/06/the-triumph-of-occupy-wall-street/395408/.

Lindahl, Hans. "Acquiring a Community: The Acquis and the Institution of European Legal Order." *European Law Journal* 9, no. 4 (2003): 433–50.

Lippmann, Walter. *The Phantom Public*. New York: The Free Press, 1997. First published by Macmillan, 1922.

Lipset, Seymour Martin. Introduction to Robert Michels, *Political Parties: A Sociological Study of Oligarchical Tendencies of Modern Democracies*, translated by Eden and Cedar Paul. New York: The Free Press, 1962.

Lipset, Seymour Martin. *Political Man: The Social Bases of Politics*. Baltimore: Johns Hopkins University Press, 1981.

Liucci-Goutnikov, Nicolas, Galeries Nationales du Grand Palais (Paris), Établissement Public de la Réunion des Musées Nationaux et du Grand Palais des Champs-Élysées (France), and Centre National d'Art et de Culture Georges Pompidou (Paris). *Rouge: art et utopie au pays des Soviets*. Paris: Galeries Nationales du Grand Palais, 2019. Published in conjunction with an exhibition of the same title, organized by and presented at the Galeries Nationales du Grand Palais, March 20–July 1, 2019.

Lloyd, Moya. "Performativity and Performance." In *The Oxford Handbook of Feminist Theory*, edited by Lisa Disch and Mary Hawkesworth, 572–92. Oxford: Oxford University Press, 2014.

Lord, Christopher, and Johannes Pollack. "The Pitfalls of Representation as Claims-Making in the European Union." *Journal of European Integration* 35, no. 5 (2013): 517–30.

Lukes, Steven. *Power: A Radical View*. London: Macmillan, 1974.

Lupia, Arthur. "Busy Voters, Agenda Control, and the Power of Information." *American Political Science Review* 86, no. 2 (June 1992): 390–403.

Lupia, Arthur. "Shortcuts versus Encyclopedias: Information and Voting Behavior in California Insurance Reform Elections." *American Political Science Review* 88, no. 1 (1994): 63–76.

Lupia, Arthur, and Mathew D. McCubbins. *The Democratic Dilemma: Can Citizens Learn What They Need to Know?* Cambridge, UK: Cambridge University Press, 1998.

MacFarquhar, Larissa. "Chimamanda Ngozi Adichie Comes to Terms with Global Fame." *New Yorker*, May 28, 2018. https://www.newyorker.com/magazine/2018/06/04/chimamanda-ngozi-adichie-comes-to-terms-with-global-fame.

MacGillis, Alex. "Who Turned My Blue State Red?" *New York Times*, November 20, 2015. https://www.nytimes.com/2015/11/22/opinion/sunday/who-turned-my-blue-state-red.html.

Mair, Peter. "E. E. Schattschneider's *The Semisovereign People*." *Political Studies* 45, no. 5 (December 1997): 947–54.

Manin, Bernard. *The Principles of Representative Government*. Cambridge, UK: Cambridge University Press, 1997.

Mansbridge, Jane J. "Rethinking Representation." *American Political Science Review* 97, no. 4 (2003): 515–28.

Mansbridge, Jane J., James Bohman, Simone Chambers, Thomas Christiano, Archon Fung, John Parkinson, Dennis F. Thompson, and Mark E. Warren. "A Systemic Approach to Deliberative Democracy." In *Deliberative Systems: Deliberative Democracy at the Large Scale*, edited by John Parkinson and Jane J. Mansbridge, 1–26. New York: Cambridge University Press, 2012.

Mantena, Karuna. "Another Realism." *American Political Science Review* 106, no. 2 (2012): 455–70.

Manza, Jeff, and Fay Lomax Cook. "A Democratic Polity? Three Views of Policy Responsiveness to Public Opinion in the United States." *American Politics Research* 30, no. 6 (2002): 630–67.

Marchart, Oliver. "Institution and Dislocation: Philosophical Roots of Laclau's Discourse Theory of Space and Antagonism." *Distinktion: Journal of Social Theory* 15, no. 3 (2014): 271–82.

Marchart, Oliver. *Post-Foundational Political Thought: Political Difference in Nancy, Lefort, Badiou and Laclau.* Edinburgh: Edinburgh University Press, 2007.

Marcus, George. "Democratic Theories and the Study of Public Opinion." *Polity* 21, no. 1: (September 1988): 25–44.

Marin, Louis. *On Representation.* Translated by Catherine Porter. Stanford, CA: Stanford University Press, 2001.

Markell, Patchen. Review of *Philosophy and Real Politics*, by Raymond Geuss. In *Political Theory* 38, no. 1 (February 2010): 172–77.

Mason, Lilliana. *Uncivil Agreement: How Politics Became Our Identity.* Chicago: University of Chicago Press, 2018.

McAlevey, Jane. *No Shortcuts: Organizing for Power in the New Gilded Age.* New York: Oxford University Press, 2016.

McCloskey, Herbert, and John Zaller. *The American Ethos: Public Attitudes Toward Capitalism and Democracy.* Cambridge, MA: Harvard University Press, 1984.

McConnell, Christopher, Yotam Margalit, Neil Malhotra, and Matthew Levendusky. "The Economic Consequences of Partisanship in a Polarized Era." *American Journal of Political Science* 62, no. 1 (2018): 5–18.

McConnell, Elizabeth A., Patrick Janulis, Gregory Phillips 2nd, Roky Truong, and Michelle Burkett. "Multiple Minority Stress and LGBT Community Resilience Among Sexual Minority Men." *Psychology of Sexual Orientation and Gender Diversity* 5, no. 1 (2018):1–12.

McKean, Benjamin. "What Makes a Utopia Inconvenient? On the Advantages and Disadvantages of a Realist Orientation to Politics." *American Political Science Review* 110, no. 4 (November 2016): 876–88.

McKean, Benjamin. "Who Needs Rights? Justice and the Precariousness of Social Order in the Political Realism of Raymond Geuss and Bernard Williams." Paper presented at the Annual Meeting of the American Political Science Association, Seattle, WA, September 2011. Available at https://ssrn.com/abstract=1901266.

McQueen, Alison. "The Case for Kinship: Classical Realism and Political Realism." In *Politics Recovered: Realist Thought in Theory and Practice*, edited by Matt Sleat, 243–69. New York: Columbia University Press, 2018.

Mead, Lawrence M. *Beyond Entitlement: The Social Obligations of Citizenship.* New York: Free Press 1986.

Medearis, John. "Disenchantment versus Reconstruction: Lippmann, John Dewey, and Varieties of Democratic Realism." In *Politics Recovered*, edited by Matt Sleat, 140–65. New York: Colombia University Press, 2018.

Mendelberg, Tali. "From the Folk Theory to Symbolic Politics: Toward a More Realistic Understanding of Voter Behavior." *Critical Review* 30, no. 1 (2018): 107–18.

Mettler, Suzanne. *Soldiers to Citizens: The GI Bill and the Making of the Greatest Generation*. Oxford: Oxford University Press, 2005.

Mettler, Suzanne. *The Submerged State: How Invisible Government Policies Undermine American Democracy*. Chicago: University of Chicago Press, 2011.

Mettler, Suzanne, and Joe Soss. "The Consequences of Public Policy for Democratic Citizenship: Bridging Policy Studies and Mass Politics." *Perspectives on Politics* 2, no. 1 (March 2004): 55–73.

Metzl, Jonathan M., and Anna Kirkland. *Against Health: How Health Became the New Morality*. New York: New York University Press, 2010.

Michels, Robert. *Political Parties: A Sociological Study of Oligarchical Tendencies of Modern Democracies*. Translated by Eden and Cedar Paul. New York: The Free Press, 1962.

Miller, W. E., and D. E. Stokes. "Constituency Influence in Congress." *American Political Science Review* 57, no. 1 (March 1963): 45–56.

Monaghan, Elizabeth. "Making the Environment Present: Political Representation, Democracy and Civil Society Organisations in EU Climate Change Politics." *Journal of European Integration* 35, no. 5 (2013): 601–18.

Montanaro, Laura. "The Democratic Legitimacy of Self-Appointed Representatives." *Journal of Politics* 74, no. 4 (October 2012): 1094–1107.

Montanaro, Laura. *Who Elected Oxfam?* Cambridge, UK: Cambridge University Press, 2017.

More in Common. "Our Publications." Accessed February 18, 2020. https://www.moreincommon.com/our-work/publications/.

Moses, Robert, Mieko Kamii, Susan McAllister Swap, and Jeffrey Howard. "The Algebra Project: Organizing in the Spirit of Ella." *Harvard Educational Review* 59, no. 4 (1989): 423–44.

Mouffe, Chantal. *Agonistics: Thinking the World Politically*. New York: Verso, 2013.

Moyn, Samuel. "Antitotalitarianism and After." Introduction to Pierre Rosanvallon, *Democracy Past and Future*, edited by Samuel Moyn, 1–30. New York: Columbia University Press, 2006.

Moyn, Samuel. "Claude Lefort, Political Anthropology, and Symbolic Division." In *Claude Lefort: Thinker of the Political*, edited by Martín Plot, 51–70. Basingstoke: Palgrave Macmillan, 2003.

Moyn, Samuel. "On the Intellectual Origins of François Furet's Masterpiece." *Tocqueville Review* 29, no. 2 (2008): 59–78.

Moyn, Samuel. "The Politics of Individual Rights: Marcel Gauchet and Claude Lefort." In *French Liberalism from Montesquieu to the Present Day*, edited by Raf Geenens and Helena Rosenblatt, 291–310. Cambridge, UK: Cambridge University Press, 2012.

Mulieri, Alessandro. "Exploring the Semantics of Constructivist Representation." In *The Constructivist Turn in Political Representation*, edited by Lisa Disch, Mathijs van de Sande and Nadia Urbinati, 205–23. Edinburgh University Press, 2019.

Muller, Edward N. "The Representation of Citizens by Political Authorities." *American Political Science Review* 64, no. 4 (1970): 1149–66.

Mulvey, Laura. "Visual Pleasure and Narrative Cinema." *Screen* 16, no. 3 (1975): 6–18.

Mutz, Diana C. "Status Threat Explains Trump." *Proceedings of the National Academy of Sciences* 115, no. 19 (May 2018): E4330–E4339.

Näsström, Sofia. "Democratic Representation Beyond Election." *Constellations* 22, no. 1 (March 2015): 1–12.

Näsström, Sofia. "Representative Democracy as Tautology." *European Journal of Political Theory* 5, no. 3 (July 2006): 321–42.

Neblo, Michael A. *Deliberative Democracy between Theory and Practice*. Cambridge, UK: Cambridge University Press, 2015.

Nelson, Thomas E., Rosalee A. Clawson, and Zoe M. Oxley. "Media Framing of a Civil Liberties Conflict and Its Effect on Tolerance." *American Political Science Review* 91, no. 3 (1997): 567–83.

Newkirk, Vann R. "How *Shelby County v. Holder* Broke America." *Atlantic Monthly*, July 10, 2018. https://www.theatlantic.com/politics/archive/2018/07/how-shelby -county-broke-america/564707/.

Newport, Frank. "Americans Still Think Iraq Had Weapons of Mass Destruction before War." Gallup, June 16, 2003. https://news.gallup.com/poll/8623/americans -still-think-iraq-had-weapons-mass-destruction-before-war.aspx.

Olson, Mançur. *The Logic of Collective Action: Public Goods and the Theory of Groups*. Cambridge, MA: Harvard University Press, 1965.

Packer, George. "Hillary Clinton and the Populist Revolt." *New Yorker*, October 31, 2016. https://www.newyorker.com/magazine/2016/10/31/hillary-clinton -and-the-populist-revolt.

Page, Benjamin I., and Martin Gilens. *Democracy in America? What Has Gone Wrong and What We Can Do about It*. Chicago: University of Chicago Press, 2018.

Page, Benjamin I., and Robert Y. Shapiro. *The Rational Public: Fifty Years of Trends in Americans' Policy Preferences*. Chicago: University of Chicago Press, 1992.

Pateman, Carole. *Participation and Democratic Theory*. Cambridge, UK: Cambridge University Press, 1970.

Payne, Charles M. *I've Got the Light of Freedom: Organizing Tradition and the Mississippi Freedom Struggle*. Berkeley: University of California Press, 1995.

Peterson, Paul E. "Forms of Representation: Participation of the Poor in the Community Action Program." *American Political Science Review* 64, no. 2 (1970): 491–507.

Phillips, Kevin. *Emerging Republican Majority*. New Rochelle, NY: Arlington House, 1969.

Phulwani, Vijay. "From Order to Organizing: Rethinking Political Realism & Democratic Theory." PhD diss., Cornell University, 2019.

Phulwani, Vijay. "The Poor Man's Machiavelli: Saul Alinsky and the Morality of Power." *American Political Science Review* 110, no. 4 (2016): 863–75.

Pierson, Paul. "When Effect Becomes Cause: Policy Feedback and Political Change." *World Politics* 45, no. 4 (July 1993): 595–628.

Pitkin, Hanna Fenichel. *The Concept of Representation*. Berkeley: University of California Press, 1967.

Pitkin, Hanna Fenichel. "Representation and Democracy: Uneasy Alliance," *Scandinavian Political Studies* 27, no. 3 (2004): 335–42.

Piven, Frances Fox, and Richard A. Cloward. "Collective Protest: A Critique of Resource Mobilization Theory." *International Journal of Politics, Culture and Society* 4, no. 4 (Summer 1991): 435–58.

Plotke, David. "Representation Is Democracy." *Constellations* 4, no. 1 (April 1997): 19–34.

Popkin, Samuel. *The Reasoning Voter*. Chicago: University of Chicago Press, 1991.

Porter, Robert. "Where Government Is a Dirty Word, but Its Checks Pay the Bills." *New York Times*, December 21, 2018. https://www.nytimes.com/2018/12/21/busi ness/economy/harlan-county-republican-welfare.html.

Rancière, Jacques. *The Ignorant Schoolmaster: Five Lessons in Intellectual Emancipation*. Translated, with an introduction by Kristin Ross. Stanford, CA: Stanford University Press, 1991.

Rehfeld, Andrew. "Towards a General Theory of Representation." *Journal of Politics* 68, no. 1 (2006): 1–21.

Roediger, David R. *The Wages of Whiteness: Race and the Making of the American Working Class*. New York: Verso, 1991.

Rosanvallon, Pierre. *Le peuple introuvable*. Paris: Gallimard, 1998.

Rothstein, Richard. *The Color of Law: A Forgotten History of How Our Government Segregated America*. New York: Liveright, 2017.

Rouaud, Christian, dir. *Les Lip: l'imagination au pouvoir*. France: Les Films d'Ici, 2007.

Rubenstein, Jennifer. "Accountability in an Unequal World." *Journal of Politics* 69, no. 3 (2007): 616–32.

Rudé, George. *The Crowd in History: A Study of Popular Disturbances in France and England, 1730–1848*. New York: John Wiley & Sons, 1964.

Runciman, David. "The Paradox of Political Representation." *Journal of Political Philosophy* 15, no. 1 (2007): 93–114.

Saward, Michael. "Making Representations: Modes and Strategies of Political Parties." *European Review* 16, no. 3 (2008): 271–86.

Saward, Michael. "Representation." In *Political Theory and the Ecological Challenge*, edited by Andrew Dobson and Robyn E. Eckersley, 183–99. Cambridge, UK: Cambridge University Press, 2006.

Saward, Michael. "The Representative Claim." *Contemporary Political Theory* 5, no. 3 (2006): 297–318.

Saward, Michael. *The Representative Claim.* Oxford: Oxford University Press, 2010.

Saward, Michael. "Shape-Shifting Representation." *American Political Science Review* 108, no. 4 (2014): 723–36.

Schattschneider, Elmer Eric. *The Semisovereign People.* Reprinted with an introduction by David Adamany. Fort Worth: Harcourt Brace Jovanovich, 1975. First published by Holt, Rinehart and Winston, 1960. Page references are to the 1975 edition.

Schickler, Eric. *Racial Realignment: The Transformation of American Liberalism, 1932–1965.* Princeton, NJ: Princeton University Press, 2016.

Schneider, Anne L., and Helen M. Ingram. "Introduction: Public Policy and the Social Construction of Deservedness." In *Deserving and Entitled: Social Constructions and Public Policy,* edited by Anne L. Schneider and Helen M. Ingram, 1–33. Albany: State University of New York Press, 2005.

Schneider, Anne L., and Helen M. Ingram. 1997. *Policy Design for Democracy.* Lawrence: University of Kansas Press, 1997.

Schumpeter, Joseph A. *Ten Great Economists: From Marx to Keynes.* San Diego, CA: Simon Publications, 2003.

Schwartz, Nancy L. *The Blue Guitar: Political Representation and Community.* Chicago: University of Chicago Press, 1988.

Schweber, Howard. "The Limits of Political Representation." *American Political Science Review* 110, no. 2 (2016): 382–96.

Scott, Mark. "Cambridge Analytica Did Work for Brexit Groups, Says Ex-staffer." *Politico,* July 30, 2019. https://www.politico.eu/article/cambridge-analytica-leave-eu-ukip-brexit-facebook/.

Severs, Eline. "Representation as Claims-Making. Quid Responsiveness?" *Representation* 46, no. 4 (2010): 411–23.

Severs, Eline. "Substantive Representation through a Claims-Making Lens: A Strategy for the Identification and Analysis of Substantive Claims." *Representation* 48, no. 2 (2012): 169–81.

Sewell, William. *A Rhetoric of Bourgeois Revolution: The Abbé Sieyes and "What Is the Third Estate?"* Durham, NC: Duke University Press, 1994.

Shapiro, Isaac, Danilo Trisi, and Raheem Chaudhry. "Poverty Reduction Programs Help Adults Lacking College Degrees the Most." Center on Budget and Policy Priorities, Feb 16, 2017. https://www.cbpp.org/research/poverty-and-inequality/poverty-reduction-programs-help-adults-lacking-college-degrees-the.

Shklar, Judith. *American Citizenship: The Quest for Inclusion.* Reprinted ed. Cambridge, MA: Harvard University Press, 1995.

Sides, John, Tesler, Michael, and Lynn Vavreck. *Identity Crisis: The 2016 Presidential Campaign and the Battle for the Meaning of America.* Princeton, NJ: Princeton University Press, 2018.

Sinclair, Betsy. *The Social Citizen: Peer Networks and Political Behavior*. Chicago: University of Chicago Press, 2012.

Sintomer, Yves. "Les sens de la representation politique: Usages et mésusages d'une notion." *Raisons Politiques* 50, no. 2 (2013): 13–34.

Sieyes, Abbé Emmanuel Joseph. *What Is the Third Estate?* Translated by M. Blondel and edited, with historical notes, by S. E. Finer. New York: Prager, 1964 (1789).

Sleat, Matt. "Introduction: Politics Recovered—On the Revival of Realism in Contemporary Political Theory." In *Politics Recovered: Realist Thought in Theory and Practice*, edited by Matt Sleat, 1–26. New York: Columbia University Press, 2018.

Sniderman, Paul M. "Taking Sides: A Fixed Choice Theory of Political Reasoning." In *Elements of Reason: Cognition, Choice, and the Bounds of Rationality*, edited by Arthur Lupia, Mathew D. McCubbins, and Samuel L. Popkin, 67–84. New York: Cambridge University Press, 2000.

Sniderman, Paul M., Richard A. Brody, and Philip E. Tetlock. *Reasoning and Choice: Explorations in Political Psychology*. Cambridge, UK: Cambridge University Press, 1991.

Sniderman, Paul M., and Sean M. Theriault. "The Structure of Political Argument and the Logic of Issue Framing." In *Studies in Public Opinion: Attitudes, Nonattitudes, Measurement Error, and Change*, edited by Willem E. Saris and Paul M. Sniderman, 133–65. Princeton, NJ: Princeton University Press, 2004.

Soroka, Stuart N., and Christopher Wlezien. *Degrees of Democracy: Politics, Public Opinion, and Policy*. Cambridge, UK: Cambridge University Press, 2010.

Soss, Joe. Panel comments delivered at the Annual Meeting of the Western Political Science Association, Los Angeles, 2012.

Soss, Joe. "Making Clients and Citizens: Welfare Policy as a Source of Status, Belief, and Action." In *Deserving and Entitled: Social Constructions and Public Policy*, edited by Anne L. Schneider and Helen M. Ingram, 291–328. Albany: State University of New York Press, 2005.

Soss, Joe, Richard C. Fording, and Sanford F. Schram. *Disciplining the Poor: Neoliberal Paternalism and the Persistent Power of Race*. Chicago: University of Chicago Press, 2011.

Squires, Judith. "The Constitutive Representation of Gender: Extra-Parliamentary Representations of Gender Relations." *Representation* 44, no. 2 (2008): 187–204.

Stears, Marc. *Demanding Democracy: American Radicals in Search of a New Politics*. Princeton, NJ: Princeton University Press, 2010.

Steffens, Lincoln. *The Shame of the Cities*. New York: McClure, Phillips & Co., 1904.

Stone, Deborah. "Foreword." In *Deserving and Entitled: Social Constructions and Public Policy*, edited by Anne L. Schneider and Helen M. Ingram, ix–xiii. Albany: State University of New York Press, 2005.

Sumner, William Graham. *What Social Classes Owe to Each Other*. Idaho: Caxton Press, 2003. First published by Harper & Brothers, 1883.

Sunstein, Cass R. "Preferences and Politics." *Philosophy and Public Affairs* 20, no. 10 (1991): 3–34.

Tajfel, Henri. "Experiments in Intergroup Discrimination." *Scientific American* 223, no. 5 (November 1970): 96–103.

Thomassen, Lasse. "In/exclusions: Towards a Radical Democratic Approach to Exclusion." In *Radical Democracy: Politics Between Abundance and Lack*, edited by Lars Tønder and Lasse Thomassen, 103–22. Manchester: Manchester University Press, 2005.

Tocqueville, Alexis de. *Democracy in America*. Translated by George Lawrence. New York: Harper Perennial, 1988 (1835).

Truman, David. *The Governmental Process: Political Interests and Public Opinion*. New York: Knopf, 1951.

Trump, Donald. "Inaugural Address: Trump's Full Speech." CNN, Turner Broadcasting System, January 20, 2017. www.cnn.com/2017/01/20/politics/trump-inaugural-address/index.html.

Tucker, Joshua A., Andrew Guess, Pablo Barberá, Christian Vaccari, Alexandra Siegel, Sergey Sanovich, Denis Stukal, and Brendan Nyhan. "Social Media, Political Polarization, and Political Disinformation: A Review of the Scientific Literature." Working paper prepared for the Hewlett Foundation, 2018. https://papers.ssrn.com/sol3/papers.cfm?abstract_id=3144139.

Valentine, Jeremy. "Lefort and the Fate of Radical Democracy." In *Claude Lefort: Thinker of the Political*, edited by Martín Plot, 203–17. Basingstoke: Palgrave Macmillan, 2013.

Urbinati, Nadia. *Democracy Disfigured: Opinion, Truth, and the People*. Cambridge, MA: Harvard University Press, 2014.

Urbinati, Nadia. *Representative Democracy: Principles and Genealogy*. Chicago: University of Chicago Press, 2006.

Urbinati, Nadia, and Mark E. Warren. "The Concept of Representation in Democratic Theory." *Annual Review of Political Science* 11 (2008): 387–412.

VanderVelde, Lea S. "The Labor Vision of the Thirteenth Amendment." *University of Pennsylvania Law Review* 437 (1989): 138–206.

Von Hoffman, Nicholas. *Radical: A Portrait of Saul Alinsky*. New York: Nation Books, 2010.

Waddell, Brian. "Class Politics, American-Style: A Discussion of *Winner-Take-All-Politics: How Washington Made the Rich Richer—and Turned Its Back on the Middle Class*." *Perspectives on Politics* 9, no. 3 (2011): 659–62.

Wahlke, John C. "Policy Demands and System Support: The Role of the Represented." *British Journal of Political Science* 1, no. 3 (1971): 271–90.

Walcott, John, and Mark Danner. "'The Secret Way to War': An Exchange." *New York Review of Books*, July 14, 2005. https://www.nybooks.com/articles/2005/07/14/the-secret-way-to-war-an-exchange/.

Walker, Jack L. "A Critique of the Elitist Theory of Democracy." *American Political Science Review* 60, no. 2 (1966): 285–95.

Walker, Jack L. *Mobilizing Interest Groups in America: Patrons, Professions, and Social Movements*. Ann Arbor: University of Michigan Press, 1991.

Walker, Jack L. "The Origins and Maintenance of Interest Groups in America." *The American Political Science Review* 77, no. 2 (1983): 390–406.

Walker, Jack L. *Sit-Ins in Atlanta*. New York: McGraw-Hill, 1964.

Weissberg, Robert. "Collective vs. Dyadic Representation in Congress." *American Political Science Review* 72, no. 2 (June 1978): 535–47.

Wenman, Mark Anthony. "What Is Politics? The Approach of Radical Pluralism." *Politics* 23, no. 1 (2003): 57–75.

Weymans, Wim. "Freedom through Political Representation? Lefort, Gauchet and Rosanvallon on the Relationship between State and Society." *European Journal of Political Theory* 4, no. 3 (2005): 263–82.

Williams, Bernard. "Realism and Moralism in Political Theory." In *In the Beginning Was the Deed: Realism and Moralism in Political Argument*, edited by Hawthorn Geoffrey, 1–17. Princeton, NJ: Princeton University Press, 2005.

Williams, Melissa. *Voice, Trust, and Memory: Marginalized Groups and the Failings of Liberal Representation*. Princeton, NJ: Princeton University Press, 1990.

Williamson, Vanessa, Theda Skocpol, and John Coggin. "The Tea Party and the Remaking of Republican Conservatism." *Perspectives on Politics* 9, no. 1 (2001): 25–43.

Woodly, Deva. *The Politics of Common Sense: How Social Movements Use Public Discourse to Change Politics and Win Acceptance*. Oxford: Oxford University Press, 2015.

Young, Iris Marion. *Inclusion and Democracy*. New York: Oxford University Press, 2002.

Young, Iris Marion. *Justice and the Politics of Difference*. Princeton, NJ: Princeton University Press, 1990.

Zaller, John. *The Nature and Origins of Mass Opinion*. Cambridge, UK: Cambridge University Press, 1992.

Zerilli, Linda M. G. *A Democratic Theory of Judgment*. Chicago: University of Chicago Press, 2016.

Zerilli, Linda M. G. *Feminism and the Abyss of Freedom*. Chicago: University of Chicago Press, 2005.

Index

Aberbach, Joel D., 178n143

Abrams, Samuel J., 11–12, 14–15

Achen, Christopher H.: autonomy and, 73; contrarian arguments and, 56; critics of, 165n25; Dahl and, 55–56, 166n35; *Democracy for Realists* and, 5, 51, 88, 165n25, 166n35; folk theory and, 36, 54, 57, 73; groupiness and, 56, 63, 166n45; group theory and, 56–57; identity and, 56–57; manipulation and, 182n51; Mettler and, 68; realism and, 5, 51–57, 68, 73, 88, 182n51

Adichie, Chimamanda Ngozi, 186n107

adjudication, 45, 50, 161n85

advocacy groups: manipulation and, 96, 98; mobilization and, 19; public opinion and, 1, 137; realism and, 52, 63, 66, 78; responsiveness and, 1, 151n46

Affordable Care Act, 67

Against Democracy (Brennan), 5, 54–55

Aid to Families with Dependent Children (AFDC), 30, 32

Alhstrom-Vij, Kristoffer, 52

Alinsky, Saul, 49–50

Amenta, Edwin, 31

American National Election Studies (ANES), 55, 147n3, 153n78

antagonism: articulation and, 132–34; competition and, 125, 138; vs. democratic antagonism, 130–31; identity and, 130; mobilization and, 132–33; vs. pluralism, 131; plurality and, 136; polarization and, 15; realism and, 74, 77, 88; responsiveness and, 12, 14–15; Schattschneider

and, 77, 88; sharp conflict and, 139; social movements and, 128–31; use of term, 130

apathy, 75, 80, 82–83

articulation: equivalence and, 132–34; feminism and, 131, 135; hegemony and, 125, 131, 133–34; plurality and, 123, 125, 130–36; vs. pluralism, 139; representation and, 123, 132–33; rights and, 132; speech act theory and, 194n71; use of term, 131–32

Atlantic Monthly, 65

Atwater, Lee, 48

audience: constituency and, 3, 46–48, 96–97, 102–3, 161n84, 162n93, 174n48; manipulation and, 96–97, 102–3; realism and, 174n48

autonomy: constituency paradox and, 41; education and, 41; manipulation and, 93; Mansbridge on, 41; plurality and, 133; radical democracy and, 133; realism and, 73–75, 88; responsiveness and, 4

axis of evil, 97

Bachrach, Peter, 78, 175n63

Back of the Yards Council, 49–50

Baker, Keith, 127

Baldwin, James, 113

Ball, Terence, 93, 95

Baratz, Morton S., 78, 175n63

Bartels, Larry M.: autonomy and, 73; contrarian arguments and, 56; critics of, 165n25; Dahl and, 55–56, 166n35; *Democracy for Realists* and, 5, 51, 88,

CPSIA information can be obtained
at www.ICGtesting.com
Printed in the USA
LVHW112309170322
713623LV00014B/481

9 780226 804507